BOOKS TO BYTES

BOOKS TO BYTES

Knowledge and Information in the Postmodern Era

ANTHONY SMITH

BRITISH FILM INSTITUTE

bfi

BFI PUBLISHING

First published in 1993 by the
British Film Institute
21 Stephen Street
London W1P 1PL

The British Film Institute exists to encourage the development of film, television and video
in the United Kingdom, and to promote knowledge, understanding and enjoyment of the
culture of the moving image. Its activities include the National Film and Television Archive;
the National Film Theatre; the Museum of the Moving Image; the London Film Festival; the
production and distribution of film and video; funding and support for regional activities;
Library and Information Services; Stills, Posters and Designs; Research; Publishing and
Education; and the monthly *Sight and Sound* magazine.

British Library Cataloguing in Publication Data.
A catalogue for this book is available from the
British Library

ISBN: 0-85170-401-8
       0-85170-402-6 Pbk

Cover by Cinamon Designs.

Set in 9 on 11.5 pt Utopia by
Method Limited, Epping, Essex
and printed in Great Britain by
St Edmundsbury Press Ltd, Bury St Edmunds, Suffolk

Contents

Acknowledgments

I am grateful to all of the journals and organisations which have permitted me to publish in this collection lectures and papers originally commissioned by them. They are named at the start of their respective sections.

In particular I want to thank Dr Stephen Graubard, Editor of *Daedalus*, who has inspired as well as published several of the pieces. I am most grateful for the many conversations we have held over the years. I must acknowledge in the same way and to the same extent the enormous debt I owe to the Gannett Center for Media Studies at Columbia University in New York (now known as the Freedom Forum Media Studies Center) and in particular to Dr Everett Dennis, Jane Coleman and John Pavlik, for plying me with countless invitations, boundless hospitality and endless encouragement.

The Arts Council of Great Britain via its Secretary-General Anthony Everitt is to be thanked for commissioning me to write and then generously allowing me to re-publish the discussion paper 'What Are the Arts For?'. I am grateful to many friends, including Colin MacCabe, Richard Paterson, Ian Christie and Shusha Guppy, whose talk and encouragement played a part in the composition of many things in this book.

Introduction

These essays and lectures have all been prompted by the desire to understand how our new machinery of information and communication is altering the way our minds and personalities evolve; and also to understand how some of the informing institutions of society – journalism, the arts, broadcasting, libraries – need to be thought about and governed in the light of what I see as changes in the operations of the self. The two groups of essays which form this book were composed for a variety of purposes and occasions, but emerge from the same train of thought and were written with this publication in mind.

The starting-point for the train of thought was the realisation that all of the processes of the intellect and of the emotions (including the terms themselves) have been steadily recategorised and reconceptualised in the course of the industrial era. Today with the pervasive spread of a completely new generation of information machines and a new phase in industrialisation perhaps they will be again. Where the *passions* were visible operations of the personality, driven by forces of nature, the *emotions* of our age are essentially disturbances of the mind to which individuals are privately prone. There have been swaps between rational and irrational qualities of mind, and a new emphasis on the distinction between the verifiable and the mysterious.

As calculation and the devising of theory became operations conducted through the creation and circulation of text, so rationality turned into the supreme mental quality of industrial society and imagination became the supreme quality of art and culture. Where explanations of human behaviour offered by religion were once considered *natural*, they came to be categorised as *supernatural* and other explanations had to be found, for example, for hysteria, in order to remove the element of mystery from the newly objectified perceptual world. The sequence of revolutions provoked by the arrival of and constant developments in printing rendered information something detachable from the holder of knowledge, transferable, reproducible, an object of exchange. People have now even come to see information, if not knowledge, as a constituent of wealth, as a resource of society, separable from the individuals who manage it, almost autonomous.

There have been other detachments of function and self. The arrival of industrial processes brought about the separation of the notions of work and labour, the latter being a separable, quantifiable entity, spread across society, abstracted in a way from the individuals who provide it, while the former remained a process which links the doer with the good or service provided.

It is extremely difficult to work through the lines of causality between technologies, institutions and changes in human personality. It entails a search through all of the branches of cultural study. Evidence is locatable in linguistics, semiotics, psychology but the searches almost inevitably end up in the cul-de-sac of metaphor. For example, people frequently assert that writing was an extension of memory just as a hammer extends physical energy; the arrival of printing provided a kind of physical substitute for memory. The thought certainly provides a useful image, but it is bounded by variable conceptions and shifting meanings. One finds oneself wondering whether the mental qualities in fact preceded and mysteriously inspired the shaping technologies. The dynamic of causality often seems to reverse upon itself. And yet, in the age of the computer we need access to some simple historical line which will enable us to look at the changing mental qualities and behaviours which seem to characterise the new systems of information. One comes to accept that it is impossible to say which are the causes and which the effects and also that the very notion of causality is perhaps tied to the processes of the typographic era. Though it is difficult to grapple with this notion when trying to understand the nature of our new environment of information, it is sometimes necessary to try.

If computerisation alters the nature of our grasp on information, then most certainly the industries of electronic entertainment must be altering the patterns of societies, generating a further series of conundrums of causality. As the means proliferate, the quantity of materials available multiplies, in every zone of cultural life. In societies which have been swept into the revolution in information, cultural activity becomes economically central; it is in the reshaping of desires that the economy finds its dynamic. The old labour-intensive mechanical and extractive industries cease to be the commanding heights and move to the periphery. The issue of the governance of the institutions of culture therefore becomes a major issue of politics.

It seems to me that crucial to our handling of these changes is the continued existence of the public space from which education, the arts, entertainment, broadcasting can all continue to be discussed, judged, governed. There has been a decade-long drive towards the market, and with it the spread of commercial motives for what once, in many countries, were public entities. Somehow the public agenda for education and culture more generally has to be maintained. Art is being transmuted into merchandise, but its social nature has to continue to be recognised. In maintaining public institutions in the arts and in broadcasting the climate of the whole cultural sector of society can retain its public dimension. The consumer cannot shoulder all of the burdens of the citizen.

Even though large areas of the press and the electronic media are drifting into the hands of a small number of large corporations, these still represent a small proportion of the totality of the information industries; there is still time, therefore, for a pluralism to be retained although much of this will depend largely on the flourishing of the public sector institutions to which I have referred. Only they can legitimate political oversight and keep it alive in an era of aggressive corporate growth.

Information is taking on, more and more, the characteristics of commodity. This is a phase through which our cultures are passing. During the 1980s the powerful force of computerisation entered our society, suffusing cultural and informational work. Habits and attitudes dissolved. The market became the forum of change. The consumer was inscribed as sovereign. But information is social in its nature, whatever the format to which it is technologically reduced. The consumer is another of the illusions of individualism.

PART ONE

Versions of the Self

1

Information Technology and the Myth of Abundance*

Inevitably, the culture within which we live shapes and limits our imaginations, and by permitting us to do and think and feel in certain ways makes it increasingly unlikely or impossible that we should do or think or feel in ways that are contradictory or tangential to it.

Margaret Mead, *Male and Female*[1]

What really *is* a technological revolution? And who are the revolutionaries? What are the criteria for a historical process to be so described? Where do we *look* for the results? I cannot claim that this essay will answer these questions, nor even that they are precisely enough formulated for useful answers to be provided. But it might be possible to construct a new kind of mental picture of the phenomenon of technological transformation, of its driving motivations and cultural consequences, by looking at certain aspects of current developments in information technology within a historical setting. The advent of printing had obviously 'a great deal to do' with the rise of the nation-state, and Elizabeth Eisenstein's researches and narrative,[2] as well as those of Martin and Febre,[3] have helped to fill out the picture of a late Renaissance 'information revolution'. An age in which a new transforming technology is taking hold must, almost self-evidently, express its most profound social, economic, and political changes in terms of that technology – so closely and complicatedly, that historians inevitably try, but fail, to disentangle the resulting skeins of cause and effect. Was there a drive for empire that altered the technologies of European navigation in the 15th and 16th centuries? Was imperialism a result of technology-push or economic-pull? Do the processes of 'take-up' of innovation relate to the dominant creative, emotional, and intellectual mindset of an age, so that the tracks may be found again through later research?

Such questions are the permanent concern of social history, but need to be asked also in the present, while the transforming process is under way. The intention of this essay is to suggest that there exists a great unifying social and cultural urge behind a technological revolution, particularly one that relates to information. The search for the emotional satisfactions of the vernacular

* Published originally in *Daedalus*, Vol. 111, No. 4, Fall 1982, pp. 1-16.

and the evolution of the feeling of nationhood were indeed tied to the technology of 'moving letters'. The Victorian bourgeois' obsession with the perfect mechanical reproduction of images in movement, sound and hue had some psychic link with the evolution of the representational technologies of film, phonograph, telegraph, and the wireless. Today, a surging belief in the perfect development of the individual as consumer is somehow discovering its own confirmation in the development of technologies of information abundance; but that individualism is tied also to a new imperialism or transnationalism in the growth of the phenomenon of cultural dependence of the South upon the North. The new information technology is reconfirming the world vision of the developed world, re-establishing its confidence as the primary subject of culture, as the developing nations fall victim to the cultural pressures of external data flow. Thus, if this argument works, information technology leads toward the displacement of nationhood, of national cultures.

I

We have all become modishly aware that the information environment, so to speak, of the late-twentieth-century individual is in the course of being transformed. News columns with titles that play neatly on the words *revolution, age, galaxy, shock,* appear monthly. But we remain prisoners still of an essentially Victorian idea of the requisite constituents of social change, in the sense that we tend to predicate the transformation upon the technology. We relate and chart development according to a measure of machinery, alongside the evolution of inventions. So numerous are the gadgets of the computer age (there goes an example of what is being criticised!) that the designated historic turning points – the number of 'revolutions' per decade – are too numerous to absorb, their effects too shrilly predicted for easy listening. We are paralysed by the dimensions of the transformation, partly because we have internalised a kind of Whiggian principle, by which machines 'produce' social effects of a measurable or, at least, observable variety. The trouble is that technological and social history cannot be related in this way, since the extrapolated trends shoot off the graph every time. Consider the influence of the photocopier, the coaxial cable, television news, teleconferencing, and so on. There are no anchors to cast in each voyage of speculation; every trip rushes straight toward infinity.

We would be greatly helped in the present epoch of speculation if we had available some improved metaphors for social change, something less traumatic and less overworked than 'revolution', something more intermingling of cause and effect, something that suggested less emphasis on technology and placed more pressure on social need as the starting point of technology. New technologies close gaps, resolve tensions, register the temporary shelving of problems, as well as automate jobs out of existence and fill the home with new junk. Above all, in order to reduce the current bewildering hyping of technical history, we need some explanatory models of the inventing process that demonstrate the collective, though concealed, social dialogue that almost invariably precedes the advent of a new device.

The apparatus of the modern media of information has been accumulating steadily through the century; the modern home may possess a telephone and a typewriter, a camera, a record player, a pocket calculator, a pile of disks or cassettes, probably by now a couple of television receivers, possibly a cable TV link, an 8mm film camera and projector, a device for playing video games, for receiving pay TV, for decoding teletext or videotext signals, perhaps even a video camera, and a home computer. Few people, however, are as yet aware of the linkages that exist – or that can exist – between all of these gadgets; the information revolution of the late 20th century consists very largely of the increased propensity for these text and moving image machines to converge and to interact. That propensity has been latent since Victorian times. Thomas Edison invented the phonograph as a repeating device to aid the telephone, thinking that a central office such as the telegraph bureau would record messages sent down the telephone lines and deliver the disks to the homes and businesses of non-subscribers.[4] It was not a fallacy so much as a prophecy, for we are witnessing today that intermixture of telecommunications with information storage that he envisaged. What happened in the late 1970s was a sudden increase in the potency of telecommunications and in the computing capacity of society that has made it possible for us to reap a whole series of benefits that were impossible when the same technical possibilities existed on a smaller scale. The present 'revolution', if such it is, is one of investment rather than technical innovation, of transformation of scale more than of technological horizon.

All of the devices that have emerged as discrete physical media of information and entertainment have their own industrial housing, so to speak. The century has witnessed the growth of a music industry around the phonograph and radio, a TV industry, a film industry, and telecommunications, computing, and book publishing industries. These great blocks of investment and industrial activity are currently undergoing a transformation, and in every society in which they flourish (surprisingly few, in fact, since most societies are becoming highly import-dependent in respect of media software), there is currently a reconsideration of the regulatory environment in which they operate. In some societies, the process is being labelled 'deregulation', where it is perceived as a process of removing legal constraints against inter-corporate competition. In other societies, the same process is envisaged rather as one of making new and appropriate regulations to stimulate similar releases of enterprise, often accompanied by moves to protect indigenous culture. The new devices of cassettes and disks and the new paid broadcast services entail an extremely complicated re-gearing of all the established industries that hitherto have been device-specific. In other words, it has to be possible for a set of rights and obligations that have been acquired in respect of a given artefact (say, a film made for theatrical release) to be transferred to a wider range of distribution systems (cassettes, cable television). The changing situation is bringing about a gradual alteration in the way we think about the property element in information and entertainment, and about the cultural demarcations between genres. At one level, the change consists in a series of publishing devices and promotional arrangements; at deeper levels, it must alter our ideas about what constitutes a 'book', what separates an 'academic work' from a popular one, indeed what body of data should properly be considered a book or an 'author'.

Let us consider a not unusual career for a modern work of fiction. It may begin as a novel about which an individual writer has pondered for years, or it may originate as a commission conceived by an agent or a publisher and fostered upon a writer of recognised skill. If it seems likely to sustain the investment, the finished work may be promoted, and through dextrous manipulation of the apparatus of literary review and public discussion, forced through a series of different kinds of text distribution. It will come out in hardcover and paperback, in serial fiction and digest form, and then as an even cheaper paperback. But it may also be transmuted into a set of moving images, where its basic authorship will be further dehydrated and industrialised in complex ways. A film designated for cinema distribution may in fact be shown, in widescreen format, only for further promotional purposes; the 70mm image will be seen only by a small fraction of the emerging audience, as the work passes into 35mm and 16mm gauges for distribution in various specialist systems (such as the film society network or the college circuit). It will appear in cassette form (all the framing of the original lost in the transformation to the smaller screen) and videodisk, on cable and pay TV, ending up on 'free' over-the-air television, public or commercial. At later stages in its career, the work may return to one or more of its earlier phases, but it will remain in public consciousness with greater permanency than that bulk of Victorian fiction which failed to become one of the tiny band of classics.

The new work of today faces a wider variety of audiences and enjoys a more finely calculated career. It is commensurately more heavily dependent upon promotion, and, indeed, more and more different kinds of entrepreneurs will speculate upon its possibilities during the course of its complicated life. There is a rush of newcomers to the marketplace, but inevitably, a wave of cartelisation will ensue as soon as this market is rationalised. Thus in this period of convergence of devices, a new division of cultural labour is growing up among them. At the same time, there is a search for new and appropriate forms of material, not dissimilar to that which took place when the telephone and cinematography were evolving, when perception of social role preceded each of a multitude of technical offshoots. The social impact of television and telecommunications has been much subtler and more far-reaching than that of other devices of the same era. Both telephone and cinematography were very slow, however, in gathering around them the aura of transformationism that today envelopes the offshoots of the computer and the television receiver.

In the 1880s it seemed possible that the telephone would become a medium of entertainment. In London and Paris, experimenters were to set up connections between the principal theatres and the central operator, so that subscribers could listen to plays and to the songs of the music hall. Others thought that the new medium would be a useful supplier of general information, supplementing that of the newspaper. As a person-to-person instrument, it suffered from obvious limitations: there were few people with whom one could speak, the costs were high, and established systems of social discourse inhibited subscribers from incorporating the machine into their lives. The telephone was neither intimate nor reliably private. It was often confined to small professional groups, such as the lawyers and doctors of Glasgow, who enjoyed their own separate and mutually incompatible exchanges. As an instrument of business, the telephone suffered from other limitations: it was more expensive than using messenger boys; it created tension within the national telegraph administrations (one of which actually proposed charging for the telephone according to the number of words spoken along the line). It came into use at first through a series of specialist groups: the construction teams on early skyscrapers, the police, doctors, lawyers, and so on. It grew within the interstices of society, later coming to occupy a more general public role.[5] The influence of the telephone on the development of social structures and the physical layout of societies is extremely hard to calculate and has tended to be overlooked.

Road and rail systems are more visible, and the great feats of engineering that made them possible have seized the attention of social historians more tenaciously than the invisible forces of telegraph, telephone and radio. But the areas of influence of the communication devices are themselves different: while transportation facilitated suburbanisation in the present century, communications has had a great deal to do with the changing 'images' of the different parts of a city, the constantly shifting areas of respectability and trend. Suburbanites have not been migrants on the whole; they have desired to retain the advantages of metropolitan life and to remain in constant touch with the centres of the society, while shunning the geographical core. Each device developed in the Victorian era (and later) began life in an aura of a certain vagueness as to its destined purpose. Was the telephone destined for entertainment purposes, or did it fulfil a special role in preserving social order or in providing general information? The purposes have constantly shifted, although each device eventually acquired its own clear purposes, its own 'culture'. Now, all is in doubt again, all the boundaries are moving.

Each fresh wave of new devices has registered and expressed a new stage in the evolution of city structure, in neighbourhood development, and in the structure of the family. Cinemas in the 20s and 30s released people from their homes; television in the 50s re-cemented the home as focus of the family, until in the 60s, a new politics of the family seemed to break up that tight postwar grouping. Today, the new multiple devices slice up the family and re-individualise it, permitting and encouraging a new microconsumerism, the pursuit of a fresh, but (temporarily) satisfying, illusion of individual gratification through endless freedom and 'choice'.

II

The communication and representation devices of the late Victorians were manifestations of a vast, unarticulated urge; they were an act of ideology expressed again and again, in different versions, of a machine for the perfect reproduction of the lifelike. It is worth dissecting the 'invention' of film in some detail and comparing its tortuous progress, via a complex of interactions between technique and social aspiration, with the phenomenon of today, when it is still difficult to express, in one similarly neat phrase, the nature of the parallel contemporary aspiration. There appears today to exist a latent collectivist, egalitarian consumerist urge, a prompting to break through economic and institutional constraints, toward an abundance of messages, from which a mass of individuals can draw material according to their 'personal' choice. Choice is the chimera of the age, the hypothesis of a new adulthood arising from the opportunity to 'perfect' the self as the basic mechanism of consumption. The Victorians, however, were pursuing, through their technologies of illusionism, an ideal mode in which their desire for a kind of artificial immortality could be assuaged.

The moving image was a substitute for – an extension of – the cemetery. The mass suppliers of early film cameras blatantly exploited this deep need of the age: the retention of the perfect images, in motion, of one's loved ones. One of the newspapers that reported the first public screening by Louis Lumière of his films said: 'When these cameras become available to the public, when all are able to photograph their dear ones, no longer merely in immobile form but in movement, in action, with their familiar gestures, with speech on their lips, death will no longer be final'.[6] The representation and extension through time of the human body was one aspect of the great bourgeois aspiration, but the techniques have their roots in the Renaissance, with the development of anatomical study and the growing importance of perspective as the enabling science that made it possible for the new knowledge to be recorded and imparted.

Marey's discovery of the persistence of vision in the 19th century played a similar role in the development of machines to capture, record and dissect the nature of movement.[7] But Marey was not in pursuit of moving pictures as illusions; indeed, he rejected the machines that enabled movement to be synthesised in favour of another line of invention (which included his own chronophotograph – the first camera to employ celluloid strip) that captured movement on a still frame through strobic effects. Marey and his follower Londe were both attempting to overcome deficiencies in human perception rather than create an illusion of reproduced movement that deceived human perception. They wanted to depict reality in a form that slowed down or speeded up true movement. In a sense, Eadweard Muybridge's notions lay along the same line of thought; his Zoopraxiscope succeeded in reanimating a series of still photographs taken in succession by different cameras of a horse in motion. The purpose was scientific – to dissect a natural phenomenon and to reconstitute the movement, in order to prove the correctness of the analysis. Muybridge's images were generally taken to be aesthetically unpleasing. They were to influence painting in due course, but only after delivering a shock to those artists of the traditional schools who thought that the real world corresponded to the idealised images that had been taught academically.

Earlier in the century, a flow of devices demonstrated the other half of the Victorian inspiration – illusionism. Daguerre's invention was a natural development of his skill in trompe l'oeil. At the Great Exhibition of 1851, the stereoscope had drawn fascinated crowds, since it seemed to add a dimension to still photography by supplementing a gap in the pure representation of nature. Baudelaire mocked the hungry eyes 'bending over the peepholes of the stereoscope, as though they were the attic windows of the infinite'. At the same time, the demand for the perfect illusion was being fed through non-photographic devices for creating the sensation of movement or of three-dimensional images, such as the Thaumatrope and the Praxinoscope, which depended on a disk with images that appeared to combine in motion through rapid rotation. These were representational toys dismissed by the more scientific school of Marey, since they demonstrated, but did not analyse, scientific phenomena.[8] Thus the pursuit of the Victorian aspiration for representing an image of life in its perfection veered from one line of development, in which its various manifestations were deemed to be recreational and at best educational, to another line, in which the quest was not to substitute for painting but to serve science.

It was the Lumière moving-picture show that captured the contemporary imagination in the mid-1890s. Writers as far spread as Gorky, Kipling and Henry James witnessed the show as it travelled between Spain and Moscow, Austria and America. They were presented with one-minute scenes of real-life events, unstaged but none the less contrived, through choice of camera angle, location and timing. The train arriving at a station, the workers leaving the factory, the gardener turning the hose upon himself – all became familiar metaphors that impressed upon those pioneer audiences the first collectively experienced moving images that inaugurated the great store of shared allusion which has subsequently accumulated. At the same moment, Edison's laboratory and its breakaway group, the American Mutoscope and Biograph Company, were feeding the same popular drive toward perfect representation with a series of inventions that offered short travel or anecdotal films projected in a machine into which the viewer had to peer. Edison was working to a much grander design that led him to overlook the importance of his silent camera and projecting device; he wanted to link his own phonograph invention with a film and recording technique, with stereoscopic effects added for good measure. Edison wanted to perfect a total system of representation that would perceive, record, and transmit across space, and he thus employed, in a spectacular series of electrical and mechanical inventions, the whole range of sciences that were to be worked on in the course of the following eighty years.[9]

All of the experimenters alluded to, and many others, were technicians primarily, but with a keen eye either on the audience of science or on the audience of contemporary showmanship, sometimes a little of both. The first decade of the 20th century saw a further group of experimenters who were primarily artists, such as Georges Méliès and Edwin Porter, though both had some technical background. Both saw the possibilities of developing narrative forms by means of the new moving cameras. Méliès had started as a

9

conjuror, and he drew from a line of non-realist illusionism for his film ideas, of which he developed hundreds. His stock – transformations of human beings into animals, of strange apparitions, a Jules Verne-type space journey – was the culmination of the aspirations of a Victorian conjuror. Porter, however, drew upon a realist line of narrative, breaking away from the theatre rather than from popular showmanship. He is famous for having developed the pacing techniques that laid the foundations of modern narrative cinema – the cutting, linking, and transposition of shots, and the suggestion of simultaneity through building-up a chase scene by intercutting events taking place in different locations.[10]

Behind these different lines of artistic and technical development, all of which proved ultimately interactive and intensely creative of technology, was a growing institution, cinema. Behind each movement forward – and many that proved to be cul-de-sacs – there lay a shared phenomenon that grew by accretion, based upon an audience whose perception and expectations were being progressively intermingled; each mechanical device depended upon a range of artistic conventions that had to be accepted and internalised by a rapidly growing audience if the institution of cinema was to develop. That institution itself was obliged to follow the contours of contemporary taste, to search for the city locations, the distribution systems, the pricing mechanisms, the patent and copyright devices that would sustain the new medium. The technology that emerged registers as a series of interim readings of the relationships that between them constituted, as they still do, the institution of cinema.

Of course, it is impossible to produce a perfect record of the evolution of a technology by concentrating on the interactions and dependencies – social, artistic, technical, and intellectual – since to do so would entail an analysis of an entire society. Marconi's work on radio was taking place at exactly the same moment as the work of Lumière; Zworykin was working on the basic principles of television in the same decade as the main work of Méliès. Regulatory systems for the telegraph and the telephone were being simultaneously created, and these were greatly to influence the early and continuing institutions of radio and television. And of course, contemporary developments in all of the other sciences – from biochemistry to metallurgy, optics to engineering – played their part in the evolution of the communicating technologies. None the less, those lines of development that led to film, television and radio entailed clusterings of technique that derived their impetus from the same animating aspiration, that of creating a perfect and enduring representation of the perceptual world.

III

It is rather harder to discern the central drive that unites the various new communication media that have been developed in the last and current decades from that earlier aspiration. Certainly, there no longer exists an unsatisfied craving for the mere illusionist representation of reality; perhaps a reverse principle might today be at work, whereby the techniques for suggesting reality are being pushed toward a realm of perfect fantasy in the new potential for, say, computer imaging. But there is some more general demand or perceived demand that is being stimulated and satisfied by the new media – demand for an abundance of supply and an image of the consumer as individual, arising above an ocean of materials. There is the image of a new leisure, a worklife without toil, a textured, variegated career structure. Many of the new devices are concerned with text storage and distribution as much as with still or moving images, with data processing as much as with storage. Some of the new devices appear, in the present stage of their development, to be concerned with supplying a new multiplicity of channels (cable systems, videodisks, satellite broadcasting, cassettes), while others have more to do with adding to the conveniences of the home or reducing information overload (home box office for first-run movies, videotext), or both. The suppliers of new services are breaking down, unconsciously for the most part, old traditional genres, such as the newspaper or magazine, by offering the chance to dial directly a specialist line of information; they are also providing a chance to evade the many constraints of over-the-air broadcasting with its 'paternalistic' overtones of prescribed, preselected patterns of material. The new specialist cable channels are on the whole reworkings of the public broadcasting service model, and offer the chance for a new kind of self-definition on the part of the subscriber into a class or sub-culture type, rather as the newspaper industry did in the era when newspapers of every conceivable stripe flourished.

All of the new services have broken into pre-existing monopolies of some kind, but all are searching for new monopolies of their own in order to survive – monopolies of first-run movies, monopolies of travel or business information, monopolies of high culture material, monopolies over certain geographical zones or certain social groups. With the advent, a decade or so from now, of direct broadcasting by satellite, a wholly new complication will arise, since the satellite, unlike any other transmission system devised hitherto, is capable of equal address across a whole society or group of societies.

Yet these services are, in the main, systems of supply quite separate from the industry providing material to a variety of systems reaching different layers of the audience. Thus a cable offering a cultural channel acquires its content from a multinational industry, programmes that have been created to serve a primary market elsewhere (though with an eye to further sales). The market for software is becoming many-layered, even though various homogenising market forces have already set in. The previous forms of distribution for much of this visual material continue to exist and tend still to be the primary sources of funding – the major national television networks and their independent suppliers. There are half a dozen annual markets and festivals at which the main lines of dealing and the main relationships are built up: Milan, Monte Carlo, Cannes, Berlin, New York, Los Angeles. Film festivals have created video offshoots, with new video markets in Europe and the East being established. But the dealing on individual projects continues throughout the year by means of bilateral arrangements between banks and production houses, television channels and cable organisations, Hollywood majors and publishing houses. Inevitable rearrangements of capital within the media conglomerates are taking place. A new world industry of moving-image products is emerging, highly diverse, but still dominated by the companies that established their grip over the heartland of the audience in the days of the old national television monopoly.

The material today is beginning to pass through a complex mesh of distribution systems, each one technology-specific, each with a different pricing mechanism and in a different stage of development. A European publishing house owned by an American bank, for example, will initiate a project designed as a series of films and an international book. It will pre-sell the films to a London-based television company for a price that covers a large proportion of the basic production costs. To cover the rest, it will pre-sell the same series to a US public television station or one of the New York cable stations, the London TV company retaining a percentage. The publishing house will then proceed to organise translations that will sell well, on the reputation of the British and American television transmission. The profit to the original publishing house, however, will tend to come from vastly enhanced book sales, since the whole scope of the market for the books has been transformed by the broadcasting operation. Gradually, the materials will flow into other cable and box office systems, while selling in cassette form in the education market. The product will retain strong national overtones; it is owned ultimately by the American bank, but its makers are British, and its accent will tend to be also. The same thing is happening in Paris, Frankfurt, Tokyo and Amsterdam, but five geographical locations in the developed world are coming to play an ever greater role in the world supply of moving images and, indeed, for text materials also.

The five locations are New York, California, London, Frankfurt/Munich and Tokyo,[11] places where there exist strong and sophisticated national audiences for the first-generation television materials, plus the necessary access to capital and the habit of working together on the part of a critical mass of relevant skills and institutions. It is likely that these five centres will remain at the heart of the world market for software in the entertainment and information fields. (Computer translation might eventually enable the Japanese to break also into the world text-information software market, already dominated by Japanese hardware.) There was a similar concentration in the world of book publishing a hundred years after the development of moving type, but the evolution of the newspaper, with its polycentred culture, was quite different. Quite different, too, was cinema, which, though it rapidly became a narrow market, began with a wide variety of supply centres. The developing world contains a number of major centres for film-making (India, the Philippines, Hong Kong), but these have remained largely national in the 1970s. Today, one or more of them could break into the wider world market, but probably only through major investment from the existing centres, since they are 'hampered' by the different musical and literary traditions of the East.

It is clear that two quite distinct developments are taking place. There is a new range of physical artefacts on which are inscribed images and text –

12

cassettes and disks – and these are distributed in roughly the same manner as books and gramophone records. These are, however, to some extent different from their forerunners, in that the material they offer is already familiar to the potential buyer, through the promotion and marketing of a film, of which the cassette or disk constitutes an extended line of supply. The other new media are all services rather than artefacts, although the recipient may, legally or illegally, make a physical copy of the text or image in the home. Thus the new videotext systems are publishing devices, where payment is made through the telephone company for 'pages' of material that have been received on a domestic television receiver. Some of the cable systems are paid for overall by the subscriber, as European public broadcasting systems have always been, while other cable systems or scrambled signal systems oblige the viewer to pay for each selected programme; these leave the recipient without a physical artefact, unless a domestic personal recording has been made. Policing the uses made by individuals of private recordings is, for the rights-holders, something of a nightmare, and pricing mechanisms are having to adjust for the practical impossibility of retaining rights long-term after the distribution of a new product. The owner of those rights has to consider the timing of the whole package of new media outlets, relying on industry-wide organisation for the policing of the multitude of new networks that are springing up.

It is still far too soon to see which technologies will prevail for specific purposes, to discern whether an optic fibre network set up nationwide would eventually take over and swamp all other systems of cables, microwaves, direct satellites, and broadcasting channels, in the establishment of a universal broadband domestic system, a kind of general information ring-main, like the electricity ring-main, linking every individual to the entire national and international system. It does appear, however, that Western societies are on the verge of the development of a system, or collection of systems, that, in their net effect, will tend to negate the basic principles by which information has travelled through society since the Renaissance. Even though the cassette and the videodisk operate in the same mode as books, distributed on the basis of single copy purchase by each user or group of users, the pressure of the non-artefact services is such as to suggest that the artefacts may play a diminished role in the longer term. The Gutenbergian principle is so firmly rooted in our culture that it is hard to imagine a society in which it has been abolished (and, indeed, no one is suggesting that anything like abolition is likely to occur). Rather, we are liable to witness a rapid erosion of the settled notion that information is naturally multiplied in physical copies until the number of copies approximates the number of those wishing to receive it. The Gutenbergian principle has already ceased to function in the case of broadcast material, where the opposite – or what one might call the Alexandrian principle – operates. There, a single copy exists in the originating tape or live performance, which then reaches its audience in non-material form; a physical tape can be generated by the individual recipient, but the mass multiplication of physical materials, as in the newspaper and in publishing, is absent.

One uses the image of Alexandria, because it suggests a great store of material that is deemed to be fully authentic, but available only to those who come

13

to it to choose. A modern data base is, in a sense, an electronic version of the principle where material is added to a central store according to fixed and accepted methods, and is then available to all who have the means and skills to unlock it. In the field of moving images, the world is today steadily building such a store of accredited materials, which have, most of them, been through the authenticating procedures of network transmission before becoming available through the newer systems of distribution. Unlike the materials of a great library or a computerised data base, these materials have still to be laid out as a programme by a cable company or satellite distribution company before they can be chosen; but as broadband systems develop, we are veering slowly toward some new condition in which an individual can choose electronic dissemination of a single item that was itself chosen from a vast or total store of video products. In the field of data, this condition is rather closer, if anything, as the various videotext systems slowly agree on international technical standards and interconnections. One further aspect of the steadily dissolving Gutenbergian principle is the part that distance has always played in fixing the cost of communication of any kind: this has applied equally in the case of the telephone and telegraph and the printed book. As the electronic systems emerge, it is becoming increasingly clear that distance is a rapidly diminishing factor in costs, both of collecting information and of redistributing it.

We are witnessing, therefore, a subtle transformation of the underlying principle that has sustained the information systems of human society since the Renaissance. The shift is coming about as a result of a vast number of quite separate responses of corporations to perceived demand, responses of technology to science and of science to imagination. There is no central machine generating this change, no great corporation or conspiracy of corporations. There does indeed exist a powerful, almost total dependence of the whole structure of change upon a number of giant corporations, but they are tending to grope toward the trend while trying to influence it. Their corporate needs greatly influence the pace of change, and while they often choose specific private directions for a period of time, the central pulse reestablishes its rhythm.

Despite the atmosphere of feverish change that has always beset the information media, the basic technologies and content forms have changed very slowly indeed. One may take, for example, the novel and the newspaper as direct emanations of the printing press, and note how each has changed fundamentally in form not more than, say, once in a century. Despite the enormous number of attempted means for creating moving pictures in Victorian times, the celluloid strip, which established itself in about 1897, has remained on the same gauge until today. The development of celluloid only took place at the end of the 1880s, and the earliest cameras for shooting a succession of images on a moving strip of celluloid hardly left their experimental state before 1895. And yet a piece of Victorian film can be taken in 1982 to any city on earth and screened. A newspaper printed in any language since roughly the same date will be clearly perceived to be a newspaper in any part of the globe, and many of its chief contents – puzzles, news, editorials, share prices, reviews – apprehended as such in scores of cultures where the language itself may not be known. Radio and television have developed more rapidly, but even with these, each new development – from the valve to the cathode ray tube, from colour signals and transistors to cables – has required about fifteen years to become established within the market. Forms remain stable because the market keeps them so; the public's expectations of any particular device or genre take years to develop, and these expectations, transmuted into listener, viewer, or reader habits, are the capital assets of the publishers and companies that have discovered or nurtured them.

Yet behind the kinds of material and the hardware, important trends do make themselves apparent. Two that have been at work since the beginning of the century are worth emphasising in any attempt to size up the changing information environment. One characteristic of the nineteenth-century systems and devices – from the popular reading room to the peep-show – was that the audience was expected to make no investment in the system itself; revenue was derived either from the purchase of an artefact, such as a newspaper, or from the sale of a right, such as admission to a hall or tent. Indeed, the quest of the age had been so to multiply the product that the mass audience could have access at the lowest coin available. Thus arrived the halfpenny newspaper, created as a result of expensive and diligent development of the mass press, mass distribution system, and the mass transportation system. As the century developed, however, the audience has been expected to indulge in an ever higher proportion of the total investment. Today, most of the investment necessary in maintaining a national television channel is held by the viewer rather than the supplier of the system – compare this with the theatre, or cinema, or the church.

In all of the new media, the audience's share of the investment has gone even higher, and the equipment companies have unsurprisingly been among the chief impresarios of development. The audience has to buy or rent the receiver and the recorder, the cable decoder, the videotex black box and so on. In fact, most of the new media are dependent upon there being several television receivers in a majority of homes; otherwise, there would be little hope of splitting the family as a viewing unit and thereby exploiting the potential for individual choice of material. With the arrival of direct broadcasting by satellite, the cost of each unit audience will rise substantially, since the engineering mechanisms required for switching from satellite to satellite, and thereby obtaining a wider choice, are fairly expensive. The whole expansion of the information sector thus hinges on the general expansion of the consumer economy, on the expansion at a steady rate of the consumer's propensity to invest in new entertainment systems. In the changeover from the old to the new systems, we are thus watching a very considerable switch in total investment in the resources of social communication from the manufacturer and the supplier to the audience at home.

The other important overall trend is for the gradual growth of local monopoly in any system. Information is historically torn between the condition of competition and its condition as a natural monopoly. One may cite the newspaper as a good example. Competition within the market for newspapers seemed natural, inevitable, and desirable in all democratic countries – as it still seems so today in places – so long as political circumstances made this desirable, and so long as the advertising done by mass consumer manufacturers required large slabs of display material. Gradually, television has become the channel for political material and the pre-eminent disseminator of national and regional manufacturer-to-consumer advertising. This has occurred on both sides of the Atlantic, although there are still a few European societies in which television advertising is illegal or minimal. Newspaper circulation has fallen a little in many countries, but seldom dramatically; where the total circulation has in fact fallen, the explanation often lies in the erosion of the habit of purchasing more than one newspaper as papers have become more comprehensive overall.

The markets for advertising have, however, significantly altered throughout the economies of the West. The major area of growth has been in classified advertising, especially in recession-sensitive advertising such as that for jobs and contracts. The market has therefore become more volatile, while television advertising – dependent more upon manufacturers and sellers of commercial services – has tended to be much more resilient to temporary economic trends. There is a natural tendency for a newspaper to be most attractive as a source of advertising (and of news) where it is believed to be most comprehensive in its content, and this tendency, in the context of the changes mentioned, has greatly accelerated the development of natural local monopolies among the printed press. In the United States, this tendency has occurred alongside a growth of chains and of cross-media ownership at the corporate, if not the local, level. The newspaper has thus been coaxed by states into becoming typically a local monopoly. Only a very few countries, such as Britain and Japan, have retained thoroughgoing newspaper competition, and in those cases, the reason has been the institution of national distribution, which has produced monopolisation of another kind – within social strands rather than geographic location. Even in Britain, however, with its highly competitive journalism, the same phenomena have occurred with local newspapers as in Germany, the United States, France and elsewhere.

The processes of monopoly have not set in as far as the electronic media are concerned, where cartelisation is restrained through regulation. It would not be surprising, however, if a certain clarification did not begin – in those markets with a very large number of television outlets as the new media, with their far greater promise of abundant choice – to reach the middle and lower levels of the market. The same tendency toward a single outlet has occurred in the case of cinema, though mitigated by the habit of tripling or quadrupling movie theatres – not to create wider choice, but to provide finer tuning of the audiences for the existing repertoire as they grow and shrink during the run of a given film.

I have deliberately refrained from stressing national differences of trend or of magnitude, in order to bring out the shared phenomena of Western economics. We are witnessing a cultural shift, or set of shifts, that are more subtle and far-reaching than the physical devices, the products of modern electronics, themselves suggest, but that are more deeply rooted in the continuing and the slowly evolving than is often believed. After all, abundance of choice does not in itself constitute a transformation, since an individual will make conditioned choices and will probably not greatly increase the total hours of his exposure. But the role of text in our civilisation and the development of the various skills of text are indeed in all probability today in the course of fundamental change. The management and use of a data base require quite new skills, and will emphasise different aptitudes from those required traditionally in primary education. The computerisation of text suggests that we may absorb smaller quantities of text into our lives, but it will be text that is better ordered and more appropriately selected. The term *book* will probably come to cover a narrower range of products than it now does, and the technical aids to research will soon enable a still wider range of disciplines to benefit from the boon of the computer.

One might take, as an extreme example of the kind of 'book' that is becoming outmoded, the telephone directory, where the form is used, in full Gutenbergian trappings of binding and single copy mass distribution, as the housing for a collection of data, only a tiny fraction of which is required by any individual reader. The time taken to collect the information and to reproduce it is so great that a high proportion of the material required by any individual reader is invalid by the time the finished product reaches him. As the total number of telephone subscribers rises, the proportion whose addresses change more frequently also rises. The directory is an essential body of data in urgent need of an appropriate mode in which to present itself to its readers. Clearly, the format of the traditional book is inappropriate, or will become so as soon as an alternative technology becomes as easily accessible, or where the level of accessibility of the alternative outweighs the disadvantages built into the existing mode. It is thus that the book will 'die', not through sudden technological redundancy, but through the prudent choices of those who actually require the information it carries. As the newspaper passes through its own crises of form, many of its traditional elements will probably be lost to the new electronic mode. The pursuit of information 'abundance' in this case is in reality the pursuit of a manageable modicum of relevant information.

But for the most part, the contemporary drive for abundance of choice is a besetting ideology much more than a practical need. It is more like the Victorian illusion of mechanised immortality, providing evidence for the psychic tension of the moment rather than for a social or economic need. The pursuit of plenty in the sphere of information is a psychological analogy to its pursuit in the sphere of nourishment in the developed world, where the use of food has more to do with marketing, fashion, and general culture than with biological need. Information abundance has likewise much to do with cultural identity in the late 20th century, and little to do with need. None the less, it is a motive force and a justification for an industrial evolution with revolutionary repercussions. An OECD report observes:

> The production, transmission and processing of the most varied information will be at the heart of economic activity and social life . . . through its links with data processing and telecommunications, the electronics com-

plex during the next quarter of a century will be the main pole around which the productive structures of the advanced industrial societies will be reorganised.[12]

There are plenty of documents in circulation that outline the growing disparity in the provision of information, and especially the communications technology, between the countries of the North and those of the developing South. Eighty-five per cent of existing data bases are in the North. The abundance of both hardware and software is the privilege of a tiny group of societies, who are themselves enjoying a continually increasing disparity. Information wealth grows by what it feeds upon.

Studies of the flows of data from computer to computer reveal its increasing internationalisation. The growth of international networks is growing in the wake of the establishment of effective national networks. There is a strong tendency for all data flow to be concentrated on capital cities, however, because that is where the main data users are located. But there is also a tendency for data to flow from the less developed to the more developed, where processing facilities are more plentiful and more efficient. In the least advanced countries of Europe, for example, national data flow is toward other countries. The newly emerging techniques of remote sensing and satellite distribution of data are bringing about further exponential growth and further tiltings in the international flow of data from developing to developed worlds. The cultural implications are self-evident, and the political implications easy to deduce. Behind the emblem of information foison there exists a growing phenomenon of global cultural domination, produced not by powerful armies, but by powerful international companies. The greater the stock of expertise in a society, the greater is its ability to make use of the information technology and benefit from its software. The educated society is the one best suited to prosper in the new age, and everything conspires against the society that has a deficit in its national balance of educated talent. The profusion of data through which the Western industrialised consumer indulges his or her choice, and expresses the nuances of a carefully refined and nurtured life-style, is the same oversupply that is drawn from the international data flow and jeopardises the nationhood of developing societies. We may expect in the next decades the lines of international tension to shadow the contours of data abundance.

Notes

1 Margaret Mead, Male and Female (London: Gollancz, 1949).
2 Elizabeth Eisenstein, *The Printing Press as an Agent of Change*, 2 vols. (Cambridge: Cambridge University Press, 1979); 'The Advent of Printing and the Problem of the Renaissance', *Past and Present*, No. 45 (1969), pp. 19-89.
3 Henri-Jean Martin and Lucien Febre, *The Coming of the Book: 1450-1800*, translated by David Gerard (London: New Left Books, 1976).
4 Ithiel de Sola Pool et al.: 'Foresight and Hindsight: The Case of the Telephone', in *The Social Impact of the Telephone*, edited by Ithiel de Sola Pool (Cambridge, Mass.: MIT Press, 1977), pp. 127-57.

5   See the above volume, passim, but, in particular, Ronald Abler, 'The Telephone and the Evolution of the American Metropolitan System', pp. 318-41.
6   This passage draws considerably on several essays in *Afterimage*, 8/9, Spring 1981, in particular on Noël Burch, 'Charles Baudelaire v. Dr Frankenstein', pp. 4-23.
7   E. J. Marey, *Movement* (London: 1895). Listed in *Afterimage* above.
8   C. W. Ceram, *The Archaeology of the Cinema* (London: Thames and Hudson, 1965).
9   Matthew Josephson, *Edison* (London: Eyre & Spottiswoode, 1959).
10 D. J. Wenden, *The Birth of the Movies* (London: MacDonald, 1975), pp. 19-22.
11 I am indebted for the train of thought in this section to conversations with Mr Stephen Hearst of the BBC.
12 OECD, *Interfutures. Facing the Future, Mastering the Probable and Managing the Unpredictable* (Paris: 1979).

2

The Influence of Television*

Our repertoire of working mental images does not seem at the present time to contain an apt metaphor or convenient cliché that sums up the flow of influence between a fresh technology and human society. We are free to borrow from economics the idea of the multiplier, or from scientific discourse Thomas Kuhn's idea of the paradigm collapse. Engineering and telecommunications are willing to lend us all manner of forces and thrusts, scatterings and pressures, but really nothing that provides a convincing and transposable conceptualisation of the causal influences which pass between a new form of equipment and the organised minds and bodies of people living in society.

In the case of systems of communication the omission is very deeply felt, since it is difficult in practice to talk about the coming of the telegraph, the telephone, radio and television without automatically, virtually unconsciously, suggesting cause-and-effect processes where some more complicated structure of simultaneity is probably more appropriate. Media historians almost accidentally leave a residue in the reader's mind compounded of these unargued impacts and influences. For example, Elizabeth Eisenstein in her remarkable books about the coming of print[1] leaves one with the feeling, even when one is on one's guard against easy statements of causality, that the printing press was after all a kind of autonomous pivot of the whole of Western history. In the 1980s we, too, are living through an era of great and probably rapid social and technological change, and we are daily injected with a stream of suggestion, emanating from equipment merchandisers as well as the media, to the effect that the new machinery of information, at the centre of all innovation, is itself, on its own authority, as it were, changing the contours of human societies. It has also become easy, through contrariness, to dismiss the impact of these new systems of information storage or transmission or to overlook the subtly transforming power of the bureaucracies, corporations and institutions that surround them. As quickly as one kind of influence is denied, another springs into parlance. Communication researchers, using empirical evidence rather than conjecture, have passed through phases when their conclusions all seem to converge on 'big effects' followed by phases when they revert to 'little effects', as the formulation of the questions about radio, television and advertising alter.

* Published originally in *Daedalus*, Vol. 114, No. 4, Fall 1985, pp. 1-16.

There was an era, just at the point when television started to become a mass medium, when researchers were concerned with the ways in which influence was disseminated. Elihu Katz and Paul Lazarsfeld produced a carefully worked model of the flow of cultural influence in a community.[2] The 'two-step' flow had already become a widely accepted paradigm.[3] Then the television studies started to flow, and after a period when people thought that the new medium was capable of transformation of consciousness a withdrawal from 'hypodermic' effects set in. Television in the early 1960s was thought to exercise its influence on *mores*, styles, political attitude only as one factor in many;[4] it was incapable of bringing change in itself. Filling the gap between screen and viewer there was a vast thicket of socialising forces and resistances.

Two divergent trends helped to bring back 'big effects' in the later 1960s. The McLuhanites, on the one hand, drew attention almost flippantly to the pervasiveness of television as a sheer presence: it did not bring effects because it was an effect.[5] It prepared the senses in its own way, but left them able to respond only to the medium itself. Other media had their own specific affective and cognitive ethos. We simply lived now in the shadow cast by this vast intruder into all experience, into all events.[6] On the other hand, a different research tradition was being developed, based partly upon the 'gatekeeper' and 'agenda-setting' studies inspired by newspapers since World War II:[7] there was a growing interest in the professionalisation and socialisation of producers, journalists, directors who create not influences in us so much as the information to which we as viewers react. There was also a growing school, emanating largely from France and Britain, of researchers who concerned themselves with the content of television as a text, as a signifying apparatus that enveloped the audience, as a machine that created not 'attitudes' so much as the 'realities' in the context of which beliefs and attitudes arose.[8]

As the interest in the cultural conditions of the Third World arose in the last decade the new 'big effects' wave continued to grow. The information industries of the West seemed poised to sweep away whole cultures with a vast electronic upsurge. Fear of American power and fear of excessive media influence went together.[9] In the last two or three years, however, a small reaction has set in. Students of Third World and developed world culture have come to realise that American television does not necessarily dominate the attention of audiences whose locally produced entertainment and information is reasonably competently made. The growth of production competence and the development of indigenous resources has quelled a number of fears, especially regarding South America and parts of Asia. The huge indigenous film industries of the Far East offer a hope, at least for the moment.

None the less, within the developed world the belief that most newly perceived social phenomena are the direct result of television influence is strong. Indeed, it has gone into a period of self-sustained growth, especially among political groups that have lost confidence in their own powers of leadership. Television is treated as if it retains the last surviving power of legitimisation in society, by politicians who feel their functions have been long ago usurped, blown away in a media wind.

The real problem is that there exist no conceptual tools with which to begin to handle the problem of media effects. One can take, as a parochial example, the issue of the televising of Parliament, pressure for which has existed for many years, partly out of a desire for 'modernisation', partly in the belief, held by many, that television, by amplifying the debates, would somehow improve the level and quality of political life.

In the course of 1985, the television channels started, for the first time, to transmit debates from the House of Lords (the Commons having taken for a few years a more cautious or perhaps coy view of the value of television to their proceedings). The debates look exactly as they must have done a century ago: rows of old men (nowadays a few old women, too) speaking rather slowly and sometimes rather boldly about the affairs of the moment, their actual legislative power having been removed some generations ago. Clearly, the impact of television upon the working peerage, so to speak, is going to be interesting; it is certainly going to be exaggerated. The effect of the experiment upon television is going to be interesting and similarly unmeasurable. None the less, one can predict a number of attempts to formulate the influences, to turn them into questions capable of generating quantitative answers and to produce a stream of case studies and research analyses. Upon these, political scientists – especially those who have had little cause to ponder the ineffable nature of media effects – will construct theories of historical change. We shall be told that the House of Lords has gained in power, has become a new forum of debate, under the impact of the medium of television. In one way, the researchers will be correct, in that television will have played some kind of role in helping concentrate attention upon a number of debates in the Lords that have always been well-argued, topical, and relatively devoid of party rancour. Perhaps television in this case will play the part of the 'vanishing mediator' which serves as the carrier of change but which can disappear once a society recognises and absorbs the message or lesson concerned. Statements to the effect that 'television has restored the faded power of the House of Lords' will not, however, be correct. Why?

First, because 'television', as the subject of such statements, does not exist. It is the decision of the House of Lords to admit the cameras that represents the crucial change, the television coverage itself being the result of a shift in attitude on the part of a number of people. Second, because the influence upon the viewing public, whatever it is, will be that of the content of the debates and the images of the speakers, which exist independent of the interposition of cameras. If one assumes that, in the statement concerned, the term 'television' is to stand for this gamut of phenomena, then the statement can be assumed to be true but extremely deceptive in its semantic spread. The variables can spread outwards far and wide: one might conjecture that the Lords, when they took their decision, were influenced by the newly acquired belief that the admission of cameras would enhance their influence and their public aura; in other words, that the cameras came as a result of a bid for influence. At the other end of the argument, one might say that the viewing public, starved of access to the presentations of clearly argued debates on public issues, have accepted and been gratified by the offerings of the Lords, the Commons being denied to them on television and being sub-jected in radio to damaging extractive coverage (the listeners in any case being appalled by the raucous behaviour of the elected chamber and the absence of dignified debate). The qualifying and explanatory variables multiply as one examines the bald statement of impact. Causes turn into effects and effects into causes. Is it possible, even after identifying as many of them as possible, simply to say 'television did this' or 'brought that about'?

Clearly, there are many who can write extensively about modern media happy in the casual application of causal statements. An extreme example occurs passim in a recent book, entitled *No Sense of Place: The Impact of Electronic Media on Social Behaviour*,[10] but one extract may illustrate the point:

> Television has helped change the deferential Negro into the proud Black, merged the Miss and Mrs into a Ms, transformed the child into a 'human being with natural rights'. Television has fostered the rise of hundreds of 'minorities' people, who in perceiving a wider world, begin to see themselves as unfairly isolated in some pocket of it. Television has empowered the disabled and the disenfranchised by giving them access to social information in spite of their physical isolation. Television has given women an outside view of their incarceration in the home. Television has weakened physical authorities by destroying the distance and mystery that once enhanced their aura and prestige. And television has been able to do this without requiring the disabled to leave their wheelchairs, without asking the housewife to stop cooking dinner, and without demanding that the average citizen leave his or her easy chair.

It is an overblown statement, taken I think not unfairly from a book that deals deliberately and extensively in such material. But the quoted paragraph only puts serially a range of widely held and constantly restated notions. In their sheer cumulative appearance they shock the reader (or some readers) into a cautious awareness of the problem. It is the problem of how to talk about the media without forgetting that one is talking about society, how to grapple with the overwhelming nature of the presence of television without losing one's sense of sociological proportion. The new media of this century (perhaps those of previous times, too) have been and still are presumed to be autonomous agents acting coercively upon the public, both necessary and sufficient causes of stated consequences. Social science has rather tended, especially since the upswing of interest in the media in the 1960s, to run after the discussion in search of a relevant contribution and has become caught up, inextricably, in endless regressions, constructing increasingly subtle ways of measuring phenomena that are more the result of linguistic confusions than of real events.

In many ways it is not surprising that the considerable changes in social and especially sexual *mores* in the last quarter century have been attended by an intensification of the various debates about popular culture. The tide of liberal thought has ebbed and flowed. Suspicion of the intentions and motives of commercial suppliers and exploiters has been fuelled. Supporters of public regulation have required material evidence to justify their pressures and counteract the forces of the apparently free market in cultural goods. The content of television has offered itself as an easy and tangible ground on which to conduct a large series of struggles. The problem is that statements about 'television' are as unverifiable as other statements about culture. The demand for 'evidence' is more a function of the intensity of the debate than of the potential for increasing certitude. Social science has got itself into something of a scrape in the matter of television, especially in the area of violence; none of the various sides in the argument about violence will permit social science to depart from the field, not the moral indignants, not the television executives, not the police. As the years pass, social science, weighed down with the sheer accumulation of unconvincing research, is more than ever embroiled in an argument in which it is better equipped to be observer than participant, student of form rather than referee.

At the risk of seeming parochial, one may cite a flurry of correspondence that appeared in *The Times* in November and December of 1984. The letters could have been penned mutatis mutandis in many other countries in the last many years. The exchange began when the director general of the Independent Broadcasting Authority the body set up by government which licenses and supervises nanny-fashion the fifteen commercial television stations in Britain) made a speech in which he declared that 'there is no evidence' (a fatally provocative suggestion) 'that television makes ordinary kids into violent kids'; he added the familiar cautionary variable, long asserted and always 'controlled for' by social scientists, that the more aggressively inclined may be tempted to watch a greater amount of violence than the less aggressively inclined.[11] The bevy of letters then provoked came from familiar or predictable quarters. William Belson, author of *Television Violence and the Adolescent Boy*,[12] was first into the lists, denouncing the self-exculpatory position of the public broadcasting authority. Belson's own research had shown, he assured the readers, that long-term exposure 'increased substantially' the extent to which adolescent boys engaged in violence; the evidence indicated that a multiplicity of factors along with television are involved and that 'the effects may take years to show up fully as behaviour'.[13]

The IBA has its own staff researchers and one of these, Dr Robert Towler, wrote within a week to indicate that Belson was too eager to treat as *major* the contribution of television to the complex of factors contributing to teenage violence. The increase is due to manifold causes (Belson had said this himself) within which television is placed as a mere scapegoat. Belson, argued Towler, had not tackled the question of what constitutes violence, an omission that was shortly to be remedied in a forthcoming work by another of the IBA's research staff;[14] Belson had not made distinctions between fictional violence and violence in news bulletins.[15] Belson's reply, some days later, brought out the essentially political nature of the dispute and the way in which one group of researchers see themselves as having laid siege to powerful and irresponsible institutions. His argument indicates the way in which social science, as much as any lay commentator, treats television content as product rather than process, as a definable object created by one party and taken in by another: 'If on some matter of social importance there is even a *possibility* that a public authority is allowing harm to be done to those it is meant to protect, then the truly responsible administrator within it will take steps to avert that possibly harmful outcome.'[16] The point at issue between the two social scientists is not a question of culture – which could not be handled in the same way – but of social pathology, of fixed laws of human conduct, of quantities and sufficiencies. But they have become drawn into an argument that has to be settled in the cultural sector, even though the only tools in their bag are tools of certitude.

Let me offer an analogy. Suppose the discussion had been about obesity, and one scientist had said that doughnuts, *among other substances*, are now pretty well proven, if taken over the long term, to be a significant cause of obesity among young people. And suppose the other had replied that the former should have made provision for important variables between jam doughnuts and the more healthy kind of cheese doughnuts. Then, imagine our reaction if the former scientist had replied to the effect that local health officials, charged as they are with the task of ensuring healthy products against the purveyors of unhealthy goods, should accept the responsibility for ensuring the elimination of what may be just one of a number of known causes of obesity.

The real key to the discussion lay in the letter that was published between those of the two scientists, a letter from Mary Whitehouse, whose contributions to all public discussion of this kind are de rigueur. Mary Whitehouse is as household a name in Britain as they come, seasoned campaigner as she is since 1960 for the elimination of explicit sexual representations, obscenity, excessive violence, and certain forms of moral and political dissidence from the television screen. For her, as a lay campaigner, the two social scientists were dealing in matters of proven certainty. For her, the social sciences are not sciences by analogy but zones of fixed knowledge. 'What is now most urgently needed is less talk and far more action to demonstrate the will and determination of the IBA to put into effect its published codes on the portrayal of violence.' In his speech the director general of the IBA, she averred, had been 'defending the indefensible'. As for Dr Towler, whose point about the necessity of distinctions as to what constitutes violence was lost upon her, she declared: 'Dr Towler says we must tackle the question of what constitutes television violence. Heaven help me! – as if we didn't know.'[17] Whitehouse represents a more direct form of social power behind the debate over television violence, that force in society which does not want the discussion to remain a cultural discussion, but sees the changes and deterioration in social *mores* to be the result of an activity or conspiracy. In some quarters, the objections to television violence came from the Left, in the form of denunciations of commercial exploitation of the mass audience for profit; equally frequently today the attack is from the Right, which sees irresponsible television as the chief agency of social change and which fights what one researcher sees as a last-ditch battle against the secularisation of society.[18]

There was a parallel and simultaneous debate under way, however, in another newspaper, the *Daily Telegraph*, and into this the trenchant theatre and television critic Milton Shulman lobbed an important missile. 'Anyone studying the literature would be aware that the evidence identifying television as a *major* contributor to violence, is as clearly and scientifically established as the relationship between cigarette smoking and lung cancer. It is true that there are still a few pockets of resistance to these findings, shamefully enough confined to spokesmen for television in this country.'[19] The Shulman quotation provides the key to the whole question of the involvement of social science – it is the certainty demanded of science and treacherously withheld, that is the problem for those who support 'big effects' theories of the media, the certain and applicable knowledge of chemistry and medicine. 'Violence', itself a linguistic construct, as much as 'labour' is an abstracted construct from 'work', or 'liquidity' from 'money', is felt to be as specific as a disease. In truth, it has become a kind of commodity derived from an attribute. Violent acts are deemed to be varieties of the same substance, their sameness derived from their motivation rather than from the moral values through which they are discerned. In the age of the media, 'violence' has been conveniently constructed as a term of debate but treated as a unitary phenomenon. It is not surprising that non-scientists snatch at the apparent certainties when the social scientists are themselves willing to take part in the debate on precisely the terms requested. The approximation of the answers merely infuriates and increases the demand for more precision, therefore more distinction of definition.

There are other debates engulfing the mass media in which the same patterns manifest themselves. The question of 'information flow' between the countries of the developed and developing worlds is one obvious parallel, and one just as politically charged as the violence debate, equally omnivorous of all quasi-data, bereft of relevant contextual considerations. Television has become excessively central to a series of other and quite necessary discussions about the moral condition of the world. So great are the concerns it generates and so much do they intersect with a number of other agenda items (deregulation, freedom of expression, the right to know) that there is a considerable danger that priorities get out of balance. In Britain, the first new statutory censorship body was set up to inspect and certificate all videotapes sold to the public. It is illegal to offer for sale a videotape for domestic use which does not contain a censor's certificate. All previous works were gradually put through this new media mill, at a cost of many millions in censors' time, and all this entirely as the result of the new moral panic about videotapes offering particularly violent sadomasochistic and other undesirable material. It is instructive to note that the wave of videotapes that provoked the wave of parliamentary concern (the so-called 'videonasties') disappeared from sale prior to the legislation as a result of increased vigilance by the police and courts using other existing laws. The new censorship was imposed by people who, only a month or two earlier, may well have deprecated any suggestion that a form of statutory censorship should return to Britain.

The television set, however, has become the location of compulsory participation in the society; it sits where in one sense the Church sat in previous ages, and where the school has been for a century or more. Arguments over

26

television legislation and deregulation are currently the place of outcrop of an older pressure for the control of *mores* through cultural censorship. Interestingly enough, the desire for videotape censorship even overrides, and certainly contradicts, the desire for rapid deregulation of television as an industry – though it comes from exactly the same quarters.

The evolution of the discussion in the United States over the Surgeon General's massive investigation of 1972 illustrates the conceptual spread that is presently under way in the television and violence debate. The 1982 update of the Report of the Surgeon General[20] revealed the way in which the discussion of media content had both become impossibly remote from the certainties required by the contending parties and had spread much farther afield than was envisaged when the investigations commenced. The role of television in the 1980s was, according to the update, being researched in the fields of consumer socialisation, sex-role consciousness, family life, education, etc. One may conclude that the discussion, together with 3,000 research studies undertaken between the two Reports, dissolved further into the fields of general cultural discussion and concern about values. Rather than unravel the complexities concealed within the bald premises of earlier research, the newer researchers choose to extend the notion of television influence and trace its impact upon other trends evident in society.

Naturally, correlations can be found between a phenomenon as widespread as television viewing and many other phenomena. One would expect a ubiquitous and omnivorous medium to contain *the means of influence* in a myriad fields, because it contains so great a preponderance of significant representations. What makes the underlying proposition of effects research so unsatisfying is the sheer lack of what one might call an underlying theory of personality. The influences that are the objectives of research to capture and explain are deemed to occur at the point of connection between screen and mind; so much attention is concentrated on filling that tiny gap in the complex cycles of connections between medium and society that the cultural location of the influence, the self of the viewer, has been almost casually ignored, as if it were not relevant to the project of research. If there is any viable measure of the immensity of the experience of the television medium in our time, then it has surely to lie in the exploration of the space that television's content actually enters. If one begins the search with a precise question, the answer to which is required for some other societal purpose, the answer is indeed likely to be an unconvincing confirmation of the hypothesis, rather than a dynamic discovery concerning the interaction of the period's principal engine of culture with the selves of the society as they are. Furthermore, there are likely to be 'influences' which are neither noticeable nor measurable in individuals but which inhabit only a territory of intersubjectivity or are interesting only in terms of their collective intersubjective role. Vast areas of disquisition here open up, fields that belong to disciplines that have never – perhaps wisely – chosen to try their luck with this set of questions.

There is a possible four-stream typology of the existing television effects research, one which would almost certainly be described as over-crude by the authors of the mountainous product concerned. There are two kinds which might be labelled 'personal' since they are concerned with influences upon persons: one of these tends to concentrate on perceived impact (violence research is very typical of this group) and the other upon the receiver's motivation and is often labelled 'gratifications' research, i.e. it concentrates on why people choose to select the material of a particular kind. The other two branches might be labelled 'social', in that they are concerned with the way in which the media manipulate available choices in society; of these the former can, albeit rather loosely, be grouped around the notion of agenda, the influencing of the prevailing concerns of a society, while the latter searches for the ways in which the 'text' of given media content structures in itself the dominant representations available to the audience – in other words, focuses on the medium's role as a creator of meaning.

As one works through the literature one can assign most studies to one of these piles, though some are of more than one variety and some, admittedly, do not seem to fit at all. The problem besetting all of them is that an army of politicised social critics are waiting to *use* the material for reasons of their own. All of them are clustered around the gap between screen and audience, attempting to discern transpositions, observe behavioural homologies, discover imprintations. It is at that very point of contact between medium and audience that the wedges of censorship are imposed, or attemptedly imposed, that public panic is steered. Those essentially political processes are amplified by the research, seldom assuaged, never placated or gratified. Media research has made it possible to open up debates that had been temporarily concluded in liberal societies, but to do so on ground that is both scientifically and morally shaky. The objection is not to the opening up again in new guise of the ancient debate about the role of the state in art and representation, but to its being done in these forms and with these motives.

True, each society will find a way to set up a mechanism to anchor the arts (taken in a broad sense of the term) to the state. The content of the media permeate. They soften the soul, in Plato's sense, and are in constant contest with the state as to which should play the greater role in shaping the soul. The conflict over television is like the conflict over art in that it is about rival conceptions of human nature. The difference is that the effects researchers share an unspoken and under-delineated doctrine of personality as the product of imitation rather than of internal conflict of forces. When we are dealing with questions of science pure and simple we may adopt a tighter notion of causality than when we are dealing with influences that operate within the personality, within human nature, where, if we abandoned the axiom of free will, we fall unchecked into circularity of argument: if the influences of media transcend the will or undermine judgment then our very questions have emanated from the state of mind we are examining. Our minds perform many different functions in many different ways and yet we have to treat our own natures as essentially unchanged, and not susceptible to sudden wrenchings of purpose or nature. If objective knowledge were possible concerning the shaping of the mind by the products of art or by the sending of messages or by the contemplation of mimesis, then we would be admitting to

28

a narrow version of the subject, narrowed to a mere pathology; anyone attempting such knowledge can only be asking questions too limited to suit the realities of human personality.

Moreover, the medium of television is itself not still. Neither its specific content nor its overall nature or function. If the self is too complex and too rapidly moving a target for the type of research undertaken, the medium is itself too volatile and mercurial. The status of its images within a society and within each personality change constantly, partly along with the flow of the meta-discussion about the role of television. Victorian photographs, for example, exercised an impact that is different from that of the same medium today and will be different again in a year or in a different place. Disney's film *Snow White and the Seven Dwarfs* was subject to censor's cuts in its early years because the witches were thought, in some countries at least, to be too frightening for audiences of small children; our conceptions of childhood and of the susceptibility of children have shifted sufficiently for that particular form of stimulus to be deemed untroublesome in the 1980s, but does that mean that children have changed, that adults have changed, that films have altered in the intensity of their impact? The question is unknowable, the answer can only be unreachable and unconvincing.

The techniques of professional researchers have the same limitations (and advantages) as technologies of perception: they limit the perspective of those who use them and can also limit the perception unless the user takes account of their *essential* narrowness. The photographer's equipment enables him to observe minutely and retain an impression of a flat surface; much can be learned with the use of the camera. It can even suggest the roundness and multidimensionality of the reality at which it points, but it only does so in a world of users who fully grasp, and accept, its limitations. Every generation of technologies of perception has left behind a newly reduced version of the human mind or limited image of the world. At the turn of the present century people began conceptualising the mind as a particularly complicated telephone switchboard; today we see it as a kind of computer. To the 17th century it was a kind of clock. Galileo's telescope enabled him to see mountains on the moon, and oceans on the planets; it enabled him to see how the physics of the heavens was a continuation of the physics of the earth, but it left him with a view of the earth and its inhabitants that was more mechanical than before. 'It demechanised the sky but mechanised the earth.' It took until Darwin's age for man to return, as it were, to become a part of nature. 'What must be denied', wrote Lynn White, 'is that mathematics, measurement and quantification provide much insight into the deepest problems and experiences of our race: courage and cowardice, affection and hatred, generosity and greed, charm and repulsion, courtesy and boorishness, awe and mockery – and so on, without end. . . About such matters we can only talk to each other, at length, carefully, trivially. We must talk patiently, weighing contradiction, balancing paradoxes, and not expecting to arrive at "laws", but rather rough consensus that draws on long experience and takes a long view at the road ahead.'[21]

But societies seem precisely to demand 'laws' and there are social scientists always ready to help construct them. In the last decades of uncertainties, many of the social and other sciences have drawn away from monocausal explanations of phenomena, adopting methods of explanation that depend upon describing contexts: of family, class, constraint. True, we need some basis for making public policy where public decisions require to be taken, but we could more honestly and more appropriately decide that the basis of our decisions lies in some albeit shakily conceived moral philosophy, not in some crude and probably self-deceptive search for the security of proof. Of course, all societies have their taboos; everyone needs the safety of feeling that *something* has been prohibited. But surely any social science should set out to help us understand why we entertain those needs rather than covertly to help sustain them. Many of the violence researchers have become so nonplussed – not so much by the unsatisfactory nature of their own results, as by the puzzling unwillingness of others to accept them – that they have constructed vast statistical telescopes, as it were, each of them growing longer and more complex in its engineering than the one before. What some do not realise is that the 'results' have been indelibly painted in advance at the end of the apparatus.

Notes

1 Elizabeth Eisenstein, *The Printing Press as an Agent of Change*, 2 vols. (Cambridge: Cambridge University Press, 1979).
2 Elihu Katz and Paul F. Lazarsfeld, *Personal Influence: The Part Played by People in the Flow of Mass Communication* (New York: Free Press, 1960).
3 See, for example, Bernard Berelson, Paul F. Lazarsfeld and William N. McPhee, *Voting: A Study of Opinion Formation in a Presidential Campaign* (Chicago: University of Chicago Press, 1954).
4 See Joseph T. Klapper, *The Effects of Mass Communication* (New York: Free Press, 1960).
5 R. Rosenthal, *McLuhan Pro and Con* (New York: 1958).
6 See Jonathan Miller, *McLuhan* (London: Fontana Modern Masters, 1971).
7 For the origin of the 'gatekeeper' concept, see Kurt Lewin, *Channels of Group Life*, p. 145. For an account of the agenda-setting discussion, see M. McCombes, 'Agenda-setting Research – A Biographical Essay', *Political Communications Review*, 1976, pp. 1-7.
8 See, for example, the selection of studies in *Screen*, Jan.-Feb. 1983 – a special edition on *Reflections on Television*.
9 For a review of the many positions taken on this issue, see the symposium published as *The Media Crisis* by the World Press Freedom Committee, Washington, D.C., 1981.
10 Joshua Meyrowitz, *No Sense of Place: The Impact of Electronic Media on Social Behaviour* (New York: Oxford University Press, 1985), p. 309.
11 *The Times*, 9 Nov. 1984, p. 9.
12 William A. Belson, *Television Violence and the Adolescent Boy* (Guildford: Saxon House, 1978).
13 *The Times*, 17 Nov. 1984, p. 9.
14 Barrie Gunter, *Dimensions of Television Violence* (Aldershot: Gower Publishing Co, 1985).
15 *The Times*, 22 Nov. 1984, p. 13.
16 *The Times*, 6 Dec. 1984, p. 17.
17 *The Times*, 11 Nov. 1984, p. 14.

[18] See Michael Tracey and David Morrison, *Whitehouse: a Study in Moral Protest* (London: Macmillan, 1978).

[19] *Daily Telegraph*, 11 Dec. 1984, p. 16.

[20] Surgeon General's Scientific Advisory Committee on Television and Social Behaviour (Washington, D.C.: US Govt. Printing Office, 1972). The update is: National Institute of Mental Health (NIMH), *Television and Behaviour: Ten Years of Scientific Progress and Implications for the '80s* (Washington, D.C.: NIMH, 1982).

[21] Lynn White, Jr., 'Science and the Sense of Self: the Medieval Background of a Modern Confrontation', *Daedalus*, Spring 1978, pp. 47-59.

3

On Audio and Visual Technologies

A Future for the Printed Word?*

Many years ago I met a man who told me that he had prepared as script-writer the first documentary ever made for British television. He had previously worked in radio and for magazines. On receiving his commission he visited the contracts section of the BBC and argued his case for extra payment. The official, to his surprise, offered him a sum not more but less than that he received for comparable work in the medium of radio. When he remonstrated the answer was: 'Oh, no, surely we pay more for radio than television for the writer in radio has to create the pictures, but in television we, the BBC, create the pictures and add them to the writer's work.' Certainly, whatever the contracts clerk had failed to grasp, she had at least identified the essentially collaborative nature of the new medium. Television was going to conjure into being, as cinema had done, a whole new range of crafts and skills, intellectual, artistic, organisational and technical, but no single one of them, in practice, would ever successfully assert its primacy.

In the technology of moving letters the printer had rapidly come to play a supporting role to the author. In the era of Gutenberg, society had developed a logocentric individualism at the heart of all its intellectual work. The printed text centred upon the author; all methods of study and instruction, the organisation of libraries, the laws of copyright, all systems of censorship and control were predicated upon the idea of textual composition as the work of named authors. The immense structural changes in society which were facilitated by the advent of moving letters occurred in a world in which the composition of text assumed the crucial moral role. Text had passed from being a mental to being a physical object; it became personal property. The distribution of text could be controlled through the licensing of printing. Industrially, text passed into the specialist hands of publishers, but the book culture of the last five centuries has been essentially a culture of authors. The film and television cultures, on the other hand, are definable more in terms of companies and institutions, production teams and partnerships. The texts, so to speak, of the age of moving images are the results of industrial processes – and these are themselves of course based ultimately upon the primary enabling function of the written word.

---

* This paper was originally delivered as one of the Wolfson College Lectures for 1985 and published in *The Written Word: Literacy in Transition*, edited by Gerd Baumann (Oxford: Clarendon Press, 1986), pp. 172-92.

The moving image media consist of a series of artefacts which bear the marks of an infinity of deals and compromises between an array of parties. All of these are in some sense creative (in that they involve the application of judgment as well as skill); all of them entail moral and often legal responsibilities; all of them are engaged, in some sense, in the act of communicating. To say, as some French film critics of the 1950s did, that the film director was or could be simply the author is to make an extremely controversial statement. The main British films of our time are producer-led rather than director-led, and in other times and places the writer or the editor could acquire the chief authorial role. It seems to me that it is the industrial nature of the technologies of audio and visual communication which provides their essential character. We are building in film, radio, the gramophone, and television a vast and new apparatus for creating and distributing meaning in society, an apparatus which is in constant evolution, but which must, in time, exert upon the sensorium a shift at least as great as that exerted by the printing press. The psychic changes are gradual and haphazard. They are observed by people whose own perceptual apparatus has itself passed through the change concerned.

It is interesting to look back at the first reception of moving images in the world, and to ask how someone immersed in the culture of the written word envisaged the changes wrought by the new medium. 'Last night I was in the Kingdom of the Shadows,' wrote Maxim Gorky on 4 July 1896 after seeing Louis Lumière's films at the Nizhni-Novgorod Fair. 'If you only knew how strange it is to be there. It is a world without sound, without colour. Everything there – the earth, the trees, the people, the water and the air – is dipped in monotonous grey. Grey rays of the sun across the grey sky, grey eyes in grey faces, and the leaves of the trees are ashen grey. It is not life but its shadow, it is not motion but its soundless spectre.'[1] This is not the excited discovery which one might have expected. Gorky was not the enthusiastic recipient of a revelation, but a rather disappointed sceptic. The fascination which had occupied many nineteenth-century minds, the dream of a medium which would reproduce life itself through a device of illusion, had been part of the attempt to break through the barriers of Victorian naturalism; the cinema pioneers had wanted to discover the secret of duplicating life, as Noël Burch puts it.[2] The Lumière brothers were doing something more than developing a mechanical device for making familiar photographic images move; they were, like many of the pioneers of cinema, trying to examine the nature of perception with a view to structuring or restructuring it. Marey had created various means for *describing* perception rather than reproducing images. He believed that Lumière had 'stripped away none of our illusions, added nothing to the potency of our vision'.[3] He believed that the research should abandon the 'representation of phenomena as we see them' and he concentrated thereafter on reproducing motion in slow form and on perfecting various kinds of stroboscopic photography. Eadweard Muybridge himself was attempting in his moving images of the running horse and the naked oarsman to analyse human perception rather than create a new device of entertainment or illusion.

The first ten years or so of cinema were dominated by a desire to do what Walter Ong has told us printing did to restructure thought. Lumière's craft developed from amateur photography; his films were an emanation in aesthetic terms from 1890s picture postcards, unposed street scenes, contrasting with the posed photographs taken by professionals and found in the home. The early film, like the postcard, was to be stared at, to be seen again and again until all the various elements converged in the mind. It was viewed quite differently from the later narrative film which was made to be seen once only. Primitive cinema was not a consumer culture. Lumière's projection began from a still frame. Gorky noticed and stressed this fact at his own viewing of the films:

> When the lights go out in the room . . . there suddenly appears on the screen a large grey picture, shadows of a bad engraving. As you gaze at it you see carriages, buildings and people in various poses, all frozen into immobility . . . but suddenly a strange flicker passes through the screen and the picture stirs to life. Carriages coming from somewhere in the perspective of the picture are moving straight at you, into the darkness in which you sit . . . all this moves, teems with life, and, upon approaching the edge of the screen, vanishes somewhere beyond it.[4]

It was not so much a case of Lumière not having learned how to frame correctly his picture of the workers leaving the factory, or the train entering the station, in order to make the information offered clear at first glance; it was a case of deliberate pursuit of a different aesthetic, according to Noël Burch, of offering a deliberately different mode of representation which was a decade later to be rejected by the new commercial cinema industry. Primitive cinema made you look at the world differently – differently from the photograph, differently from the medium which later emerged.

How different was the memory of the silent cinema in its classical period. Richard Griffith in his introduction to the postwar edition of Paul Rotha's *The Film Till Now* writes of the 'singular completeness' which silent cinema had acquired by that fateful year of 1929 when the medium was just about to disappear after the arrival of the talkies in 1927. 'To walk into a darkened theatre,' says Griffith, 'to focus upon a bright rectangle of moving light, to listen somewhat below the level of consciousness to music which was no longer good or bad in itself but merely in relation to what was on the screen, and above all to watch, in a kind of charmed hypnotic trance, a pattern of images which appeared and disappeared as capriciously as those pictures which involuntarily present themselves to the mind as it is dropping off to sleep – but which, also like those of the mind, gradually amount to a meaning of their own – this was an experience complete and unique, radically unlike that provided by the older arts or by the other new media of mass communication.'[5] As Béla Balázs wrote, looking back on the same moment in media history:

> The birth of film art led not only to the creation of new works of art but to the emergence of new human faculties with which to perceive and understand this new art . . . Now the film is about to inaugurate a new direction

in our culture . . . words do not touch the spiritual content of the pictures and are merely passing instruments of as yet undeveloped forms of art. Humanity is already learning the rich and colourful language of gesture, movement and facial expression. This is not a language of signs as a substitute for words – it is the visual means of communication, without intermediary of souls clothed in flesh.[6]

I am suggesting that a medium of communication is both an industrial technology and an attempt to reconstruct the process of cognition. In part each new technology is based upon an attempt to learn how human mental processes work but it ends invariably by reorganising those processes and thereby, I would add, influencing works of art or communication performed through other, earlier processes. The media have one history; they are an accumulation of cultural projects, not a mere succession. Within each medium there exists a series of genres and each of these has also in effect come into existence to reorganise thought or to appeal to latent emotional patterns or to satisfy a newly structured facility to absorb narrative or argument. Since the arrival of printing Western mankind has attempted through new apparatuses of observation and representation to possess the world ever more securely; the equipment for seeing the world has also been the equipment for coming to terms with it, for unravelling its mysteries, for co-opting the environment. Here is Pudovkin on film editing:

If we consider the work of the film director, then it appears that the active raw material is no other than those pieces of celluloid on which, from various viewpoints, the separate movements of the action have been shot . . . And thus the material of the film director consists not of real processes happening in real space and real time, but of those pieces of celluloid on which these processes have been recorded. This celluloid is entirely subject to the will of the director who edits it.[7]

Cinema has passed through a number of major technical watersheds, each of which has enabled a different kind of structuring of reality to take place; for example, with the development, under the directorial eye of Jean Renoir and Orson Welles, of deep focus, or the technique of *cinéma vérité* of the 1950s. Each stage has suggested an intensification of the fidelity with which the resulting illusion mirrors or suggests 'reality' but each has been a new illusionism, based upon a technical development in production and a new training of the eye on the part of the intended audience. We can today accept ways of arranging a narrative – see the extraordinary methods used by writer/director David Hare in the film *Wetherby* – which would have puzzled, perhaps dismayed Pudovkin or Eisenstein.

The Gutenbergian printing press had offered a similar restoration of seeming reality. It produced for simultaneous audiences the *ipsissima verba* of an original work. It offered an exact multiplication of knowledge. Through reproduction it offered a library without walls, as Erasmus put it, the complete restoration for one generation of the entire corpus of ancient work, which was previously available only in copies painfully constructed in the effort to preserve the information faster than the ravages of time consumed the material which held it. Knowledge ceased to be focused upon the restoration of that which had been known but lost or almost lost and became subject to a process of progressive augmentation through the easy comparison of available versions of texts. Where knowledge had been a matter of search, it became a matter for research. The roles of memory, imagination, speculation, and reasoned argument all shifted. Different mental qualities came to be prized. The intellectual skills were differentially revalued. Education has gradually caught up with new social tasks based upon the prevailing methods for storing and distributing information. 'Reading' and 'literary' have become dominant terms, ever-expanding metaphors which we are obliged to use when describing other cognitive skills, including the observation of moving image media. We speak today of 'film literacy' and 'reading pictures', suggesting that somehow the air of legitimacy acquired by the older skill should apply with appropriate amendment to the new medium. Each new technology since printing has realigned the senses and altered the nature of the images collected by the memory. Printing with its control over the language has not lost its supremacy.

The trouble with the bulk of public discussion of the media is that it is combined inexorably with discussion of social effects. Each new medium appears to possess, in the eyes of the generation whose perceptions were shaped by a previous medium or rather a previous formation of media, an uncanny and incalculable power over behaviour. The structure of public argument over cinema and over television has not been dissimilar to that over the fluoridation of water. These media – and others – have been presumed to be autonomous agents acting coercively upon the public, necessary and sufficient causes of stated consequences. Social science has rather tended to run after the discussion in search of something to do and has become inextricably caught up in the endless regressions, analysing increasingly subtle interactions between direct media effects and gratifications.

Radio, cinema and television have all taken so firm a grip upon our culture that it is easy to assign too great a causality to them, indeed to 'blame' them too automatically for every other discernible phenomenon within society. So pervasive is this easy rhetoric of social causation that it has become today almost impossible to find a way in which to discuss these media without automatically contributing to the loose but accumulating reservoir of conjecture. Every medium and every genre together with every stage within their evolution leave their impact upon the sensorium, even those which precede literacy and which therefore leave no physical reminder. But that is merely to say that they alter the opportunities of thought and feeling, not the conclusions. One may try out a very distant example, drawn from the dawn of the chirographic age. Eric Havelock[8] shows how the pre-Homeric epic worked as a tribal encyclopaedia, expressed through formulaic language and repetitions; a complete perceptual apparatus was allowed to linger into the age of the scribal culture and indeed engaged in confrontation with the new educational philosophy of the age of Plato; Homer's versified bardic encyclopaedia survives today, still metaphorically powerful while interacting with millennia of further modes of thought, feeling and imagery. The process of change is one of circularity rather than displacement. A media system exists within a set of social purposes and offers its own structure of feeling, designed to intermesh with a perceptual system.

Rather than visualising media history as a series of technological breakthroughs one might choose to envisage it as a series of technical breakdowns as the apparatus of memory and cognition fails to cope within the genres, forms, and devices available. Havelock describes the revolution in Greek culture which made Platonism inevitable: the sheer social necessity to move from concrete to abstract modes of thought exerted its impact upon the old poetic form and upon the techniques of inscription. He describes the break with the poetised tradition 'with its habit of emotional identification with persons and stories of heroes, and with the play of action and episode. Instead the philosopher is one who wants to learn how to restate these in a different language of isolated abstractions, conceptual and formal: a language which insists on emptying events and actions of their immediacy, in order to break them up and arrange them in categories, thus imposing the rule of principle in place of happy intuition . . .'[9]. There was a need, perhaps driven by conscious economic requirement, for a new kind of thinking, a new psychic activity which the intellectual techniques of the bardic age prohibited or inhibited. 'In the Homeric or pre-Homeric period,' writes Havelock, preservation of the corpus of knowledge 'had to rely on the living memories of human beings, and if these were to be effective in maintaining the tradition in a stable form, the human beings must be assisted in their memorisation of the living word by every possible mnemonic device which could print this word indelibly upon the consciousness. The devices that were explored were first the employment of standard rhythms engaging all possible bodily reflexes, and second reduction of all experience to a great story or connected series of such stories.'[10]

It is possible to track the shifting of consciousness from medium to medium only with great difficulty, since it is that very point of psychic change that those directly concerned are keenest to deny. One may cite the way in which oral traditions were repressed at the point of the introduction of printing and substantially lost. The new cognition appears at a different point in the society. The cineastes despise television at first. Newspaper journalism scorns radio until their professionalisms merge. The new medium arrives as toy or irritant, usurper or rebel. Over thirty years ago Béla Balázs wrote of the coming of silent cinema a generation before that:

The forms of expression of the silent films developed gradually, but the rate of development was fast enough and together with it the public developed the ability to understand the new form-language. We were witnesses not only of the development of a new art but of the development of a new sensibility, a new understanding, a new culture in its public . . . Many million people sit in the picture houses every evening and purely through vision, experience happenings, characters, emotions, moods, even thoughts, without the need for many words. For words do not touch the spiritual content of the pictures and are merely passing instruments of as yet undeveloped forms of art.[11]

The evidence for such change in the sensorium is hard to track down, even harder to establish in the form of satisfactory proof. One would have to say, in the case of film and television, that constant evolution in directorial technique, in the social and economic context of these media and in their inner and outer technologies (that is, the means both of production and distribution) are reflected in a number of concomitant changes in perception. The addition of sound to cinema for example transformed the medium's imagistic possibilities. Colour, anamorphic lenses, computer animation, each has opened up a whole further range of visual possibility, and left audiences trained to apply to the world a growing repertoire of modes of seeing.

Television as a domestic medium has altered all the dimensions of distance within the communications processes of today, in absorbing within itself the whole international archive of cinema; television and video wrestle with partially rival cognitive systems, each frequently taking a step towards convergence, each discovering a new exclusive potentiality. I am not certain that I agree with all of Walter Ong's list of resemblances between the new orality, as he labels our age, and primary orality: he lists 'its participatory mystique, its fostering of a communal sense, its concentration on the present moment, and even its use of formulas'.[12] The moving image media can operate also without a participatory sensibility and their formulas can shift and change very rapidly. They foster a sense of their own continuousness; their works follow in cumulative succession as if in mutual response. Television is a continuous process of transmission, almost a single text in itself, urging us to remain with the flow or be somehow excluded from the essence of what is really happening. Its essential trick – and that of radio before it – is to imply that it represents the completer version of reality, from which one's absence can only be exceptional. It is the opposite of escapist. It is the absent member of the audience who is the absconder. Perhaps it was rather like that if one missed the public recitals of pre-Homeric bardic culture.

Victor Hugo argued that the printed book supplanted the role of the cathedral because it took over the task of carrying the spirit of the people. But it was the book which in a sense splintered the medieval cathedral, as a message-bearing medium into the opinionated diversity of the printed word. To quote from Béla Balázs again, printing 'made the faces of men illegible . . . So much could be read from paper that the method of conveying meaning by facial expression fell into desuetude'.[13] In cinema and television the psyche is being offered a return to cathedral, forum, preprinted text, a return to the reading of human feature and gesture, to the transcultural rather than the intracultural dissemination of signs. But the return is within the spiral. We are the cognitive heirs of an accumulating sign tradition. And it is the specific nature of the prevailing electronic media of today which must be influencing us by altering the prevailing modes of perception.

The communications systems taken together constitute a great marshalling of the facilities of perception of individuals and of societies, but among them they entail the placing of the senses in a hierarchy: in other words the media impose a bias upon the relative status of the senses and thus influence the content of memory, which in time further amplifies the prevailing patterning of the sensorium. As subjects of experience, as potential knowers of that which is to be known, we are to that extent prestructured, though in a context of constant change. Human perception thus enjoys its own history, of which media history is a part.

The media strain and filter the information which passes through them and to some extent our non-media experience is rechecked by us through the filter of the media – and other institutions of society. But each medium has its own special experiential mesh and these have been applied in practice not separately but successively in history. Our senses learned to cope with the narrative structure of a Henry James novel and absorbed it through the multi-sensing apparatus of Henry James's sentence structure. Today the Henry James vision is available, in the case of several of his novels, by way of cinema, which completely reorganises the narrative but still offers us the characters of James and something of his artistic intention. Our memories generally can differentiate the two experiences; we might forget in which novel a character appears but we seldom mistake the memory of the film for the memory of the novel. We might decide that both are independently excellent. We might completely reshape our view of the novel under the impact of the remembered faces and costumes of the actors in the film. But though one experience is laid upon the other, they remain memories of separate media experiences, which have passed through a different arrangement of the senses, a different programming of the senses.

A number of students of communication history have compiled great historiographic systems mapping out the media epochs into three or four grand stages. Walter Ong's is certainly the most developed of these and in his book *The Presence of the Word*[14] he labels four great ages, oral, chirographic, typographic, electronic, each of them framing the epistemic possibilities of its time. What I would wish to emphasise is the extent to which each has completed a task, a complete human perceptual project, while opening up new tasks. Printing, for example, enabled us to acquire a cumulative view of knowledge, to learn the techniques of comparative criticism of different versions of the same information. With printing the whole world was quickly to acquire a calendar, a time system, inter-language dictionaries, maps and sailing charts, and, more to the point, an enduring certainty about the necessity of such things. Printing provided us with a certain training of the senses, an accepted filtering and arrangement of the knowledge that resulted and a set of permanent needs and latencies which later media have not and cannot displace or expunge. There may – or may not – be fewer people who can read today than fifty years ago but typographic culture has left its mark none the less, not just upon the skills of the senses but ineradicably upon human culture.

To dismiss the standardising power of typographic culture as 'the middle-class literacy approved by the American establishment', as Robert Pattison does in his book entitled *On Literacy*,[15] is to miss the point. The standardisation of language was an achievement without which the technologies of the electronic era would have been impossible. Pattison says: 'Electronic media are a powerful stimulant to the development of a literacy centred on the spoken word. They threaten established literacy by offering a continuous stream of vernacular raised to the level of popular art – an art without the constraints of correct English . . . Established American literacy with its emphasis on mechanical skills and its assertion of the limitations of language thwarts man's desire to feel himself fully represented in words.'[16] Let me pass over the curious modern tendency to use the words 'Americans' when the word 'people' is possibly what is meant. Pattison is guilty as are many of the apostles of the 'new literacy' or 'new literacies' of a misapplication of their liberationist instincts. The culture of voice and sound, of natural language in what Pattison calls the age of rock is built upon the culture which arose from the standardisation of language and of writing. The genitive apostrophe may be as dead as a dodo, as he says, but only in a society which has acquired other linguistic means, just as secure, for establishing the relationship between objects. A language can go off the Latin standard, as a currency can go off the gold standard, but there exists some substitute machinery for setting up norms if the language is to survive on being taught to people with other tongues. The dictionaries have been written and someone needs to use them – without necessarily imposing a tyranny upon others. Literacies, so called, live in succession and new ones depend upon old ones even if careless of them.

The quest for objective knowledge – of which typographic culture was an essential prerequisite – has not departed nor will it, however many decide to opt for the 'literacy of the ear', as Pattison calls it. Chirographic culture, as Havelock shows us in his account of pre-Homeric society, never managed quite to cut the link between the knower and the known. Writing arrived as an extension of speech; it was print that offered a substitute for speech. It imposed a standardised system, for ever, upon the task of communicating knowledge. The knowledge thus acquired and stored became accessible in other times and places and, moreover, set up expectations that the defining essence of knowledge was thus.

It could be argued that our rapidly accumulating repertoire of electronic gadgetry – from the telegraph and radio to videodisc, digital computer, and satellite – places us in a kind of transitional era between the typographic and some super-electronic stage of communication. It seems to me that the implications of the electronic stage are already becoming clear, though its hardware is far from complete. The essence of the new stage in communications is digitisation, the breaking down of all information into the basic unit of the bit, a mathematical standardisation applicable to all things which can be reduced to the condition of information. It is not dissimilar in some ways to the Gutenbergian discovery of moving letters, though it is much simpler. All objects of the senses can be labelled in terms of strings of ones and zeros, and so can phenomena of nature such as signals passing through the electromagnetic spectrum. The striking difference between the Gutenbergian and the binary-digital system is that the latter is content to register the certain from the probable. The perfection of a digital recording to the human ear is in fact constructed from readings of the waves produced by the instruments through equipment which is content to calculate the resulting sound on the basis of statistical sampling. Marey's primitive cinema devices were based upon the exploitation of Plateau's discovery of the persistence of vision, the use of a human weakness to produce a perfect illusion. Digitisation offers a similar illusion of perfection of information based upon registering the approximate.

Before the beginning of the electronic era, the various mechanical techniques of communication extended our senses in range, but did not, as it were, offer us a new sense. In the era of primary orality hearing was the chief of the five senses, where perhaps previously the sense of touch had been predominant. Hearing operates across space, beyond the line of sight, around corners, through physical substances. Writing, of course, placed emphasis upon the sense of sight; the exchange of information by way of writing was a substitute for speech and hearing in certain circumstances, and with the arrival of printing, both of words and pictures, very large quantities of information could be made available without physical presence. The various media of communication of course work through a combination of senses and refer back constantly to the data provided by other senses than the one that may predominate at a given moment.

The reproduction of images through still and moving photography provides a substitute storage for visual memory, but also offers the evidence of vicarious seeing, just as typography offers the evidence of vicarious knowing: the media enable us to employ the senses of others, but linked to our memory. No medium before telecommunications, however, that is, prior to the electronic stage, could offer us through our senses information which is carried only by means of a sense which human beings do not possess: the sensing of the electromagnetic spectrum beyond the range of frequencies registered as sight, hearing and touch. The electronic therefore offers us a new set of dimensions to information, by transmuting that information back into data retainable in the human memory and accessible through the human senses. It is the principle of digitisation married to the science of telecommunications which offers the particular extension of or substitution for the senses which is occurring in the electronic age. We are in transition to that age but are far enough into it to register at least the theoretical implications.

The mechanics of the Renaissance helped to recalculate the world for us. The universe which the perceptual tools of recent centuries helped us to compile offers a completely different conceptualisation of the environment of time and space within which the senses – and the memory and imagination to which they are tied – operate. Where in medieval thought the human being had been a microcosm, the epistemic link with the macrocosm, the new sense order of the typographic world left mankind as a perceptual apparatus, self-conscious but lost within a different, now an infinite universe designed by Newton with the help of Galileo. The human sensorium, freed from the constraints of both concentric and anagogic views of the world reached out for one perceptual artifice after another with which to explore the new spatial extension. That left the self to expand upon the newly enfranchised senses. The instruments of knowledge which now filtered the world's data both trained the senses and offered it new categorisations of knowledge, from biology to economics, from physics to psychology.

That reconstruction of the individual-in-the-universe was completed within the confines of typographic culture, before the electronic revolutions of the 20th century. The medium of print had helped to structure the senses in such a way as to pave the way for a new preoccupation with the self. The idea of the personality was the logical extension of the sensorium of the typographic age. Freud could later discover a new enabling substratum, the foundations of the new self, in the unconscious.

The structuring of the senses which the knowledge techniques of the 20th century facilitated has been aided by sources of information which go beyond the senses. The moving image technologies, radio, the gramophone, have continued the work of extending sight and sound, but the electronic media of the latter part of the century are offering something more. The new apparatus which reconstructs information in terms of binary oppositions changes the nature of the whole environment of information.

The new aesthetic discoveries of the early years of the century prepared the senses for the multi-perspectives of electronic culture; in Morse code there had been a rehearsal of the great digital transformation of codes which has arrived now in the 1980s. Mathematics and physics underwent transformations under the impact of Einstein, Heisenberg, Russell, Hilbert, which urged new conceptions of time and space to take over in the realm of memory and imagination as much as in the laboratory. The innovation in art of the early years of the century accelerated the process of transferring the new concepts to the realm of the senses. The scheme of the Renaissance had shown how to reproduce the dimensions of space in illusion within rectangles of canvas, but now it became possible for art to take on the task of offering a complete reconceptualisation of the world.

Simultaneously in the field of language studies nineteenth-century concepts of philology were being replaced and a series of language analogies made themselves available in the human sciences as models for the decoding of information. Being and consciousness separated, linked henceforth through language; consciousness came increasingly to be seen as a culturally constructed phenomenon, functioning within these new conceptualisations. Moreover, it was now accessible to the world of the economy through advertising and publicity which came more and more to be seen as central to these new cultural circumstances. Where a nineteenth-century radical would see the physicality of work as economically basic, the late-twentieth-century counterpart would increasingly emphasise the economic role of the senses; the emotional and cultural identity of human beings, as much as their labour power, had become their link to society.

The new information machines and their attendant institutions intrude deeply into the self, reshaping emotional and cultural outlook, redefining perceptual functions. Television and video arrived not really as toys and distractions, as the cinema and phonograph had done, but as workhorses of the psyche, offering as it were a complete service, swamping the separate genres of information with the sheer pervasiveness and omnipresence of the electronic moving image, searching out every issue, every place, every event, every personality, in order to build the new overwhelming perspective into the sensorium.

What is now offered in the information revolution, as the complex web of late-twentieth-century changes are apt to be labelled, is at root a digital revolution. And it is allied to the next set of changes which are occurring as the medium of television itself undergoes the process of digitisation. If we are to envisage the impact upon print culture of these alterations in the methods of information carriage, storage and transfer, we have somehow to put together in our minds some of the issues of perceptual change, together with some of the strands of technological evolution, and add some notion of the dynamic forces causing both breakdown and demand in other industries.

Digitisation offers further exponential increases in the rapidity of information processing, in the accuracy with which signals can be transmitted. Students of computer development are now suggesting that the 1990s will see a further leap forwards in the capacity of the simple data storage available domestically. With the use of cryogenically cool circuitry, computation times could be cut back to trillionths of a second. Furthermore, the arrival of such long-predicted devices as Josephson Junction Computers could reduce really large-scale computer power to suitcase capacity, thus placing large computational power in the hands of individuals; thus opens up the possibility of the intelligent book, a portable device capable of access to great libraries of material, but capable also of interrogating that material, carrying out some of the tasks of critical comparison of data. These are all aspects of what has come to be labelled the fifth-generation computer. Such devices might also be capable of making full transposition between print and speech, thereby bringing about the final stages of convergence between the Gutenbergian and the electronic modes of information storage. It is always wise to be sceptical of too grandiose predictions, and the speech possibilities of the fifth-generation computer have perhaps begun to be overcanvassed. We need to hold back the technological predictions within an approach which concentrates upon the fundamental potentialities of digitisation as a principle of organising information, while permitting other questions to be treated as issues of quantitative rather than qualitative change.

Let us look again at the Gutenbergian system for reproducing text through moving letters. Essentially, it relied on placing identical blocks of information at different points in space and retaining them through time, almost indefinitely. The new survival ability of information meant that cataloguing became increasingly difficult but concomitantly necessary. During the typographic era the development both of new subject systems and classification systems took place on a scale suitable, at first at least, for catching up with the rate of evolution of knowledge itself. The progressive augmentation of knowledge accelerated through subject classification. The unit of information in the typographic era has been the book, retrievable under two or three keyboards such as author's name, title, subject-matter. Now, with digitisation as the basic principle for capturing information, the possibilities for accessing information are increasing very considerably. The unit of information is reduced to a single nugget of knowledge, a word even, and this in an era when the search for information has been made increasingly difficult through the sheer quantity and flow of new data, not merely at the level of specialised research but also at the level of ordinary life. The search for an item of data to do with social welfare, the search for an address or a telephone number, for a medical record, or an insurance policy or a criminal's fingerprints, all such quests for information are becoming overwhelmed by the bulk of data available, at least where these functions have not already been subjected to the process of digitisation.

The telephone directory is a printed volume, or set of volumes. That is, it looks like a book, is printed as a book and has to be produced, bound, and physically delivered to homes and offices. The telephone directory is a typical example of the Gutenbergian mode of information: its existence is predicated upon the idea of multiplying the number of physical copies until they approximate to the size of the probable audience. It is still a convenient system for many genres of written material and will long remain so. It is a good distribution device for poetry, for the novel, for certain ranges of educational materials. It is not, however, any longer an appropriate device for disseminating perishable ranges of information including much scientific research. Digitisation has already occurred at the production level; it is but one leap to transfer the digital signal to an electronic mode of distribution. And that is what, in due course, must happen. With the arrival of ever cheaper systems of information transfer – most probably the optic fibre attached to public videotex systems – the telephone directory is an urgent candidate for the Gutenbergian scrap-heap. So are timetables and classified data of many kinds – not all kinds, but many. Many of the ranges of information contained in the newspaper could be effectively transferred elsewhere and, indeed, are being developed through videotex.

We have now passed into the era in which every citizen is familiar with the principle of manipulating digital information, through the devices of teletext and videotex, in airline and travel offices, public libraries, schools, and elsewhere. Before The principle can be applied wholesale a further transformation in attitude and perspective must take place. For digitised information still runs counter to established habits of mind. In need we reach automatically for a book. The personal computer is still too small a thing to transform our attitudes to information – although it is training the imagination.

Technology is suggesting two possible directions, the first towards a merger of the printed word and the moving image, the second away from the printed word to the screen. The two are by no means mutually exclusive. Nearly all printed words, books, newspapers, magazines or invoices, pass through at least one stage of digitisation. Hot metal type is very rapidly disappearing and only in the conventional typewriter does the moving letter system survive significantly in the industrial economies. The word processor, as

44

it transforms office work, will ensure that a further range of printed words will undergo this basic enabling process. The digitisation of the moving image is still in its infancy, but certain elements of the television process are now changing to the digital mode. Gradually digitisation will spread until it takes over all television, at the level of production. At the level of distribution the digitisation of television will take much longer since the bulk of investment in the existing television system is held not in the studio but in the home and the transformation of reception will take a great deal of time, especially given the establishment of video. However, the digital 'compact' sound disc is becoming a familiar object; the distinction between high-quality sound reproduction devices and high-definition television images via disc is not a great one and at some stage these might merge, possibly within a decade. Already the videodisc, which has had a very slow and shaky start, had been identified as an equally good medium for text, still and moving image, as for a combination of all three. One can envisage within a very few years the arrival, perhaps in rather specialist areas of work, of a combined text-and-video disc, a circular video-book if you like.

The real problem in the information business is the lack of development of display systems. The cathode ray tube has not undergone a fundamental redesign for many decades, although various improvements to this bulky object have indeed taken place. During the last decade and a half there have been various crises in the newspaper industry, associated partly with the high cost of newsprint, a politically sensitive commodity at the best of times, which has now run foul of the ecological lobby also. It would not be beyond the bounds of feasibility before the end of the century for some kind of general merger of display systems to take place – the arrival of a flexible disc or rectangular screen which could display all of the digitised materials. This would have considerable impact upon both the television and newspaper or publishing industries, but in the production area of both the change would be gradual. The impact on booksellers, and on newspaper and record distributors would be enormous and rapid. Happily for them, they seem all to be diversifying into one another's domains, so that publishers, independent video production companies, chains of bookstores, and newsagents are increasingly aware of their collective problems, aspirations, fears and opportunities.

I am not predicting the arrival of some new object, the 'post-book' or 'post-television' medium. Rather, I am suggesting the evolution of a range of new objects for the carriage of information, some of them able to function as devices of interrogation, of access and input as well. I do not believe – exactly why would be difficult to say – that the book as such will disappear. In one important sense, of course, the book already has disappeared, in that its production system has been in recent years completely reconstructed through the use of computerised typesetting. But it continues to look like a book and to be used like a book. However, one can now begin to imagine a different object which, though perhaps still looking like a book, could combine moving images with readable text. It might even have pages though it is more likely to be some kind of semi-conductor slab.

I have not tried to predict or describe the future of the printed word, but to give an account of the context within which that future will be determined. As media change is accelerating, the apparently simple questions of the last ten years themselves seem to be changing. We used to ask, will the book survive television? We now find that the question is rather: in what forms will printed words, pictures, and moving images converge? What kinds of new media will be distributed widely, and what genres of material will they contain? The greatest determinant of the content of a new medium is, of course, the inherited culture of the previous ones. Typographic culture by its very nature has great survival power; its materials fill our world. The institutions of education, information and government that emerged from the Gutenberg mode of information processing are equally resistant to rapid change.

There is a story that when Mr Attlee entered Downing Street in 1945, one of his younger aides suggested that No. 10 should acquire one of the new telex machines, just then on the market. Attlee dismissed the idea. The Foreign Office had plenty of clerks who could bring their telegrams across at any time. But he did agree to have one machine on a month's approval, and one afternoon noticed up-to-the-minute cricket scores clattering out of it. He proposed that the telex be retained, but always thereafter referred to it as 'the cricket machine'. We accept new modes and new technologies when they are justified by established needs. It takes time for them to generate new needs. The next generation of computers does indeed promise an intriguing fusion of the spoken and the written word, the ability to transmute languages from the written mode in one tongue to the spoken in another, and even to reverse the process. It offers us books that will converse with us, movie screens that behave like the pages of books. But such devices only emerge at a point of interaction, when the cultural and perceptual needs generated by established media stimulate more dimly felt new desires. It is an emotional as much as an industrial question that is raised. The real revolution in information is a revolution in perception as well as in the material base.

Notes

[1] J. Leyda, *Kino*, (London: Allen and Unwin, 1959), p. 407.
[2] Noël Burch, 'Charles Baudelaire v. Dr Frankenstein', in *Afterimage*, 8/9, Spring 1981, pp. 4-23.
[3] Georges Sadoul, *French Cinema* (London: Falcon Press, 1953), p. 100.
[4] Leyda, *Kino*, p. 407.
[5] Paul Rotha, *The Film Till Now* (London: Jonathan Cape, 1944).
[6] Béla Balázs, *Theory of the Film: Character and Growth of a New Art* (London: Dobson, 1952), p. 41.
[7] V. I. Pudovkin, *Film Technique* (London: George Newnes, 1933), p. 56.
[8] Eric A. Havelock, *Preface to Plato* (Oxford: Basil Blackwell, 1963).
[9] Ibid., p. 287.
[10] Ibid., p. 198.
[11] Balázs, *Film*, p. 41.
[12] Walter J. Ong, *Orality and Literacy* (London: Methuen, 1982), p. 136.
[13] Balázs, *Film*, p. 41.
[14] Walter J. Ong, *The Presence of the Word* (New Haven: Yale University Press, 1967).

15 Robert Pattison, *On Literacy: The Politics of the Word from Homer to the Age of Rock* (London: Oxford University Press, 1982).
16 Ibid., p. 202.

4

The Public Interest*

Individuals gratify their own interests; but something more is thereby accomplished, which is latent in their action though not present in their consciousness.

Hegel

There is a felt dimension of public interest in virtually all private action: from smoking to the divorce and marriage laws, from literacy to childcare, we constantly find ourselves judging private actions and personal proclivities as if we were thinking for society as a whole. But when we say that a person is acting in or against the public interest, or that a proposed government measure is 'in the public interest' or that the operations of a commercial company represent a breach of 'public interest', is there a real entity in our mind corresponding to this notion of a 'public'? Where are we placing ourselves in relation to the rest of society and to our neighbours when we use the term? These questions have become irksome, yet urgent, in this era of worldwide deregulation, especially in the burgeoning fields of telecommunications and information technology. For, quite suddenly in historical terms, a number of familiar political issues have switched their emphasis. Where the main actors in a number of countries saw government intervention as the instrument of public benefit, they now tend to place their faith in a revival of market forces and the interplay of individual motivation as a surer path to collective benefit. This is not merely the defence of the rights of private persons – it is a statement about the means for guaranteeing the general good.

This essay will consider how such arguments have been deployed, particularly in respect to telecommunications in the context of an inherited set of discourses, which have been rehearsed over several generations, concerning the public interest in the management of utilities.

All human societies have a way of expressing generalised collective needs. Each possesses an appropriate term to describe and account for its collective historic national, doctrinal or regional identity. The art and culture of each society contains in myth or legend representations of that collectivity, often linked with its religious belief. In Western culture this 'public' sphere is felt as

---

* Published originally in *New Directions in Telecommunications Policy, Vol. 1: Regulatory Policy: Telephony in Mass Media* (Durham, N.C.: Duke University Press, 1989). Subsequently published in *Intermedia*, Vol. 17, No. 2, June-July 1989, pp. 10-24.

something of an aberration, something less than, or added to, the society; we see rights and obligations as primarily based upon individuals and their families.

There are countless versions of the public sphere and diverse ways of expressing and envisaging it. We have today almost entirely eradicated the image of 'Christendom' as a supra-national and supra-continental cause but the term 'Islam' still expresses the goals and faith of a whole string of societies, which feel politically and emotionally compelled towards a sense of unison, above schism and sect. Pan-Africanism, Pan-Arabism and the European movement are other examples in our own time of movements which endeavour to create new contexts for the expression of the collective needs and goals of large territorial groups.

Every age in history creates new kinds of political emotions and finds appropriate ways of representing the interests of large groups; emerging terminology expresses the pursuit of mutual benefit through collective sacrifice and altruism. When we in the West speak of the public interest we are, half-consciously, groping for a way of referring to something highly valued, a telos or collective good normally standing in opposition to, or above, other legitimate demands and interests. We acknowledge the potential of intangible ways in which our lives may be enhanced; we recognise the presence of a public sphere which does not correspond to the mere aggregation of the desires of living individuals.

Our society of the West has in recent times accorded even higher value to the economic activity of individuals and when we speak of the 'public interest' in a Western context we are indulging in an attempt to reassert the dimension of the collective within that culture of individualism. The term 'public interest' in itself contains subtextually a sense of the existence of a natural conflict between individual and public goods, between the natural strivings of people for their own betterment and the social benefit which might ensue from a partial or temporary denial of self-gain.

There are, of course, a whole diversity of meanings for 'public interest' in the context of any single society. There is one special form of public interest entailed in projects designed to protect individuals against harms which are invisible to the victim. Environmental pollution is the characteristic contemporary example; it entails denying the economic rights or opportunities of individuals and companies in favour of the health interests of everyone. Not everyone benefits immediately, but all benefit in the longer run, by surviving. There are losers in the achievement even of this particular form of public interest. There exists a limit to the economic freedom accorded to individuals beyond which the good of all has to take precedence. None of us wants to drink polluted water. None of us wants to suffer the consequences of a depleted ozone layer, even though we may disagree as to the immediacy of any present danger. The supreme example of this manifestation of public interest is of course defence. Where human beings have to work together to preserve their very society or to protect their health, a strong and very fundamental sense of public interest comes into operation. Some such areas (for example, control of water supplies) have come into question in the course of the present political re-evaluations, but in general the retreat from government regulation has not come to affect such crucial aspects of society.

There is a somewhat different form of public interest where the collectivity of individuals can never hope to benefit, except in a very long-term, tribal sense. Most people agree, for example, that a society enjoying universal education is superior to one which does not. However, not all individuals would agree to contribute to the cost of achieving this in the immediate present. Universal education, therefore, enjoys a weaker, though still widespread, support as a collective public good. Where it is achieved it is not on a basis of universal acclamation, but on the basis of the coercion of a minority. Society as a whole, over the course of time, values the phenomenon of universal education. There are many instances of public interest discourses of this kind, which are pursued in the political sphere generally through long periods of public debate and persuasion. They are not an expression of survival needs but are seen as desirable objectives in societies which have passed through a certain political evolution, not necessarily a radical one. German and Italian cities and states developed sophisticated requirements for opera, theatre and art galleries, at a time when the United Kingdom and the United States continued to regard these entirely as matters for private commerce. Societies have to acquire a certain view of cultural activity and of the public interest before providing arts facilities comes to seem a proper function for the state to undertake.

In the course of history, our society has reinterpreted and concretised these and other manifestations of the debate about the nature of the public and its 'interest'. In fields as diverse as transportation, education, public health, care of the deprived and provision for the arts, Western societies have permitted the notion of public interest to spread, sometimes leading to the formation of public services for the free or inexpensive provision of the benefit concerned. Sometimes these services have seemed to be more appropriately organised through the use of government-regulated utilities where the enterprise itself remains privately owned. It began to seem desirable and economically possible to express the developing views of the nature and objectives of the public interest in a wide variety of fields which had been previously considered the domain of individual need or individual taste. All Western societies have passed through a long era of such thought and policy-making. Gradually the state has come to accept the responsibility for carrying out the roles assigned to the 'public', whether directly operating a necessary service, regulating its operations within the private sector, or merely making national or regional policy in the field concerned. During the course of the century, a vast proportion of economic activity in all Western societies (irrespective of whether they are formally wedded to utilitarian or socialist doctrine) has been swept into public discourses, if not into direct state ownership.

Today, however, Western societies are beginning to consider the argument fundamentally, sometimes to unravel it or turn it on its head. In its new version, people have come to question whether the benefit of the collectivity of individuals is, in practice, fulfilled by the attempt to meet needs on a collective basis. The discourse of consumerism has replaced in arena after arena the discourse of public interest leading to ownership or regulation. If society is conceived as an overlapping series of providers of goods and services and recipients of these services, not divided by class or rank, but by an infinity of criss-crossed lines of responsibility, then the nature of the 'public' shifts accordingly. We are all consumers and we nearly all have something to offer other consumers. There is thus an important shift taking place in our whole concept of the public in Western economies as they pass into a new phase of evolution.

There has long been, for example, a public interest argument in favour of municipally run buses in certain countries and regions in order to ensure that people at all levels of income enjoy cheap and reliable transport, arguable in the interests of welfare and of the economy as a whole; there now comes into place a reverse argument, still a 'public interest' argument, to the effect that the same individuals would benefit more from a purely market-based, non-regulated, transportation system in which privately operated bus and train services offer reduction in fares and improved service. Both versions of the argument can be rehearsed as public interest positions, not as 'basic survival' positions but as examples of the weaker public interest position – the one which is most susceptible to the contemporary shift from 'public service' to 'consumer satisfaction' thinking.

There exists in the field of telecommunications an important instance which demonstrates the kinds of ambiguity and tension hanging between the two kinds of public interest mentioned. Telephone service is a better service the more individuals have access to a telephone. It is better financially as well as socially. Universality of service has therefore long been a key policy in telephone administrations, whether run by private companies or by the state – a prime example of public interest discourse leading to the establishment of state-run or state-regulated companies.

However, in the context of the new telecommunication technologies, a different view has come to prevail: the process of developing new services is accelerated not by, or not only by, the pursuit of universality, but by encouraging equipment suppliers and individual subscribers to make individual choices of equipment and innovative adjuncts to the basic service. Here the industrial need conflicts with the pure consumer interest. So crucial is the new technology of information to the wider process of retooling and computerising Western economies that great government and judicial pressure has been brought to bear upon the existing corporations working in the field to ensure that they compete vigorously and innovatively. A new kind of public good has been invoked which reverses the logic of the previous view. The new public good is an economic one: we all benefit from living in a competitive and updated economy and the degree of benefit we gain from government intervention designed to free the market is greater than the gain from society continuing to pursue a welfarist view of provision. To achieve the new public interest entails the coercion of a minority, those whose economic interest, whether they are suppliers or customers, is satisfied through a continuation of the previous welfarist system. Thus subscribers have to acquire their own

51

instruments, for example, where previously they were supplied, but they now have access to a diverse market of differentiated kinds of instrument.

Telecommunications in all its manifestations throws up issues of this kind. This is partly because the existence of the state was one of the necessary pre-requisites for the establishment of the earliest telecommunicated services – the telegraph; it meant that telecommunications became a very early theatre for the rehearsal of modern arguments concerning public interest and society equity. The administration of telecommunications became inseparable from the administration of defence and land-usage planning, and also from the more generalised debates about how to regulate markets, about the nature of 'natural monopolies'. The history of the telegraph and its offspring acts as a kind of commentary on the history of modern ideas about the nature of the public interest.

In many countries today, we are witnessing a considerable alteration in the prevailing public philosophy concerning the role of the state in industrial organisation and in the provision of cultural facilities; the era knows itself as an age of deregulation, aided by a widespread reinstatement of liberal economic theory. Quotations from Mill and the Utilitarians have become suddenly plentiful again in political speeches and in the public addresses of business leaders. 'People understand their own business and their own interests better, and care for them more, than the government does, or can be expected to do,' says Mill in *Principles of Political Economy*. This view is more deeply rooted than its expression in a mere economic context suggests. It emerges from Mill's beliefs about the nature of the autonomous self: '. . . there is a part of the life of every person who has come to years of discretion, within which the individuality of that person ought to reign uncontrolled either by any other person or by the public collectively.'

The modern movement in economic belief borrows its inspiration more than any direct influence, however, from these perfectionist views of Victorian liberalism, although parallels of expression are uncannily consonant with the deregulators of the 1980s. 'The mass of adults are so well acquainted with their own interests and so much disposed to pursue them that no compulsion or restraint put upon them by others for the purpose of promoting their interest can really promote them,' sounds off James Fitzjames Stephen in his tract *Liberty, Equality, Fraternity*. The present-day movement has far more than a political antiquarianism behind it, more than the passionate echoes of an easier world, and it would be wrong to assume that these ideas are actually the ones driving forward the changes in telecommunications. The new thinking about telecommunications and the revival in liberal economic theory are synergetic but coincidental, not derivable from the same source.

The deregulatory movement in telecommunications has much to do with the sheer material necessities of the new information technology as it begins to exert its impact upon the networks and switching systems, upon new ways for distributing and storing signals, than it has with the revival of nineteenth-century economic doctrine or, rather, with our contemporary attempt to purify economic thinking of the Keynesian dross, accumulating over two generations.

The reorganisation of the telecommunications industry has now become a continuous process with no particular end in sight; it is being undertaken in the light of a felt understanding of the public interest as much as of new ways to accumulate corporate profit. Two main US agencies – the Department of Justice and the Federal Communications Commission (FCC) – have embarked upon the crusade in the light of their different remits, to keep competition open and untrammelled by the fusion of diverse interests within a single corporation and to regulate the usage of public airways in the interests of diversity. The corporations concerned are by no means always gratified by the processes through which they are obliged to pass: the two agencies between them delve more deeply into internal corporate affairs in the era of deregulated competition than in the preceding era of regulated monopolies.

There is a structural political drive behind the movement, as much as a drive to profit for its own sake. In US telecommunications, the deregulation processes centre on the goal of ensuring the presence of a technically dynamic industry; they are a means to this end rather than a purely ideological objective. The United States feels that it has to measure up to the forward thrust of West Germany and Japan. Deregulation, the removal of government agencies from the process of management, takes place alongside the confirmation of government in its role as anti-monopolistic goad. In the United States there has been a similar fusion of the ideological with the new industrial practice. Economic thinking has been transformed in favour of private sector initiative in many parts of Western Europe as well as Australia and New Zealand. In all these there are noticeable ironies present in the confluence of liberal economic thinking with the pursuit of the wider and historic industrial objectives.

Can one label these attempts to move the emphasis from public to private sector as actions in the 'public interest'? Radio and television have been in many ways the anvil on which modern attitudes to old questions of public interest have been hammered out. European social democratic and conservative thought, as well as American, has been profoundly influenced by the argument over where the sectoral divisions between government and private should lie in the field of broadcasting. It is arguable that the welfare dimension once attached to an activity can never really be removed. Even after radio and television franchises are sold or auctioned or awarded by lottery, there still remains a residue of the original discourse of public interest, including the possibility that society or state will one day decide to revert to a different form of allocation.

The process of deregulation is a very different historical project from the process of regulation; arguably, it leads to a greater presence of the state, more constant forms of vigilance and a more powerful bureaucracy than in the society of liberal 'public interest' values which gave rise to the allegedly over-regulated entity. That is why it is important to observe the industrial rather than the doctrinal exigencies lying behind the series of changes we witnessed around the globe in the 1970s and 1980s.

The key to the argument which has raged in respect of broadcasting, television in particular, is aptly expressed in a statement by Walter Lippmann made in 1960, after the television quiz scandals brought about a wave of distrust in the governance of the medium: 'We must not forget that the economic interest of the companies, which require bigger audiences for bigger revenues, is against any serious or lasting effort to use television for its higher possibilities.' There lies a profound disillusionment behind the attitude of Lippmann and those who shared his view of the infant medium in the 1950s and 1960s. His generation of thinkers about (and regulators of) the electronic media had all been educated under the spell of the Social Darwinists who had exerted much influence over early twentieth-century sociology.

In Europe and the United States alike, a socially optimistic view had been taken of information media since the development of the penny press back in the 1870s: they felt that information media could help the process of evolution away from *Gesellschaft*, the society of loosely anchored anomic individuals, prey to every lurking propagandist, towards a more communitarian society of informed individuals. Robert E. Park made the journey to Germany before World War I to learn the latest ideas of the students of *Zeitungswissenshaft*, the newspaper 'science' which had filled the minds of many Europeans with a late-Victorian intellectual optimism. The press had reached a stage in technical advance and industrial organisation which rendered it a new tool of social engineering; the new society had to use this instrument to achieve more than the benefit of its individual members. Information could provide the missing unity between personal freedom and social responsibility. It could fill the gap left between philosophical liberalism and the new sociology.

When the media industries, however, became corporately established and began to weave the web of accumulated capital from which the media of today have grown, it rapidly became clear that their mode of operation belied the prophecy that they would become a tool of social betterment. The expressive function of the press took precedence over its referential function. It was emotion, not intellect, which predominated in the modern modes for communicating ideas. In France, Gabriel Tarde and Gustave Le Bon had pioneered their over-schematic but rather influential views about the excitability and manipulability of crowds by demagogic speakers who had discovered how to play upon the tendency of people gathered in large numbers towards mutual imitation. In Italy, too, the criminologist Scipio Sighele saw the modern crown as vulnerable to the criminal mind.

Sociology in the period from 1900 to 1920 was an expression of a growing social disillusion, one which came to characterise the whole of the human sciences as the century moved on: the disillusion was centred on cinema and the press, whose operations during the War had seemed to confirm the most passionate of the social pessimists. The crowd psychologists, with their strictures on the excitability of the modern urban crowd, seemed to have won the argument, judged by the evidence of the years of total war.

Walter Lippmann had himself experimented with this range of notions, though transmuted through the ideas of Cooler and Dewey, in some ways an American counterpart of these European writers. The latter had all emphasised the organic nature of a society; they had been trying to see how individuals became socialised rather than how they exercised the individual freedoms conferred by society. They discovered a relationship between individual and society which was now modulated by the media. Mechanically created flows of information held self and society in a single grasp and facilitated, it seemed, the continuities of a social being rather than the static wants and needs of individuals.

Much later, in the television age, when Lippmann came to revisit these issues, he reverted to these older conceptions: 'Because of the discrepancy between the People as voters and the People as the corporate nation, the voters have no title to consider themselves the proprietors of the commonwealth and to claim that their interests are identical with the public interest.' The People, in his latter sense, were for Lippmann an organic entity, composed of the people not yet born, as well as the people who were already dead. A society was obliged to pursue, he therefore argued, the interests of the individuals composing future generations as well as those of whom a community temporarily consisted. 'This invisible, inaudible, and so largely non-existent community gives rational meaning to the necessary objectives of government.' Lippmann then takes issue with the Benthamite view of the social world: 'The interest of the community then is, what? – the sum of the interests of the several members who compose it.' Contrary to Jeremy Bentham, 'the people' is not the aggregate of living persons who vote in order to serve 'their pleasures and their security' (in Bentham's phrase) and where factions contend for immediate advantage in the struggle for survival and domination.

American thinking in the first decade or so of television was still suffused with notions of this organic public interest, one in which information media played a facilitating part. Television did not exist only to gratify immediate needs, but to help the whole process of historical evolution.

The creation by Lyndon B. Johnson of a public television service (using spectrum allocations specially set aside by the FCC a decade before) was an expression of the continuing workings of this view of society within American media politics. It was a view that was to become tarnished with the jibe of paternalism. It was suspect for social manipulation, for socialism, for Luddism even, but the pressure for openness within the operations of the FCC itself and for the continued extension of cash and spectrum opportunities for public television were remnants of an extinct but coherent view of society, one which gave space for the interposition of a public interest in the workings of private media capital.

What we are working with today is a survival of some of these strands of thought, but in the context of a society dynamically determined to alter the terms by which public and private interests define their roles within the play of the economy. A great curtain of suspicion has come to shroud the workings of public monopolies on both sides of the Atlantic and around other oceans, too. The focus of disillusion is not human nature, which had so let down the sociologists of an earlier generation, but the systems of administration devised by government. We are no longer content that the regulators can go unregulated and we have found no fresh device, no new way of regulating them without the interposition of the market. The alteration is still socially driven and still in pursuit of an updated vision of a public interest.

Many, however, are the new demands made today upon this term by new international and continental authorities, as well as all manner of national and regional government institutions, and a considerable confusion arises. For one thing, the public does not necessarily any longer inhabit the same society as the speaker. It is no longer easy to say who is to be the judge of interests public or private and by what social instrument either is to be safeguarded.

A risible, but somewhat typical, example of the complexity of public interest issues in our era is to be found in the story of the 'Europlug'. The twelve countries of the European Community have developed a new two-prong electric plug. It is slightly wider than the plugs used in France and West Germany, which although slightly different from each other, are generally found mutually compatible. The new Europlug corresponds to no standard currently in use, but a single cheap, safe, continent-wide (or EC-wide) device would enable a kettle bought in Hamburg to make tea in London. What is more, it would make it possible for all the electrical goods of the twelve countries to be manufactured with plugs already attached – to the great benefit of the consumer and of safety. But if the Europlug had been designed within the existing standard of any one country, it would have given manufacturers in that country an unfair advantage over all others. It has therefore been necessary to choose a design which no one presently uses so that the new implement will leave everyone equally disadvantaged. This means that every member country will have to retool and refit.

There also exists, however, a Worldplug project; an international worldwide standard plug is simultaneously emerging from another set of committees. It is not compatible with the Europlug. If the Europeans are to be real citizens of the world they might, it could be argued, decide to be the first to adopt the Worldplug while abandoning their national plugs. But their main project for now is to establish their European identity and therefore to construct a kind of electrical autarchy in Western Europe, with a view to hindering Japanese and US goods seeking European markets.

The Europlug problem entails an inextricable intertwining of industrial, social, political and economic objectives. It is an identity problem, looked at from one standpoint. It illustrates the loss of clearly visible symbols of public interest, but also of the very objectives of public interest. The plug problem will ultimately be resolved, of course, after an army of bureaucrats and politicians have worked on it for years to disentangle the skein, but only then as a result of trade-offs and deals in a dozen other spheres. Somewhere in the miasma, however, the theorists of the last three centuries would all succeed in finding remnants of all of their theories somewhere at work. They would not agree precisely where. At one end of the spectrum of ideas and beliefs there would be the purest of libertarians, recommending that all of the industrialists in all of the countries should be forced to compete until the best and most serviceable standard plug emerges; at the other end would be the pure planners, arguing that the plug problem is soluble and that plugs are inherently perfectible, given fully representative committees and sufficient time. The latter would be inherently saying that within each individual and each society involved, there exists a 'best' version of the self, that version that strives to serve rather than to possess, which, if given the chance to determine the outcome, would produce a safe, improved and internationally acceptable plug. One version of the public interest argument finds its fulfilment in the free play of the ego; the other demands free movement of the superego.

In the history of telecommunications, there is no shortage of examples of complex multi-dimensional dilemmas of the 'plug' kind. The decisions taken in the United States, Europe and the Soviet Union in respect of line standards for television, the grand quarrel of the 1950s and 1960s over the choice of system for colour television and the present-day melodrama over the choice of modulation method for satellite broadcasting are all examples of the Europlug kind, where the interplay of the actors' motives and interests is backed by the interplay of implied doctrine. Such international issues occur very frequently in coded form, and the code can often be embedded in the equations of electrical engineering rather than in the acerbities of geopolitics or diplomacy.

At the same time there exists an underlying and new techno-industrial logic, a pattern of necessary (industrially necessary) interconnections which partly challenge and partly support the doctrinal and motivational patterns. The telecommunications system has a natural 'yearning' for interconnection of all kinds. It is evolving from the uniform centralised network to a more open, poly-centred pattern. An exchange of functions between federal and state levels of government in the United States mirrors, but in reverse, the European shiftings of function between Brussels and the twelve member capitals. The technology itself appears autonomously as it were to be demanding to reformulate its whole interconnective capacity into a pattern of decentralised networks; a political pluralism would seem to be the counterpart. However, the change requires the presence of extremely centralised and determined government to put it into effect. Throughout the societies which are attempting to reconstruct their economies around these profound industrial shifts, the paradox is felt: a new economic pluralism requires a tremendous central power to drive it onwards and overcome the powerful inertia of existing interests.

The project of privatisation of state-owned or state-operated utilities is widespread. It is an expression of a new centralising state authority as well as, simultaneously, the expression of a new pluralist consumerist impetus. The newly released and more freely moving capital is the engine of the great retooling of industry but also of altered conceptions of society and social value. It is, in one sense, a world phenomenon defying the boundaries between nations, empires, continents, as these have been understood as foci of identity and of loyalty. Ideology, in a sense, is replacing territory as the locus of patriotism. Our compatriots have become those who most deeply share our convictions.

Throughout the history of industrial society, the proper role of the official or government sector in production, and the protection of the inhabitants of society as workers and consumers, has probably been the chief political debate. Indeed, most of our political life has revolved around, or flowed from, the various interim judgments made by parties and national classes on this question. Only in the age of advanced telecommunications (that is to say, when the computer was sufficiently developed to enhance the telecommunications pattern and interact with it) has the debate significantly shifted its terrain. Where there existed a century-long evolution of growing government regulation and control in public utilities, a changing wave of opinion has reversed the long trend, impelled by a revival of older strands of liberal economic thinking.

All sides and all shades of the argument over the role of the state in communications use the terminology of 'public interest'. In the past century, it was economic liberals who marked out the marketplace but began to erect a number of intellectual barriers, safeguards against excess: gradually the latter overtook the former. When broadcasting arrived in the 1920s, the climate was prepared for statist thinking of many varieties and a newly trained postwar managerial elite was in place, anxious to experiment with modern political and executive ideas, especially in respect of an instrument which was potentially a powerful tool of mass education.

Today's economic liberalism has gone back to the starting point, but in a context of significantly different values. Where nineteenth-century pioneers treated the open market as a valuable means to acquire certain benefits for society, the modern economic liberal tends to see the untrammelled market as an end in itself. There is thus a tangible shift between the two from a deontological to a teleological view of market forces. It may be only a phase as new political converts to the cause make manifest their dedication to free markets. During Victorian governance, in the United Kingdom at any rate, of the new communication utilities of trains and telegraphs there was envisaged at one time a private developmental stage followed by a publicly owned mature industry. Private capital would give way to public at a future stage in the growth of the two industries. The railways of the mid-19th century, and the telegraph, also helped to establish and encourage the thriving capital market: intending entrepreneurs came to parliament to persuade it to legislate the necessary systems of wayleaves for these new communication and transportation networks to develop. But most of the legislation envisaged a time when the franchises would be called in and a national, or even nationalised, and socially owned railway and telegraphic system would come into existence. Today in the case of the UK and France's Channel Tunnel, a project of comparable scale, funded by corporations but subject to national legislation in two countries, a similar rubric is being employed: the private entrepreneurs are given a period of time in which to develop their investment, after which the ownership of the project reverts to the state.

The regulatory systems which followed or accompanied the Industrial Revolution were deeply embedded in contemporary thinking about national development. The public, however conceived, clearly lived within national borders and was subject to national jurisdiction. Its interests were visible rather than abstract. In Europe and elsewhere, the nature of the

electromagnetic spectrum itself dictated a consciousness of a kind of international public interest, expressed at first through the International Telegraphic Union (originally established to cross the borders of a group of
German states), the most ancient of global organisations, predating the
United Nations by a century. The United States, because of the dynamism
of its growth and because of its sheer size and situation between two great
oceans, has not felt the presence of the ITU as a structuring force in its national
planning and decision-making.

Only in the era of satellites and the scarcity of slots in the geostationary
orbit has the United States been brought to recognise the tensions and conflicts contained within the counsels of the ITU. In crowded Europe there has
been greater collective need for careful organisation of spectrum use and this
has transcended even the political divisions of the continent into socialist
and non-socialist camps. Today, we are seeing the first stages of the attempt
to knit together the regulatory processes of the twelve countries of the EC, in
their efforts to create a bloc which can compete in equipment production
and in the provision of value-added services with Japan and the United
States. In the field of telecommunications, therefore, the twelve have been
attempting to seek out and identify the areas in which conceptual and juridi-
cal barriers to the free exchange of services will have to be removed.

Despite the relative homogeneity of thinking about broadcasting in Western Europe, complicated problems remain to be solved. For example, each
country has devised its own system for supervising the content of advertisements – a few countries still ban television and radio advertising altogether,
although such prohibitions are unlikely to survive very long. The control of
advertising reaches the sensitive heart of public interest values and it has
been difficult, though not impossible, to devise a lowest-common-factor
approach to the problem, which will leave the twelve with an intensively regulated but unified system for supervising the content of advertisements in
channels which are sent out across national boundaries by intent (Europe
has long learned to survive the transmission of television signals which cross
frontiers accidentally).

Unification is more difficult in the area of programme content. Sweden, for
example, will not permit the representation of violence in its programmes,
especially programmes for children, but it takes a more permissive view – in
comparison with the rest of Europe – of the representation of sexual activity.
In the United Kingdom, legal constraints on the representation of explicit
sexuality have been steadily growing as a variety of special interest groups
have become increasingly active and have caught the attention of government. Statutory censorship of videos has been introduced and this has been
followed by the establishment of a Broadcasting Standards Council to create
'codes' of taste in matters of sex and violence, possibly covering even news.
These new institutions are additional to, not substitutes for, the bodies which
previously concerned themselves with such matters. Cinema, too, is increasingly vigilant in arranging the various levels of age-range certification. The
deregulatory climate in the economy is being accompanied by a strongly regulatory climate in respect of the depiction of anything affecting morals. It is at

this point of apparent contradiction that the 'new' public interest discourses are meeting their greatest tests.

It could prove to be somewhat difficult to encourage a multiplicity of competing channels in cable, satellite and conceivably further terrestrial television while simultaneously constraining those programmes which most encourage audiences to sample the newly enfranchised production industries. It seems to many in the film and television industries that government is trying to move in two opposite directions at the same time. It will take much time in negotiation (and legislation) for these tensions to be resolved. What will emerge, because it has to, is a new internationally accepted definition of how the public interest is in future to be represented at the point of programme production in what is becoming the world's largest and most dynamic single market.

The interests of the public are no longer necessarily, of course, the interests of the nation concerned. It is here that one of the main shifts occurs, to a great extent as a result of the needs of telecommunications production and networks, but also as a result of changing production organisation generally. The deregulation of telecommunications' administrations in Europe has been advocated and conducted partly to guarantee the continued existence of jobs and investments that might otherwise be undercut by more vigorous competition. At the same time, it has become clear that no national economy can any longer think of itself as secure within any particular set of borders. International competition is forcing a new division of labour between societies at different levels of development and a new search for rationalised markets which entail the abandonment of whole ranges of national belief and assumption. The nation state was a source of emotional and economic refuge; today it is often a hindrance. In several regions of the world – Western Europe, the Comecon countries, areas of Africa, Southeast Asia – it is slipping away, leaving a new generation to ponder its identity.

Right across the spectrum of positions in regard to public interest there lies a shadow of ambiguity and contradiction. In all of the societies which are attempting to establish for themselves a position in the new international telecommunications equipment industries, a new rethinking is under way: philosophers and political theorists have lost the sense of where to place the public interest in the modern context – in the market or in the enlightened state. Business sees it buried in the historic rights of free enterprise and market freedom. But politicians and civil servants are apt to be more sensitive to the needs of deprived groups and the painful process of switching public goods from people who have grown to expect them to those who might benefit from the results of free market competition. As a group they therefore tend to cling to some part of the accepted notions of earlier decades.

The whole drive behind deregulation in the United Kingdom and the United States is fuelled by powerful doctrine. It is as if society had come to be seen as a subset of the economy. The felt need is for ownership to be social and widespread but by way of stock-holding; for industry as far as possible to be self-supervising and for official interference to be effective but minimal. What is difficult to observe is the ways in which telecommunications as an industry is demanding or necessitating this alteration of attitude and the extent to which an accident of political history is now shaping this important set of industries. It may be possible in twenty or thirty years to disentangle the skeins of influence but, of course, by then the historian will be peering at the process through further layers of public policy and public belief.

However, the historian of the future might also be living in a society in which the state, smaller in size and personnel than the apparatus of the 1970s and 1980s, exercises powers paradoxically more extensive and intrusive than those which prevailed during the post-World War II era of 'big government'. For the new wave of economic liberalism is not functioning within the context of an industrial competitiveness which it defends and upholds; it is struggling in a radical way to create the conditions of competition which correspond with its doctrinal predilection. So that in the case of the reorganised AT&T, for example, an unfinished debate continues among American policy-makers as to whether the successor group of companies are 'competitive' in the predetermined sense. The FCC can never be certain it has created an ultimate 'natural' market or whether, like a piece of clockwork machinery, the market has to be wound up again every few years by a regulated reconstruction of the industry, after intervention by the Department of Justice.

To carry this kind of responsibility, the regulatory agencies have to undertake more than was once envisaged for them. They are no longer able to act as a kind of usher of the economy. The Justice Department and the Federal Communications Commission have to delve deeply into the corporations concerned, analysing their pricing structures, their investment initiatives, corporate alliances and their research and development practices. The result is that United States government has acquired a greater power over United States corporations than, say, the average Western European government enjoys over its still-nationalised Postal, Telephone and Telegraph Authority (PTT). Deregulation makes for smaller government but often with greater powers and more interfering habits.

It is worth recalling the situation of the 1920s, when broadcasting was first industrialised after a decade or two of existence largely as a military tool. On both sides of the Atlantic, radio provided an archetypal new industry of the interwar industrial economy, exemplifying the prevailing doctrines then governing the state-versus-industry practice. In the United Kingdom, the Post Office (which controlled the telephone and the radio regulatory system) was among the first organisations to adopt modern management techniques. In establishing the BBC, the Post Office, the government and the radio pioneers saw themselves as providing a grand rehearsal for new industrial organisational methods. Government in the early 1920s concerned itself with spectrum regulation (through the Post Office); it decided which companies were to participate in radio, it oversaw technical standards and it decided how much the listener had to pay. But it set up a BBC that rapidly established itself as the first of a whole generation of nationalised monopolies which gradually took over a large proportion of the industrial manufacturing economy. The BBC painfully created for itself an area of editorial independence (never complete, never sufficient) in response to a very open and permissive government licence. The relationship has remained uneasy and somewhat experimental but the two sides learned slowly to remain within their allocated spheres of authority, the government accepting in time that the monopoly broadcaster had to be left in substantial editorial control, within parameters which were constantly reviewed by parliament. The institutions of broadcasting gained a satisfactory independence but at the cost of constant public investigation, reform and reorganisation, not as much as in France perhaps, but enough to keep the management of the moment nervous about what might happen next (but never did).

In the United States, the 1927 Radio Act similarly defined the point at which the technical exigencies of broadcasting, the necessary avoidance of signal interference and the establishment of appropriate controls over content intersected. Section 29 specifically forbade the licensing authority (then the Federal Radio Commission) from interfering with free speech, although the same clause stated that 'No person within the jurisdiction of the United States shall utter any obscene, indecent or profane language by means of radio communication.' It was clear, furthermore, that the pioneer entrepreneurs had to be constrained in respect of the amounts of spectrum they used and in respect of the power of their transmitters. There had already developed a 'chaos of the airwaves' caused by the unconstrained greed of the early practitioners of radio. Herbert Hoover, the Secretary of Commerce, articulated the doctrinal dilemma posed by radio between general public benefit and private enterprise, and in the 1927 Act he established that the US radio station occupied a role as 'trustee' of the public interest. The formula of 'public interest, convenience, necessity' which the 1927 Act employed to express the objectives of this public stewardship which was conferred upon radio licensees was borrowed from public utility legislation; its vagueness left scope for half a century more of debate.

The presence of the First Amendment provided the bedrock for free expression in broadcasting in the United States but did not remove the need for debates comparable to those taking place in Europe over what constituted the proper uses of radio and television. But it avoided the European-style confusion over where editorial authority lay – not in the Commission but in the hands of the entrepreneurs concerned in the industry. There existed a tension between private corporation and government regulatory authority and growing linkages between the two as the industry expanded. Just as the BBC turned out to be the prototypical nationalised industry in the United Kingdom, the FCC, as established by the 1934 Communications Act, experimented in the nature of a new style of relationship between government and industry in the United States. By the time of the 1934 Act, a new situation prevailed; the Communications Act of that year reflects the greater readiness of US government to intervene in the economic process in support of the public interest: where the 1927 Act reflected the relationships between government and industry which had been established during the war, the 1934 Act was the offspring of the New Deal.

The public interest dimension in broadcasting was supported by a series of practices, especially affecting news and public affairs programmes and

programmes designed for children; these came to encompass, most promi-
nently, Fairness and Equal Time for advocates of opposing views. But from
the publication of the 1946 Blue Book, a reasoned expression of official programming policy, drafted largely by Charles Siepmann, a consultant to the
FCC, to the more complex attempts in the radical 1960s to introduce a 'right
of reply' to advertisements, the industry vigorously argued that all such rules
interfered with the First Amendment rights of broadcasters. There was thus a
permanent tension in American broadcasting between what might be
labelled constitutional and 'public interest' positions. There developed a
solid constituency for reducing the freedom of network controllers in the
interest of a socially caring commitment, lobbying – for example – for protection of children against excessive advertising and the portrayal of violence;
for more obligatory local programme origination, unpaid public-service
announcements, and news at prime time.

Many of the battles were won, in fact, temporarily at least, especially in the
1960s, but gradually the new mood of competitiveness, added to the
increased intra-industry competition brought about by cable and satellite
channels, accompanied moves to abolish the doctrines which most interfered with the free scheduling needs of networks and stations. Until PBS was
established by the Johnson administration, America had no European-style
public television but in the large foundations it was to possess a counterpart
public-interest institution. Through this sponsorship, Ford, Markle and
Mobil Oil brought into being some of the materials which only public funding provided in countries with different public philosophies.

Most television observers have emphasised the contrasts between US and
European attitudes and issues but looking back over the decades perhaps
one should rather be struck by the similarities: producers could and did move
fairly easily between the various systems. It would have been virtually impossible, however, for a producer from the US or any Western European society
to work within the culture of Soviet or South American radio and television.
The television cultures of America and Western Europe in the 1950s, 1960s
and 1970s derived a great deal from the constitutional structures of broadcasting established before the war. On one side of the Atlantic there existed a
series of powerfully established national institutions, some of them in competition, others monopolistic; on the other side there had emerged three
immense networks drawn from many hundreds of licensed local stations but
operating under rubrics which for a time grew very precise and demanding in
their insistence on an interventionist guarantee of the public interest.

Of course, in both cases the 'public' was seen as a passive, undifferentiated
mass. Only in the 1970s and 1980s did a fresh set of doctrines emerge and a
new structure begin to evolve in France, the United Kingdom, Italy, Germany
and elsewhere of a thoroughly different kind. The supplying corporations,
whether functioning in the highly charged competitive atmosphere of the
United States or the more monopolistic context of Europe, were few. The
audience was seen and described and analysed as a 'mass' audience; the
'public interest' at work in radio and television was located in society, outside
the viewing audience. The viewers were to be 'protected' from excessive

violence, from misleading advertising, from biased news coverage in order to preserve the structures of democratic society. The individuals comprising a society existed, in effect, in two separate manifestations: first they were viewers and listeners and therefore part of the passively receiving mass audience, but secondly they were citizens, members of a 'public' whose 'interest' lay in the preservation and protection of cultural, constitutional and social forms.

What is being argued here is that in the debate over how to establish the cultural institutions based on telecommunications (which has lasted from the 1920s until now) Western societies have largely been experimenting with different interim solutions to the problems posed by their heritage of nineteenth-century liberalism. In radio and television, private and public sectors are locked together in a condition of interdependence. However, the industries and institutions have their responsibilities divided up in different ways depending on the prevailing state of the debate in the society concerned. Only where a fundamentally different doctrine lies at the root of a system (for example, where a party or an individual operates control over the media as the instrumentation of a cause or ideology) have fundamentally different kinds of broadcasting culture developed. In the 1980s we have started to 'harmonise' broadcast regulations in Europe; such an operation would have been unthinkable in a Western Europe which was divided into ideological camps.

The public interest has been similarly ideology-bound in the area of common carrier telecommunication services. Until the break-up of AT&T, the United States enjoyed a publicly supervised, but privately capitalised, monopoly which was obliged to offer certain prescribed standards of service. European PTTs based their telecommunications services inside traditional postal organisations, which can trace their institutional ethos ultimately back to the message systems of the Holy Roman Empire. Message sending and signalling by electronic means felt like different approaches to the same activity and the maintenance of equitable and reliable standards has always seemed hard for Europeans to keep separate from public control. In this respect the most-stressed public good has been the goal of universality and equality of service, to which end monopoly has been judged essential.

At the height of its power, the British Post Office could and did place orders for equipment on a scale which determined the survival of vast industries. Officials who were essentially part of the civil service, rather than members of the industry concerned, exercised powers which were remote from parliamentary scrutiny as well as from market control simply because of their high level of technicality and their vast scale. The separation of telecommunications from the postal service and its eventual privatisation within a (partially) competitive marketplace seemed the only way for a sense of the public interest to intrude into this zone of extreme and unpoliced private power.

As the state postal and telecommunications monopolies of Europe began to disappear in the 1980s, there remained the desire that the whole of society should benefit from modern telecommunications by ensuring popular access to modernised instruments and services at competitive prices. It would be perfectly fair to say that there was an accidental synergy between the process of modernisation and the advent of a powerful, new political right in British politics. However, the sheer political determination and radical energy which lay behind the privatisation of British Telecom required the grit which ideological commitment alone could provide; one can only speculate as to what might have happened if a different faction of the Conservative party had been triumphant in the 1978 election.

Sceptics point out that BT retains a vast geographical quasi-monopoly, subject to a certain amount of competition, no longer the sole supplier and manufacturer of terminal equipment, certainly subject to the vigilant scrutiny of a new and tough supervisory Office of Telecommunications, but still a unified national body controlling networks in telephone, telex, facsimile, radio and television transmission (and much of cable also), videotex and data links. It is notionally no longer a monopoly but in its geographical totality, and in its industrial muscle, it remains one of the largest enterprises operating under a single board anywhere in the European economy. One further ideological twist at a future general election and it could be renationalised without the difference being immediately apparent.

We are apt to be so fascinated by the novelty, and often the sheer flair, of the thinking of the new radical right that we lose sense of the continuities of thinking that are still at work in defining public policy. The goal of the 'natural' marketplace has long been pursued, at each stage in the evolution of liberal thought. Locke envisaged a world of separate individuals pursuing their judgments and wills but held together by their objective common needs: language linked them and obliged them to mean the same things by the same words; the laws of nature caused them to share an outlook on the environment, on their bodily needs, on their evaluation of goods and physical priorities.

In the 1980s we have seen a new breed of politicians in all of the free economies willing to articulate again, after a gap of nearly a century, an older strand of market ideas, which they *feel* to be 'pure' and derived unpolluted from the text on the spirit of Adam Smith. We have seen in the Reagan era chairmen of the FCC who have tried to define the public interest as 'that which interests the public' – suggesting by implication that only in the free choice of channels and programmes can the ideal be achieved. The Peacock Report on the pricing of broadcast services in the UK went through a similar process of thought and ended up declaring that in the slightly longer run all regulation could be shed and substituted by the pay-per-view system, in which the public would and should simply purchase programmes one at a time or through subscriptions for single strands or channels. This goal could only be reached when the supply of telecommunications channels was so plentiful as to be analogous to the free availability of paper in publishing. Technology could render spectrum scarcity a thing of the past, a brief historical interruption. It is going to create a pure and open market for cultural goods, and it should be the purpose of governments to encourage that development by all means, so that there would no longer exist a technical or economic requirement (though other reasons might remain) for such institutions as the BBC or for regulatory bodies supervising commercial broadcasting to exist.

However, this outcrop of freemarket thinking in the 1980s is much more an attempt to follow the contours back to a society in which complex problems were more easily solved than it is a radical innovation. Indeed, it is most consciously archaistic in its expression, a return to a language which could be spoken plainly and understood, a rejection of the kind of technologised socialism which has ended up in big bureaucracy protected by big government and wrapped in public-service terminology. As has been said, the difficulty is to see the extent to which this development within public philosophy is a 'natural' superstructure to the new technologies and their host industries.

Perhaps the language for describing the shift of doctrine has been badly chosen. We are not really dealing with an extension of competition or an intensification of accountability of enterprises through the market, so much as with a general reorganisation of enterprises. What was shown to be impossible in the 1970s, with the development of international enterprise and with the presence of very powerful labour organisations in many countries, was a process of plain reorganisation in the methods of production and regulation (in telecommunications and elsewhere). Recourse to the processes of deregulation and the selling of state-owned enterprises came to seem to be the only way of forcing reconstruction. The direct consumer benefits of competition are apparent but trivial, and sometimes negative; what we have now seen, however, is an entry of large sums of fresh capital into institutions which had previously tended to deter the investor. We are also seeing a reorganisation of the labour force geographically, industrially and in terms of skills available.

At the same time, new functions and new services have emerged from the computerised reorganisation of the financial services industry. In the era of the computer, capital tends to be written off, through rapid obsolescence, at a faster rate than in the mechanical and extractive industries. Different industries requiring different forms of state regulation have come to play central roles within the economy. The older industries have become peripheral and the new communications-related industries have become the new heights of the economies of the West.

This far-reaching and rather complicated economic project was possible only with the help of some form of state direction, but the essential process of reorganisation had to occur in the private economy. Hence the paradoxical nature of a change which leaves the state with apparently greater power over more intensely competitive private industries. Moreover, the telecommunications retooling has necessitated complex and enlarged participation by financial institutions, all in the private regulated sector.

The present transformation might turn out to be a phase rather than a destination. One should recall that the evolution towards the civil and moral rights of groups was the main theme of the 'new politics' of the previous decade; it continues to flourish beneath the 1980s reversion to free market theory as a dominant theme of politics. There was in that decade a strong return to a sense of human rights as against material acquisition; there were, and are, articulate environmental politicians; the women's movement found its way into mainstream political fora; community movements and workers'

66

control pressure groups were functioning throughout the OECD countries. In the 1970s, the public interest would be deemed to lie at the resultant of the forces generated by these vociferous groups and tendencies. Today these are regionally active in politics and continue to exert influence within the major parties. In some European countries they have manifested themselves as national parties in their own right. Perhaps we shall see a new 1990s trade-off between the possessive values of the free-market theorists and the socially developmental values of the forces surviving from the previous 'new' politics of the 1970s.

For within liberal theory the pendulum has constantly swung since the 17th century between two juxtaposed views of human rights and public interest. On the one hand there were Locke and Bentham who saw property as a natural right and an emanation of the individual as autonomous being; for them the maximisation of possessions and possessiveness itself were the bedrock of the freedom of a liberal society. On the other hand, Paine, Mill and the writers of the United States Constitution all belonged to a tradition which set the atomic individual slightly to one side and built its view of the liberal society upon aggregated benefit more than upon the natural rights of the individual. The shock of the experience of industrial society forced the establishment of a welfare state not merely in the interests of those at the bottom of the ladder, but in the name of a shared general public interest. Urban drainage systems impinged upon personal property but in the name of society's advancement.

The followers of Hayek and other freemarket theorists of the present day can see the pendulum swinging back to the other strand of liberal thought, now that the particular perils and injustices of early capitalism are attenuated. Perhaps it is not a pendulum swing so much as a special corrective mechanism operating in the evolving liberal society which might be followed by a renewed interest in the solution of society's problems by shared aggregative measures lying beyond the grasp of the atomic individual.

Of course, at one level, all policies, plans and purposes on the part of government in respect of telecommunications are manifestations of the public interest. It is in the public interest that private interests are given the opportunity to invest and compete in the new technologies in the new environment. It is in the public interest that a large section of the spectrum is reserved for military use. The imposition of content rules in common carriers and in respect of broadcasting occurs in the same public interest, but so does the removal of that very regulatory apparatus at a later stage. Public interest is a field in which parties struggle to establish policy. Public interest implies the invocation of social purpose in all matters in which there remains a territory of discussable collective policy within a society.

From regulated monopoly to perfect competition, from privacy to personal security from access to fairness, all the traditional causes (and their countervailing policies) are requisites of public interest, although they arise in different groupings and patterns and in different emphasis in different societies. The United States has conducted most of its reforms in the name of choice and diversity; the UK has only half-heartedly pursued this aim, but

67

has rather attempted from decade to decade to supplement existing provision in radio and television in the interests of stated cultural purposes – breaking a monopoly, creating regionally based signals, offering opportunities to independent producers. The United States has been investment-led in its policy-making, Europe has been production- and politics-led. That pattern survives the changing environment of multiple technologies of distribution.

That environment is characterised partly by the pervasiveness of new forms of communication, partly by the relaxation of inhibitions which made the inherited system a series of hurdles among which would-be entrepreneurs and communicators have had to pick their way. The public interest was defined in terms of prohibitions. Today it is being steadily redefined in terms of permissions: permissions for common carriers to offer voice, data, images and for broadcasters to offer message systems; permissions for institutions which possess networks to maximise their use and invent value-added services to inform, entertain or enhance commercial effectiveness.

In a world of total, or almost total, interconnection of common carriers and the elimination of traditional barriers between different kinds of message, are there new 'natural rights' emerging which constitute a fresh internationally acceptable statement of the liberal view of public interest? It is worth the attempt, perhaps, to state what would have to be some of the common elements within the Western economy.

First, governments would have to accept that the unimpeded carriage of messages is a primary social good, and that the elimination of scarcity no longer constitutes a case for controlling content of messages, either by rationing bandwidth to approved parties, or by interposing prohibitory agencies. This might be acceptable in the United States but would have difficulty gaining acceptance in the United Kingdom, France and elsewhere, certainly in the foreseeable future. It would not, however, be impossible at a moment when there really did exist a profusion of signals on a scale which made interference, say, on grounds of obscenity, impractical.

Secondly, governments and governed would have to accept that information and entertainment now necessarily must be permitted to flow from societies other than one's own. It would be necessary to accept propaganda – religious, political, moral – or what seemed to be propaganda; there would be an obligation to political quietude; there has never existed in Western Europe the demand to jam radio signals from beyond the frontiers, although there has been in respect of unlicensed domestic signals. US audiences are not used to casually picking up Radio Moscow or Radio Cairo in English a millimetre on the dial from their favourite station. But it is consonant with the new environment of international access and inter-connectedness that obligations remain with the governed as with government not to inhibit the flow of content from satellite or from cable, whatever the provocation. It is likely, for example, that some Moslem countries would object to a principle of this kind, since the exclusion of printed and visual material of many kinds is felt to be crucial to the moral well-being of society.

Thirdly, governments are becoming more aware of the centrality of copyright legislation to the potential prosperity of their information-based industries. There are no final or completed formulae available. Constant revision and reform of copyright is the only means by which this group of industries and services can make progress. Only government can hold the ring and discover the points of balance between the constantly changing needs of competing enterprises. The new technologies exert subtle and far-reaching alterations to the ways in which law impinges on the flow of information. There is no single 'correct' solution. What offered a reasonable intellectual freedom in the case of the printing press does not provide for the same intellectual and industrial benefits in the era of the moving image and of computer-held information. Just as a careful balance between the needs of corporations, government and individuals has to be held in the case of privacy, so a similar balance has to be struck between the desserts of publishers and authors and the demands of intellectual and educational access.

Fourthly, government has a responsibility to regulate in such a way as to multiply the possibilities of interconnections of all kinds. Rather than acting as a kind of marshal between systems, it has, in the new environment to ensure that systems exist in fruitful mutual juxtaposition. It is hard to see how this objective can be guaranteed without the presence of a powerful regulatory system and regulatory *mission* within government.

The first of these four aims can be achieved by societies through constant vigilance, but to ensure that society actually acquires a growing set of highways and networks permitting the free-flow of messages from the new unregulated institutions necessitates positive action on the part of authority.

There is a further, fifth, goal which similarly requires an interventionist approach on the part of government: that is to ensure that all citizens, all inhabitants, are actually as a matter of practice provided with access to the new instruments. One cannot ignore the inseparability of social freedoms and systems of communication. The fact that the marketplace allows the networks to grow and makes the new technologies practical does not in itself mean that the equipment and services it carries automatically reach the whole of society. A society cannot enjoy a free market in goods and transport unless all the inhabitants enjoy actual access to roads, and are permitted to move without hindrance wherever goods and resources are being supplied or demanded; by the same token, the practice of economic (and social and political) freedom is impossible in our time without access, in practice as well as principle, to the means of communication. That has implications for education as well as for markets.

Finally, there remains a paramount requirement for all of the inherited cultural and political freedoms to survive. That remains a *sine qua non* of public interest. We have seen since the 1920s, even in the United States, a complex growth of hindrances and limitations in media of the freedoms enjoyed since the 18th century in books and newspapers. There have usually been very good reasons for each separate restriction – from crowded airways to suppression of pornography – but taken as a whole our freedom of expression (in most countries of the West) is less than it was at the turn of the century. The United Kingdom perhaps offers the most disappointing case where fresh intrusions into publishing freedoms are arriving, at present, at the rate of one a year, an accumulating and slowly asphyxiating mesh of statutory censoring and classifying bodies, investigating councils, reviewing committees. There is much to be said for each of them, nothing for all of them. Nations will have to practise internally and internationally what they preach and benefit from commercially. Yet in the 1980s, the small group of societies with a free press and open publishing has actually grown in number, and that is not unconnected with the same technical exigencies of late-twentieth-century technology which have so greatly altered the industrial scene.

Clearly the new telecommunications environment has arisen from, and is characterised indelibly by, a commitment to free commercial practice. The commitment to cultural freedom has wavered at times during the process of change. Any definition of public interest has to be founded upon a restatement of the human freedoms that gave rise to the debate and its paradoxes over the centuries.

5

Nations*

We can all write down our emotional addresses beginning with the self and ending with the universe. Our personalities exist within a series of circles of identity, moving outwards from individual through familial and national towards the ethnic, the surrounding civilisation, the human species. However, the circles are concentric and the lines of influence move inwards through the spiral as well as outward. There are no individuals and no crowds – only ways of looking at people through the prism of prevailing ideas about individuals and crowds.

In reflecting on the changing circumstances of culture in the late 20th century it is useful to look at one in particular of those circles of identity – the nation, which has for several generations now acted as *a*, or perhaps *the* focal point of our cultural lives. We experience and receive information and entertainment through the vernacular and today, largely by means of technologies which have been steered through the industrial system by regulatory systems stemming from the national state. The legality which underpins the content of modern culture is national. So is the emotional legitimation.

A child growing up almost anywhere in Europe in the last years of the 20th century is offered not so much a choice between, as a contrived confusion of simultaneous identities. He or she will have a gender which is available for experiment, a family perhaps, though very possibly some additional temporary parents as mother or father passes through a succession of marriages. The child will learn to recognise and use its vernacular but quickly realises that English hovers around the television set, compelling and universal, whatever the mother tongue. It will rapidly begin to notice the symbols of national identity from flags, coins and stamps, but will rapidly become familiar also with a multiplicity of pigmentations and ethnic groups in the streets and squares of almost every town and village. Quite quickly it will learn that there exist institutions which are broader than those contained within the national state; it will learn that in the broader world there exist a variety of institutions which bear upon the identity of nations and peoples, such as the United Nations and the European Community. It will be taught about the tensions between regional, national and international as political concepts. It will discover that for every loyalty there is a countervailing rival: for a Swede

---

* This paper was originally delivered at a symposium on Postmodernism at the University of Pittsburgh in July 1986.

there is the sense of being Nordic, for a Scottish child the sense of (sometimes) being British; a German child will discover the global ideological divide between East and West more rapidly than any of the others, while an Irish child will discover that religious beliefs and practices are bewilderingly entwined with political identity. An English child will never quite be sure what to *call* its country. Only in the sportsfield will these manifold 'belongings to' suddenly seem clear and real; whenever a question is asked about them, they all seem to dissolve into further questions. It is a world in which everyone seems to talk incessantly about these various layers of identity, but every one of them disappears into a fog of dispute and speculation, under pressure of questioning.

None the less the sense of nationality is a crucial balancing point for the emotions between self and family on one side, and international and pure humanity on the other. The decline in the purely political aspects of nationhood has not necessarily reduced its cultural, and therefore emotional, importance. The nation offers the self a major part of its history, and does so by employing all of the senses and the memory of the senses.

What are the sounds and images which evoke for us in this final lap of the 20th century the sense of adherence to a nation? Does an Italian feel that confirmation of identity at the sight of a plate of steaming spaghetti; or at the finely spun outline of a Lamborghini; at the first stirrings of a Verdi overture, or at a postcard reproduction of the Sistine Chapel ceiling? All of these are now part of 'international culture' and they are apt to evoke a sense of the Italian in non-Italians. They are part of the national world consumer market which requires national sounds and impressions to validate goods. which would otherwise be indistinguishable. When you slip a Burberry off the clothes hanger in Bloomingdale's menswear floor, you hold in your hand an object – probably identical in most of its qualities with the rival Japanese, American, Korean and French raincoats which surround it – which evokes a rainy English day, suffered in a curling Dickensian fog. The price differentials will reflect this superficial fulfilment of our striving towards that sense of authenticity, which helps to fuel the consumer economy. It is somewhere in the relationship between objects which have been detached from their experiential environment and the perceptions and expectations which we bring to them that our modern sense of nationhoods resides. The objects may not have been manufactured, for they can be places or even people – they exist as elements of our perceived environment, but they share the circumstance of being split away from their own aura, their own phenomenon and, in recognising them as symbols, we attempt to restore the fission. In doing so we, in a literal sense, naturalise the objects by nationalising them. They become whole, at least in the moment between our recognition of them and our consumption of them.

Perhaps nowhere is this aspect of the operations of nationhood so clear as in tourism. For the tourist both participates in and obscures the discourse of nationhood. The British, for example, are used to being the object of the gaze of Americans; right through the 19th century American tourists were helping to build the international myth of the British and re-intensifying thereby its actual practice within Britain and by Britons abroad. In the period since World War II the American touristic observation of Britain has intensified in its phenomenological (and economic) significance, and Britain has invested intensively in heightening the effects of its own imagery while extending the apparatus and organisation of American tourism. Without tourism, for example, the pageantry and ritual of the monarchy would have evolved very differently. The industry of tourism is one of the most important of machines of representation at work in the world. It exists at the precise point at which national, regional, ethnic identity becomes global, where the global economy feeds upon, fashions, reifies national identity – and in consuming it destroys or transmutes it.

Tourism is of course, far more than economic activity – it is an employment of the emotions, both those of the subject and the object of tourism. It works constantly to define and redefine national symbols and adjusts national reality. As one city or region becomes overexploited or filled up, new zones and experiences are opened up and their mythic content brought out. The organisation of tourism is itself a signifying practice, an exercise in the objectification of selfhood and also in the authentication of material desires.

Tourism today is one of the mass media. That is to say it is an organised industrialised means by which representations of ideas and values are circulated and amplified or attenuated. The granting of the sense of 'being there' and of 'having been to see' is an important gratification of the human desire to possess through seeing. It is perhaps a humanising or even democratising of the imperialist emotion – the simple desire to possess other cultures.

However, the most powerful form of tourism today is the counter-tourism of the presence of foreign cultures in one's own. There are today a number of powerfully articulated fears of the impact of better materially endowed cultures upon the smaller or less wealthy. Small island cultures are blotted out by planeloads of visitors in search of sunshine. Micro-economies are obliterated or distorted by the arrival of retirement colonies.

But tourism is also a metaphor for the much greater inter-cultural dislocation which is today felt to be the result of the flow of television programmes. They are themselves, in a way, a special form of counter-tourism. There exists a growing fear throughout Europe of the implications of 'transborder data flow' in all its forms but as manifested in particular by the success of American television in the European markets now opening up in cable and satellite, as well as conventional television. The fear of cultural imperialism is a more interesting phenomenon than the actual practice. The belief that television programmes can take possession of the self in such a way as to asphyxiate nationhood, especially of pre-industrialised societies, is a necromancy of the intellectuals. A diet of *Dallas* is thought to be 'natural' in Brooklyn, but dangerous in Newcastle and destructive in Dakkar. The hypodermic view of media effects has largely been abandoned in respect of industrialised societies but – in a string of books and studies and in UNESCO – is still flourishing when the impact of television on the developing world is under discussion.

Can a steady diet of American soap opera deprive a Swedish child of its Swedishness: does the relative paucity of indigenous mass entertainment compared with that of a foreign nation cause Italy to feel less Italian, or for that reason, to find it harder to maintain its national economy under local control? The complex of causes and effects simply stuns the logical processes of the mind: it is impossible to think through the myriad of variables that are contained within the communication process, the totality of human interactions which constitute culture.

A sense of the lost cause now hangs over the cultural imperialism debate, as the cultural and linguistic issues have been swept up into the larger industrial issue. There has been a change of focus between the 1970s and the 1980s. We live in an age in which the computer and the telecommunications network has taken over a very large number of the functions of the previous systems for disseminating image and text. The English language is, almost everywhere, accepted as the language of information technology. However, the major centres of design, conception and manufacture of the apparatus of this new kind of industrial revolution are not in Europe but in the East, and on the Pacific coast of the United States. Europe is an important market for the information economy but not its initiating source. Many of those services and industries which tended to define the mental borders of the national state (the railway, the postal service, banking, steel, the motorcar industry) have either become relatively less important or have become subject to foreign or international domination anyway. The size of an individual country does not necessarily prevent its being the source of international supply – Swedish vehicles compete with French, German and Italian in a world market – but none of these could survive in a single country or probably even a single continent. The financial services which are essential to the new international culture and the new economy are increasingly transnational. Throughout the sphere of the material base, the national is taking second place; there is a group of core nations functioning within the new economy, a group of secondary production nations (many in the Third World), while the rest are struggling to define themselves and their roles in relationship to the changed situation.

One strand of current discussion searches for continental culture. Suddenly the politicians and EEC officials are starting to talk about European values. Europe is a geographical term and, insofar as it has shared, or shared in, a cultural history divided between two global political camps. Until now there has existed no consciousness of being European in the face of America, or Africa or Asia. Many of the issues of nationhood within the European nations stem from political anxieties about how to integrate large Asian, African or South European and South American populations within the broader national culture. France shares more history with its Algerian population, than it does with say Norway or Wales. The real mixing of European cultures has taken place not in Europe but in America.

It is not surprising that several new 'consciousness-projects' have started up since the discussion of the American 'threat' to European national identity commenced: there has been an experiment with the ideas of using the Mediterranean as the locus of a special culture, of its own indigenousness, as it were. This does not seem to have a great future as a project, since so many of the countries involved are pursuing political causes which lie completely outside the concerns of the Western European countries. There has also been a recent experiment with 'Latinity', a concept based upon the notion that France, Spain and the Francophone and Spanish-speaking Third World nations constitute a kind of cultural autarchy. This has its intellectual and political attractions, but it runs counter to the sheer fact of American power in South America (also in French Canada), and the still unresolved destiny of the new states of Africa.

Today's debate over 'transborder data-flow' are vigorously fought. There exists a well-aired and politically well-entrenched fear that, in the wake of American television products pouring into the minds of the European young, there will take place a breakdown of national consciousness leading to the loss of political autonomy. The cultural ministers of the EC have for several years now been considering plans for subsidising some kind of trans-European enterprise for stimulating European mass entertainment programmes. The French Minister of Culture, Jack Lang, in the first part of the Mitterrand era, took a lead in trying to inject, not merely into European official thinking, the belief that some kind of cultural bulwark against the United States could be constructed. There have been fears that not only the Third World but the powerful nations of Western Europe themselves are vulnerable to the insidious forces of 'foreign' (i.e. American) television. The example of Canada has quickened the debate, since its case is particularly acute (if one shares the basic fear) for the majority of its English-speaking population live within antenna-shot of the American television networks, while its French population is protected against the outpouring by reason of their language. It is important to look back at the roots of the cultural nationalism which seems today to be about to succumb to transnational or global forces. We all share the sensation at some level, though we may resist some of the political aspects of the debate.

The immediate forebears of the European nationalisms of the last century who provided the models and the language of present-day cultural nationalism were the philologists of two hundred years ago. They initiated the vortex of issues by studying the tribal roots of legend and song in Europe. They fed their researches into a political movement which urgently required emotional material to back the contemporary political yearning for the creation of nation states. Composers of the 19th century – and the 20th – wove traditional airs and peasant tunes into the symphony and the concerto, which evolved as a kind of industrialisation of the popular culture. Orchestra, opera house, public education system, popular library – these evolved as the cultural machinery of the modern nation state, working to construct the new politics upon a linguistic, musical and mythological vernacular. However, the nationalist paradigm was riddled with contradictions in the cultural as much as in the political sphere: where the Austro-Hungarian Empire, for example, had been administered in the Latin language, the yearning for the vernacular led to the replacement of Latin by German, bringing out the latent conflicts between the many national groups within that Empire and opening them to later attempts at German domination. The contradiction between nationalism as a democratising force and nationalism as an imperial force, worked its way through into controversies over education, religious teaching, maintenance of regional cultures and so on. Britain was enveloped in both forms of nationalism, its imperial manifestation satisfying itself for a couple of generations by its leadership of an 'English-speaking world' while a number of unsatisfied micro-nationalisms (Wales, Ireland, Scotland) festered away inside.

The problem with the new argument over nationalism and culture is that it takes place at a time when the technologies which transport popular culture, and the industries which carry them, are international by nature. The film industry is irreversibly dominated by Hollywood, which is coming now to dominate also the market in television software. We do not live at a point in time when we are *discovering* national values in the content of popular culture, but merely trying to hold back what is felt to be an imminent floodtide of American production, the waste product of the American domestic market. It was possible during the last decades to maintain, even enhance, the sense of national solidarity in cinema, radio and television, by constructing a controlled, regulated or nationalised indigenous industry; today, however, there exists an international market for software and the need, for industrial reasons, to permit a deregulated set of modern information networks to evolve. To exclude the American 'avalanche' can be achieved only at the price of a general economic backwardness. France has attempted to build an indigenous electronics industry to accompany a gallicised information and entertainment industry, but it will be harder and harder to maintain it in future and impossible for every nation in Europe to maintain its own cultural autarchy by such means.

It is unsurprising, therefore, that a movement to create a European base for software production has emerged, though it is difficult to see the cultural basis for this. For many European countries, Britain especially, America is far less 'foreign' a country than their immediate geographical neighbours. Ties of history and links caused by emigration patterns mean that almost every country of the continent has a stake, and in a sense, can find a kind of expression in America, which it could not find by trying to absorb the cultural production of adjacent countries. Only Scandinavia has been able to form a transnational set of cultural linkages which seem and feel 'real' in historical terms, but to imagine the actual content of a trans-European mass culture is impossible. The clear fact about the American popular product is that it does indeed offer an aura of accepted Western cultural values, far more than the soap opera of other European societies; the American product is familiar, the European exotic. American mass television culture has found the formula by which a myriad of national and tribal audiences around the world can become involved in a film or video narrative from within their own emotions; the American product conjures a recognition of its meanings from widely different audiences and, conceivably, in the process alters or undermines the structures of values or, at best, of social and material desires, of the receiving cultures.

But of course there are powerful reasons why politicians in Europe have started to support cultural and artistic and entertainment work which would help to sustain a sense of the national. Politics itself is rooted in the national – the electoral system is part of national culture. The major institutions of culture and learning, from libraries to television stations are rooted in national legality – though today on the brink of electronic internationalisation. The nation remains the legal and political substructure for most cultural institutions. It is the basis of the political argument for subsidising the arts. It is used to help educational systems maintain the onward flow of the heritage. It is part of the defence of political sovereignty despite the increasing dependence on a global economy. All governments agree to protect aspects of national culture as a strategic concern. It is an aspect of territory. But they will choose different symbols and different tactics.

In Bulgaria in the 1960s the authorities started an attempt to stop about three-quarters of a million ethnic Turks from speaking Turkish and from wearing the *shalvari* or Turkish trousers, and to give up their Turkish names as well as Islam itself. One Bulgarian publication of the 1980s described this process as part of the struggle 'for Bulgarian nationhood, and for the development of a new awareness, way of life, customs and traditions'. One of the principal means employed by the Bulgarian authorities to encourage the Turkish community towards a complete sense of its Bulgarian nationhood consisted predictably in prohibiting listening to radio broadcasts from Turkey. Those were the unacceptable techniques of communist-led nationalism. But how are Western techniques different? Take a document of the Canadian Radio and Television Commission (CRTC) which, in a ruling designed to force a commercial broadcasting company to produce more 'Canadian' drama declares:

> It will be a condition of the renewal of the CTV network licence that 26 hours of original new Canadian drama be presented during the 1980-81 broadcasting year and 39 hours of original new Canadian drama be presented during the 1981-82 season . . . The primary orientation should be on Canadian themes and the contemplated production should be intended for telecasting in the peak viewing periods of the evening schedule.

Why this need to contrive the sense of nationality through media iconography? Is it not similar to forcing the wearing of a garment?

There is clearly a widespread belief based on fear that the cultural behaviour of large groups decides the survival of national governments and political autonomies. The Bulgarians feared that the Turkishness of their ethnic Turk compatriots prejudiced the completeness with which they can develop as a Bulgarian nation within their national (and ideological) boundaries. The Canadian telecommunications regulator has absorbed the contemporary fear of the effects of cultural 'imperialism' to the point of insisting that an intending broadcasting body shall compose fresh *drama*. How does theatre emerge from edict? Can Canadianness, or Bulgarianness for that matter, be contrived by statute? Are institutions which exist to sustain national cultural identity or autonomy the cause of or the result of national consciousness? If a culture is not backed by the mere instincts of the population, then is it national or is it culture?

The nation state which emerged – somewhat to the surprise of political prophets and historians – as the primary political force of the 20th century, finds itself today defending cultural homogeneity after abandoning economic, political, diplomatic and often military exclusivity. In the least policeable field, that zone of life which is closest to the emotions and to our individuality, it is rather strange to find the state so insistent, when sovereignty of all kinds has long been happily surrendered to the EC, the United Nations, Comecon, the European and World Courts, and a host of trans- and multinational enterprises and institutions. America too is not immune to the same insistence, and even in the United States with its multitude of ethnicities, there are anxieties expressed whenever a newspaper or a TV channel or a film company passes into danger of foreign control. Perhaps we are witnessing a final spasm of the national movements of the 19th century. Perhaps this is all a last attempt by local elective elites to hold on to a sense of importance, a bureaucratic protectionism disguised as a national emotional need.

No two nations exist as nations by reason of the same theory of nationhood, nor by the same criteria. Some see themselves as the genetic outcrop of an ancient clan or tribe, while others proclaim their identity on the basis of a fusion of cultures achieved only in the recent past. Some date their nationhood by dynasty, while others base it upon a revolutionary break with monarchical institutions. Some are founded on territory and the speaking of a language, while others treat their nationhood as essentially portable and are content to speak the language of, and use the institutions of a host (not necessarily hostile) community. What all of them, however, share is a sense of a culture-in-the-present, something which nourishes or supposedly nourishes the sense of adhering to a group. Those customs, traditions, beliefs, attitudes, skills, which are deemed to constitute essential elements of the nationhood concerned are defined by their oppositions: the essential requirements of the nation tend to be the very things which are, at a given moment, under threat. Nationhood, therefore, has evolved as a discourse; it is a debate about the requirements of being a nation.

A nation is a culture or a society which has seized upon the discourse or discourses of nationalism as being structurally essential to it. Thus there are no definitions of nations as the subjects of historical experience, only observations of the progress of internal and external tensions which fuel discourses. In the Republic of China more people are learning English than the entire population of the United States; in France the thought of so much English being spoken would occasion great public concern. In West African societies tribal languages survive and flourish while English is the official language of the public world. In Quebec the spread of English in the public sphere is deliberately held in check. There are no set ways of being a nation, only debates about the identity of national groups.

None the less nations of all kinds, and based upon however divergent a range of ideologies, have at their disposal the same library of national sentiment. The emotions all overlap on a scale from Homeric patriotism to Nazism and every age has expanded the range and made it more subtle. Every layer of political experience has left its affective mark upon national anthems, the design of flags and pageants and the evasions and declamations of public inscriptions. National sentiment is the residue of national struggles and the raw material of the continuing debate about the nature, origins and destiny of the nation concerned. Armies of historians have, since the birth of political nationalism, in the many versions which flourished in the last century, helped to select and modulate the emotions which attach to the world's nations and nationalities. The imagery of the nation is itself, of course, in constant motion and passes through the many stages between proclamation and repression.

Anyone who reads the later and generally unsung stanzas of Britain's national anthem, calling upon the Almighty to 'scatter the enemies' of the monarch, is aware of the ways in which sentiment shifts in meaning or ceases to be emotionally and politically satisfying as time passes. But sentiments attached to patriotic identity also arise from the internal tensions and struggles of classes, regions, dynasties, which exercise their impact upon the language of patriotism, purifying it, corroding it, overstimulating it. One generation's expression of patriotism (Britain's other anthem 'Land of Hope and Glory' is another relevant text) can suddenly appear to the next as an expression of imperialism and therefore be socially divisive; but, one generation further, with the ending of a colonial empire it returns as a pure, poetic expression of geographical patriotism. The final lines 'God who made thee mighty, make thee mightier yet' implying something industrial, intellectual or spiritual, rather than territorial or militaristic.

There is a constant evolution, repression and resurrection of symbols entailed in national histories. Renan said it was necessary for nations – '*oublier bien des choses*'. The Chinese told their satrap to the south that its name was Viet Nam two centuries ago, an appellation rejected by the leaders of that people. The Chinese later decided to call the area Annam (the South), as if it existed in relation only to the Chinese. Yet within some generations the name Viet Nam was the one proclaimed by nationalist revolutionaries as the true name of the country and Dai Nam (= the Great South), which had been used by local officials for much of the 19th century, fell out of use. The history of national symbols is a history of improvisations applied within a debate about identities.

The economic transformation which is occurring as a result of the arrival of information technology is also at the heart of other transformations, shifts in many forms of identity, personal, familial, national, international. The information economy is fuelled by constantly changing wants and expectations, and constantly refashioned emotions and loyalties. The nation in its countless self-defining forms remains notionally the basic unit of the world as society, but its cultural dimensions are in the process of being tested to the point of destruction with the advent of satellite, advanced cable and an international market for cultural goods. The weaknesses and self-contradictions of nationhood are being progressively exposed. Language, creed, political system, historical tradition, none of these any longer follows the lines of the nation. Today we feel more acutely the falseness of the quest for such unities and therefore find the goal of nationhood fading as a motive force.

Yet clearly the sense of nationality will remain as one of the series of layers of identity within each individual. We shall continue to share the consciousness of skin colour, of gender, of race and ethnic origin, of faith, language, continent, class and ideology; we shall find, amid this multitude of units of belonging not so much a unique mix for each individual, more a sense of the temporariness of the self, of its essential improvisation, for every element of identity is itself but an idea of who we might be, not a destiny but a choice, not a definition but an attempt to define ourselves. At the core of our being is not a certainty but a wondering; not a truth but an enquiry.

6

Revolution or Evolution?

The Social Consequences of Technology Convergence*

It has become increasingly difficult of late to say what is meant by the term 'information society' – that once simple and optimistic phrase used to describe the general social impact of the computer and telecommunications. As the 1970s and 80s progressed, these new technologies produced different aspects of this long-predicted state of society. And with each aspect came an apparently completely new definition of the topic as a whole.

For more than twenty years now, people have been welcoming the imminence of a new stage of industrial society, or if not a new stage, then at least a reorganisation of work and leisure, arising from the coming of advanced information technology. They were referring to the new era of devices which were then beginning to emerge from the convergence of the computer and telecommunications. All sorts of social and attitudinal changes were ascribed to this new generation of technology and many others were predicted.

During the 1980s, dramatic events started to occur in parts of the world where for generations the inhabitants had endured a tyrannical and wasteful aberration of industrial society. It was a society in which most people had long failed to receive their share of the wealth and the social freedoms that the rest of us enjoy. Many quickly attributed the changes in these societies to that same proclaimed information revolution, even though the collapse of communism had never been foretold to occur as a result of an information society. Russian friends arrive nowadays wanting videos and personal computers, travellers from central Europe turn up enviously eyeing our telephones and fax machines, and we slip into discussing perestroika and the collapse of communism as if they were another effect of the information revolution.

Since the late 1960s, governments, scholars and industrialists in what we used to call Western democratic societies have been possessed by the idea that through the mixing of computer and telecommunications technologies an explosive force of social change could be unleashed and a new stage of industrial society achieved. Many governments have decided to specialise in the information revolution, and have built excessively high public expectations of its potential.

---

* This paper was originally delivered at a Technology Studies seminar at the Freedom Forum Media Studies Center, Columbia University, New York City, in October 1991.

Many people hoped that information technology would turn out to be a kind of all-purpose panacea. At the point of convergence of computer and telecommunications technologies many long-accumulating problems of Western democratic societies might suddenly become soluble. Automation would take a giant leap forward and develop a different kind of role from the simple labour-saving and cost-cutting of the 1950s. Massive computing power and instant communication would alter the very methods of production and the nature of work itself. Inexpensive long-distance communications could inaugurate a work-at-home movement, thereby reducing or ending altogether the traffic jams clogging the cities of the world. As distance became less of a cost factor in the information business, so it would in physical transportation, since an ever-larger proportion of the cost of manufactured goods consists of the information element – the research, marketing, distribution and advertising costs.

Information was turning into a novel form of resource, and could be conceptualised as an ingredient in the creation of all goods and services. Thus the cost-structure problems of traditional manufacturing seemed to be diminishing.

This new economic resource would partly replace the industries of manufacturing and extraction as the main realms of employment. One could envision the totality of the databases and bit-streams of the world as social and economic resources. Somehow these would be measured for accessibility, purity and quality; they would be a new factor in calculating the wealth of nations.

New global networks would spread words, images, scientific and medical data, and news and entertainment cheaply, profusely and instantaneously to every kind of audience, from mass to specialised. Moreover, they would do so in the newly possible interactive mode; people could answer back technologically, express their needs and vexations through the new networks and thus democracy itself would be rejuvenated by a technologically powered process of social consultation. The poor and the sick would receive better treatment. Women and ethnic minorities would have a better place and enjoy fuller recognition in this newly re-formed economic realm because they could quickly possess, among other things, the newly required skills. Old problems were being perhaps rather facilely linked to new opportunities.

Furthermore, there were to be important changes in the whole style of our societies. The information workforce of the future would not be composed of proletariats but of unclassifiable white-collar workers. A new bourgeoisie seemed to be springing up, international in character, having no particular social class as its progenitor. In Britain, the newly successful entrepreneurs seemed to speak demotic English. People were defined by their style more than by social origin.

And it was style that drove the engines of the consumer economy, invigorated by the continual shifting and refining of individual needs. The free market would be expanded and intensified with rededicated dynamism and the interplay of individual preferences would determine the distribution of wealth and profit.

Important changes in the home would follow. The home would become the centre of economic and cultural life when the new networks would permit shopping from domestic terminals as well as the selection of information and entertainment from a global store of materials. Later, 'smart cards' would multiply personal access to goods and services of all kinds and would permit instant gratification of the demands stimulated by print and electronic media.

The computer-and-telecommunications revolution was to be another industrial revolution, or a new stage in the industrial revolution, sweeping away old social relationships as it proceeded. The ideological conflicts of centuries would wither away as the new pragmatism of the information workforce gradually took root.

This new stage has been given many labels, many of them beginning with the prefix 'post' – postindustrial, postmodern, post-Gutenberg – all of them expressing the same sense of a newly discovered space in which technique would converge with human needs and a new cultural zone for making and remaking the self.

Much of this prophecy has been well founded. Many of the changes that I have listed are coming about. Telecommunication networks are transforming the economic and social worlds. Market economics is the religion of the decade. The means of communication are multiplying precisely as predicted, but somehow that element of the dream that was to be revolutionary is not being fulfilled. The profusion of channels is not turning us into a vastly educated democracy. It is not even noticeably expanding the number of people who want to multiply the cultural influences to which they are subjected. The number of the illiterate still seems to be growing. The widening array of available choices seems to make possible a narrowing in the choices that an individual actually makes.

There has also been a failure in the political consequences. The availability of increased knowledge about, say, the ecological crisis has not made politicians any more willing to work towards global solutions. They are not entirely unwilling, but the flow of information itself has not noticeably altered the constraints within which they function. The seizure of oil resources by a foreign army will cause governments to move fast, but the knowledge of the effects of acid rain brings about no instant mobilisation of national resources.

We have learned that information does not act autonomously. It is not an agency but rather one of many instruments of history. Truly large-scale political change has, in fact, occurred in those societies that enjoy the least information, where telephone and fax are still the utmost of luxuries. My point is that information technology has not, despite all the anticipations expressed and the enormous quantity of capital invested, revealed any particular and reproducible line of social effect.

Perhaps the most important of the delayed or falsified predictions is that changes in the geography of work have not come about. Perhaps there are more consultants working at home, but the roads are clogged with new flows of commuter traffic. And new office blocks are rising on every horizon. The analogies that were drawn in conferences during the 1980s between the coming of new, cheap and accessible telecommunications devices and the printing revolution of the last century simply do not hold. Information technology has not brought in its wake a transformation in education or in the physical organisation of society. It has not altered the rhetoric or conduct of politics, and still less the content of politics.

None the less, hundreds of computer applications have indeed become deeply inscribed in daily life and in our normal working expectations. Word processing and ticketing and billing procedures are now virtually invisible in the sense that we use these services without noticing the presence of the technology as such. Many computer applications – the pocket calculator, for example – have virtually become standard extensions of our physical or mental capacities. But to justify the term 'revolution' you need to find a real and widespread transformation in fundamental aspects of our social structure.

The word 'revolution', we sometimes forget, is just a metaphor. When it was first applied to human affairs, it still held a reminiscence of fortune's wheel, the turning of which restored a given state of affairs. A revolution was something that put things back to where they were. The Glorious Revolution of 1689, which brought William and Mary to the throne of England, was one such bringing back. It was the French Revolution of 1789 that first attached to the metaphor the sense of a thorough transformation in the social order. When the British began to speak of an industrial revolution in the 19th century – at first in lower case and only much later in upper case when it became an official term of history – it was in order to point up a contrast to the bloody revolutions that had occurred on the continent of Europe. The Industrial Revolution was offered as an explanation for the absence of a political and social revolution.

The industrialisation of manufacturing was not a revolution in the same sense as the changes that followed from the storming of the Bastille; it was in fact an extremely slow evolution in technological circumstances that, when looked upon with the full benefit of decades of hindsight, seemed to have been a revolution. Therefore, when we talk today of an information revolution we are applying a metaphor to a metaphor. The very term has distorted our expectations.

However, we are evidently passing through a massive change in prevailing technology, which does appear to be bringing in its wake changes in attitude perhaps more profound than those that have occurred in other periods of ten or twenty years since World War I. But every two or three years the defining aspects of this great change alter. Every time we look at this 'revolution' we find a different way of describing it.

At this moment, for example, the emphasis of concern is on the process of convergence, that is, the synergy of different technologies or elements within a technology, and the concomitant linking of corporations and institutions. These changes appear to warrant various legislative and constitutional reforms or, rather, they demonstrate the outmoded nature of present legal arrangements that had seemed eternal only a year or two ago. We are also witnessing the process of globalisation, the restructuring of great corporations around the world to fulfil commercial purposes that are mysterious often even to those directly involved. The emergence of great global corporations, about which I shall say more later, is occurring simultaneously but for quite different corporate reasons – so different as to make generalisations about them hard to formulate.

Defining the Information Society

The thought that communication as it has been variously defined marks a new stage in industrial society is a fairly old one and one that has been expressed in many ways. People have seized upon different technologies as the essential instruments of the transformation. Quite different defining characteristics have been selected in the course of attempts to describe what is happening to us. I shall dwell for a moment on a number of them, but my list is not exhaustive. My point is that one gets a new information revolution for each machine or, rather, each phase in the technology that one happens to choose.

Television was thought by many to be revolutionary in its impact. It was claimed that television constituted something much bigger than a new phase in the development of mass culture, which had already begun with the phonograph, the cinema and radio. There was a tendency, especially in the 1960s at the high point of enthusiasm for Marshall McLuhan's concept of a global village, for the whole change to be thought of as cultural rather than technological in nature. Students and intellectuals were thought to be the new revolutionary class. A cultural revolution was under way within a communications revolution. European cultural analysts of the 1960s described a change in capitalist society that was being led from within the cultural superstructure, while American writers on the subject tended to describe a change that was being brought about by innovation within the technological infrastructure.

Within the societies of Europe and North America, the prevailing areas of concern in the early television era were the social problems of the time. Was it the content of television that was causing the wave of teenage crime and the slackening of the moral code? Since advertising evidently had economic effects, there ought to be clear and traceable social effects. But after years of research it appeared that there were not any, at least not the kind of effects for which social scientists had been searching. There seemed to be highly complicated indirect effects, reconstructions of the social and political agenda through television, the remaking of identity through the representations of gender, class, nationality and ethnicity. These were not specific to the new technologies, instead they were continuations in a long line of cultural observation. The search for special and transferable characteristics of an information society, insofar as mass communication and entertainment technologies defined that society, seemed to end up in a dense forest.

There was one part of the forest where it seemed easier to look for this special technology-based cultural change. One powerful focus of research was developmental change, the process of modernisation in traditional societies. There, the television, telephone and radio were all thought to be the harbingers of real social change, the catalyst for the transformation of whole societies.

In developing countries, during the first era of television, there evolved new elites characterised by their cultural and often economic dependence upon interests in the West. There was, therefore, a kind of optical illusion of social change visible from the West. But development, as it had been envisioned, did not occur. The aspirations of people who came to live in cities altered a great deal, and terrible problems of environmental degradation and pollution began to emerge, but modern communications did not bring about the implantation of that nexus of attitude and industry that should have produced a Western-style prosperity.

We learned that society and consciousness precede economics. The same entertainment material, the same telephone system, the same formats in radio and television, bring different gratifications to different kinds of lives. They reapportion prestige and alter relationships, but they do not transform a receiving society in the sense of remaking it to correspond to the ways of the donor society. In time, Third World countries produced their own cinema and television industries without necessarily adopting the same forms of social change as the donor societies of the West.

It is interesting to note that when some East European countries decided that they wanted to create a free economy and a democratic system, they did it not as a response to new technologies but as a result of the collapse of the old regime. Perhaps degeneration, disillusion and collapse are the only really transferable principles of history and are more powerful than the positive forces of knowledge and innovation.

Developing Information Highways

In the 1970s, a different kind of technological change became visible on the horizon. Now it was the telephone – that ancient collection of wires that passed through the majority of homes and businesses – that became the focus of attention, rather than television. It was clear that a new generation of networks was being constructed that would bring about low-cost broadband communication. These new networks would permit the easy distribution of commercial information as well as entertainment material and advanced telephony along the same highways. Instead of a few terrestrial television transmitters there would be multichannel systems and subscription channels for specialised information. The problem was how to create this new set of information highways and trunk systems throughout a society.

Some of the new signal-distribution methods were completely novel and required something more sophisticated than analog signals. They would depend upon the digitisation of text, sound and image – in essence, the reduction of all information to the condition of computer data. A new generation of computers was arriving that would encode and decode the materials. But to bring about this change entailed very great institutional and legal changes, which took some time for politicians and corporations to understand.

An enormous investment sunk in the world's telephone systems, which had evolved since Victorian times, would be thrown away. New computerised methods involved the rapid writing off of considerable quantities of capital. There were difficulties encountered in the choice of the highways themselves, since there were brand new coaxial cables and undersea cables for long-distance traffic available. But new microwave links were opening up, and optical fibre, which became a practical reality very rapidly, was already an object of active experiment in the late 1970s. The revolution in the then rather neglected instrument of telephony was crucial to all that has subsequently occurred.

It was impossible for a government, any government, almost by its nature, to find the right legislative path from prevailing to potential circumstances. Only the free play of market forces and great battles between industrial titans would result in the creation of this necessary new system. Deregulation was the inevitable tool. Therefore, in societies with a high degree of national ownership of telecommunications, there also had to be a long and difficult process of privatisation in order to enable dozens of competing judgments and motivations to be brought to bear on these issues. An industry that had grown under careful official tutelage had to be released into the chaos of the marketplace, in order to produce greater, indeed vitally necessary, public benefit.

With the new broadband systems in place, there could be a new industrial revival in the countries of the north and south. But it would entail a political and social shake-up, country by country, a shake-up that seemed so daunting as to be worth labelling a revolution. The most powerful vested interests, in both public and private sectors, would have to be tackled. They would not like it. They would insist on preserving their interests. The process would be profoundly political and would both test and reshape the operations of politics in many countries. It was that essential ingredient of far-reaching political change needed to bring about technological change that was the real essence of the information revolution to come.

A wholly new and quite unpredicted evolution in political doctrine developed to fuel the changes. A new set of telecommunications highways was created in many countries. New industries followed from them. In Japan, to take the most dynamic example, a new world economic power was born from the union of computer and telecommunications. In Britain, to take a less dynamic example, several million new jobs have been created – a substantial gain, though less than the millions of jobs that had been lost through de-industrialisation.

But politics was the real engine of change. Thatcherism and Reaganomics both had their imitators (although not always their overt admirers) in socialist France and Australia and Islamic Turkey. It will be many decades before historians can trace the linkages between the new market ideology and the computer revolution. But without the ideological fervour that fuelled such events as the break-up of AT&T and the privatisation of British Telecom, the rest of the machinery of change would never have started up. It required an intensity akin to that of the building of the railways in the 19th century to force the pace of change, but fervours of that kind require governments with strong wills to push them into being.

The information revolution, if that is what it really was, involved a unique alliance of governments, ideologists and technology at a time when Western consumer economies were in a bad way, needing some sort of boost. What is still impossible to determine is whether the economic changes brought about the ideological and cultural ones or vice versa. What makes all those schools buy computers and then force small children to learn by playing with the new computer toys? There was – and still is of course – a social adrenalin at work, the result and cause of countless television programmes and newspaper articles, congressional and parliamentary debates and hundreds of volumes of pop sociology.

Just as the railway pioneers discovered an untapped and unexpressed demand for low-cost mass travel, so did the computer and telecommunications industries, in their re-formed guise, lay bare a huge seam of public interest in a retooling of industrial society, whose viability depended upon a mass preparedness to participate.

In the nineteenth-century cheap-printing revolution, most of the necessary investment was confined to the industry of the press and its distribution system, although a political will and national investment in mass literacy were also necessary. In the world of modern communications, a much larger proportion of total investment is in terminal equipment. It is, therefore, the users who have to be persuaded to spend their money. It is the mass public, at home and in business, that has to make the real investment in the new systems. A radical shift in consumer preferences is required to make the technological changes come about. In other words, the revolution has to occur within the mind and outlook of consumers.

Information as Resource

Many observers of the changing scene envisaged information as a kind of constant and renewable resource: the contents of a society's combined data stream could be judged for sophistication, flexibility and accessibility and the quality of its research. Information could therefore be treated as a new measure of social wealth.

The trouble with this very attractive notion is that information is not really *sui generis*, even when transmuted by digitisation into a single technical condition. Text is not really homogeneous when it emerges as data any more than it is when inscribed on paper. The existence of computerised taxation and pension records, police records and insurance and health data are obviously a good guide to a society's administrative modernity. But many more questions need to be asked about the availability and handling of records and databases before it is possible to judge the state of a nation's data stream as 'advanced'.

The newly emerging information economy grows as information of all kinds is spread through a society's services and institutions. But the treatment of information, as if it had become a resource of its own, like water, forests, farm produce or the education system, is another example of a metaphor being over-extended into indicative language. The metaphor may be a useful way of arresting attention, of making people look at familiar phenomena in new ways, but it is ultimately misleading.

If you do develop a homogenised mental image of information as a singular phenomenon, a different picture of the information society as a whole emerges. It is a society in which information becomes a kind of cash crop and we are all defined as its consumers. Differences of value between the preferences of one group of consumers over another become harder to emphasise. Everything comes to seem of similar value. In your evaluation, reading *War and Peace* is no better or worse than reading pulp fiction. All information about persons seems to turn into a commodity. All knowledge and research that is made to pass through the electronic pathways and storage systems passes also into personal possession and ceases to be social in nature or national in ownership. Knowledge that is free if collected through traditional methods now costs money and is, therefore, subject to market valuation.

As a method of conceptualising the essence of the information society, this new image of information is a new secularising, reifying and commodifying process. But it has contributed something to our picture of the state of society. In academia and in the media, an egalitarianism of the text has emerged that shocks traditionalists. The old canons of literature have been shelved. We study our own culture as a source of meaning, rather than pursuing the excellent as a means of attaining a progressive refinement of taste. The change in style is also part of the information society.

A further definition of the information society frequently offered during the late 1970s and early 1980s was an argument based on the shape and size of the workforce. Observers noticed that it was possible to divide work into two broad categories – information and non-information. You could then count the numbers of workers passing from one category to another. It appeared that the number of information workers had grown by the 1960s to half of the total workforce in the United States and certain other countries. And it seemed that an easily checkable and portable definition of the new society had been isolated.

Gradually, however, certain paradoxes became apparent. The adoption of information technology tended to reduce, not expand, the number of people employed in handling information. And even though many more people were using computing in one form or another in their work, they did not appear to be developing the same consciousness. After all, people who used typewriters have never defined themselves as a group because of their use of the typewriter. People in the travel business did not feel any closer to people in the banking business merely because they both had to be fairly adept in interrogating international databases.

The workforce theory of the information society has, therefore, gradually faded away. But for a time it had seemed to be telling us something about the changing nature of our society.

Computers and the Culture of Procedures

There are, nevertheless, aspects of what one might call the mental training that goes with the use of computers. These aspects are significantly altering the way we think and feel. There could still be a great deal of mileage in this strand of thought, which is a recent addition to the discussion.

Computers impose upon us a culture of procedures. They are almost smugly infallible pieces of machinery. They insist that we move through a series of ordered and layered instructions and that we think about the information we provide and extract in ways that suit the strict and 'ordered mind' of the computer in all its forms. It is not surprising that one writer, James Beniger, has labelled the phenomenon of computerisation the 'Control Revolution'.

The propensity towards human error has been present and made manifest in industrial society in cruel and destructive ways. Chaos, accident and loss were the constant companions of economic growth. The sheer problems of organising production, bookkeeping and commerce in the 19th and early 20th centuries sent inventors in search of new ways of maintaining managerial order. Among the developments of earlier stages of industrial civilisation were methods of what today one would call information processing. These were physical rather than mechanical means, organisational techniques and the paper storage of information generated by the running of stocks and the control of the flow of work and production; yet these catalogues and bookkeeping systems were the forerunners of the computerised systems of a later day.

The computer is in a sense simply the mechanisation of bureaucracy. There are, therefore, human continuities between the physical hierarchies of the last century and the systems of today. It is not surprising that with distributed computer power there often comes a democratisation of, for example, the whole culture. Human organisation is itself a form of information processing.

There are other ways in which the computer helps to reveal the human machinery that it displaces and encodes. For example, the traditional methods of printing by movable type go back to the 15th century. They have now been virtually replaced by electronic means. But it is those methods that gave rise to our ideas about the nature of authors, indeed, to a kind of sacralisation of the text around the notion of the author.

In academic practice, research is an interdisciplinary, collaborative process that passes across continents and across generations. However, the exigencies of publishing and of academic organisation have caused a culture or cult of individualism, or rivalry, of even a kind of hero worship and national competitiveness to be incorporated into research. In the era of the international database, that culture is progressively reduced in meaning. Of course, investors in research require returns, individual discoveries are protected and copyrights and patents maintained, but behind the scramble for knowledge, there lies an emerging realisation that, looked at through time, it is all in truth a vast collaboration.

Knowledge is social and global in character, though it has been pressed into the moulds of individualism and nationalism. Through the operations of the computer one can see how the trick was done.

The old knowledge culture was built around the notion of the text as a singular and eternal phenomenon. The new conception is based upon an infinity of versions, subject to permanent interpretation. The text is never complete, but eternally interim. All our certainties turn into provisional suggestions.

The protean character of knowledge is parallel with style, the driving force of the information-age economy. But that ever-altering sense of what constitutes knowledge reflects a modern psychic state, a different way of handling certainty and doubt. Our intellectual lives are a constant evolution of disillusionments, each one an enrichment and an advance, none of them being the product of a single mind or group of minds.

It would be wrong to speak as if the computer had caused that change in our state of mind. But it has been the necessary accompanying instrument of the change, a change that is itself far from completely evolved. As the byte replaces the slug of type as the basic unit of stored or transmitted knowledge, the text to which they both contribute has shifted from a sense of fixity to the condition of infinite revision.

Knowledge as it appears in books and papers continues to look as if it is a fixed material, but the processes of publishing belie the shift of consciousness that has taken place. In one field of learning after another the profusion and approximation of the database has a greater sense of reality than the printed text, out-of-date as soon as it appears.

Globalisation and the Ownership of Information

The phenomenon of multi-ownership of text – in the moral sense at least – is not too hard to assimilate. However, the implications of globalisation of ownership of information resources are still to be revealed. It is a new phase in the evolution of the information society and it might in time impose its own special character upon our culture more vigorously than any other.

The international process of merger and deal was first fully visible in the 1986-7 period when the economic cycle was reaching its peak. New consortia drawn from operators and users, computer vendors and equipment suppliers had sprung into being. Software suppliers in a series of media started to look for international link-ups. Hardware producers searched for software partners in order to consolidate their position and software consortia looked for hardware to make their empires more solid. By the mid-1980s so many telecommunications enterprises had been privatised that there existed a whole new demi-monde of businesses looking for acquisitions, scrambling to occupy the first positions in a new global league.

There is no visible established pattern of globalisation or corporate diversification. The picture is one simply of scramble. There is now a $320 billion annual market in telecommunications alone, and the strategy of certain companies is to fight for a place in what might become a small league of supercarriers that link a larger number of smaller and more local operators. AT&T, British Telecom, Nippon Telegraph and Telephone Corporation (NTT), Deutsche Telecom, France Telecom and US Sprint are the major entities in the field. All of these organisations are attempting to build intelligence into their network operations in order to enable themselves to seize the initiative in a global market for simple public-processed information.

As the international linkages become more competitively priced, the market grows and plans are developed for new transatlantic cables and satellite linkages, which will make inexpensive international telephony and data processing possible throughout the world.

Globalisation is the objective, and the means tend to consist in breaking the taboos that surround the building of monopolistic practices. Railway companies are pressing for permissions to use their land for establishing networks. Waterways and canal companies are joining in. The internal communication traffic of the great multinational corporations offers a vast new market and the global operators are all attempting to break into it, even though this entails following the multinationals far from the telecommunications companies' national bases. Where regulation has until now separated the sale of information and entertainment from the operating of networks, it has gradually become evident today that no such division is pure or unqualified or eternally acceptable.

In the United States, the first major breach was federal Judge Harold H. Greene's decision to permit the Baby Bells, which emerged from the deregulation of the AT&T corporation, to sell screen-based information to consumers. What appears a major affront to the traditional divisions of function in the United States has been common practice in European countries for some years. With the ability of wire and radio frequency to carry text as easily as video, it has been impossible to maintain separations of function that once appeared essential on grounds of political morality. The European Postal, Telephone and Telegraph Authorities (PTTs) have long been operating public-information services, albeit often acting only as common carriers themselves. Increasingly it has seemed that money is to be made only when the carrier processes and offers information services directly.

There are telephone company privatisations imminent in Asia, Latin America and Eastern Europe, which will add further energy to the international scramble. The same regions are also currently starting to license satellite and mobile communications as well as domestic cable systems. They are also privatising many of their broadcasting utilities. The seven US Bell operating companies are already full square in the business of providing entertainment and information. In these newcomer regions they will find themselves competing with corporations with which they are in alliance elsewhere. The position is complicated. For example, in Britain, Cable and Wireless Plc runs Mercury Communications Ltd, which works in competition with British Telecom; it owns a transatlantic cable (PTAT) with its partner US Sprint. But Sprint is finding other ways into the British market and is trying to work with British Waterways and other companies who compete with Cable and Wireless' Mercury telephone system.

The confusion of loyalties spreads across the globe. Cable and Wireless also holds a monopoly franchise for lucrative digital networks in Hong Kong – as well as in various former colonies of Britain – which, as they deregulate, will be attractive to Sprint. And on it goes.

Globalisation is one of the many simultaneous transformations taking place in the information and media fields, but the process is far from complete. In fact, it is so incomplete that one cannot see clearly any of the eventual shapes and formations. Indeed, so small a proportion of the total world industry is as yet actually concentrated in multinational firms that the whole process may turn out to be a misnomer or a tendency towards something else. At present, however, globalisation is the label for the accumulation of 'synergies' and company linkages of the 1980s.

Some predict that there will eventually be six immense companies controlling the culture and communications of the entire world. The air transport industry seems to be developing this way. It is more likely, however, that there will be a dozen or so companies, most of them still unknown to us by their eventual names, that will own a combination of hardware, software and communication linkages, and these will exploit the combined converging power of their assets to achieve a global cultural impact. We might admire the results. We might hate them. It is far too soon to tell. The companies themselves do not yet know who they are.

After all, in the present decade there are several completely new media technologies likely to spring into existence, high-definition television (HDTV) prominent among them. This medium may require the secure collaborative power of a movie company, satellite linkage, theatre ownership and hardware manufacture just to come into practical existence. The convergences that are presently sending shivers down the spines of American constitutional purists are nothing compared to what is to come. As with other aspects of the information economy, the big challenges are faced more in the political and legal worlds, than in the technological.

The Lunar Society

In the 1780s, a group of extremely learned and insightful individuals used to meet in an English Midland town once a month on the night of the full moon to discuss the changes then taking place all over England in the areas of science, manufacturing and commerce. Benjamin Franklin was sometimes present. The others were inventors, scientists, men of letters. They met on the full moon because it was easier to find their way home afterwards in the dark. They were called the Lunar Society.

They discovered a series of fascinating processes which were then under way. Much later, a school of history came to call these processes the Industrial Revolution, although that image did not appear in the minds of these contemporary observers, who speculated on such issues as whether the population was rising or falling, and whether steam power could be used to pump water out of flooded coal mines.

They had no single phrase with which to describe the changes going on around them and although they were living through the very midst of the change, it was impossible for them to see its full scope and eventual nature. The word 'revolution' was unknown to them in its twentieth-century metaphorical usage. Similarly, it is far too soon for us to see the essence of what is changing around us, although we see it in so many different manifestations and although we are certain that it concerns information.

In *The Man Without Qualities*, Robert Musil offers a useful observation: 'Our history is made up of the fact that every time we fulfil just a little of an idea, in our delight we leave the greater part of it undone; magnificent institutions are usually bungled drafts of ideas.' Musil was speaking about the ideas of individuals, but the observation also works on the grander scale of social ideas.

Every society gets hold of an idea with which it tries to rebuild itself from time to time, but it always fails to implement the whole vision or bungles the process of working it through from draft to reality. Sometimes the result of the process turns out to be an appalling tyranny; sometimes just the sense of a generational failure. But sometimes the bungling is a happy deliverance from something far worse. Perhaps that is as much as we should hope for.

PART TWO

The Life of Institutions

1

Contemporary Knowledge and Contemporary Journalism*

We are living at a time when the *means* of knowledge are all in a state of transition – indeed, when the major transformations under way within our economies are emerging from the changes which are influencing the means of knowledge. In the 1960s a furious debate took place in the arena of journalism concerning the validity of a function or technique described as 'objectivity' and the balance of view at that moment was that objectivity was somehow 'over'. Michael Schudson says the very word became a term of abuse.[1] What lay behind this decline of faith in (and within) many parts of the journalistic community was a growing distrust of certain forms of professionalism, of groups of people who claimed, by reason of their role and collective techniques, to hold in their hands a power of legitimising certain ranges of knowledge. The change taking place two decades on derives from a kind of flowering of intuition born of that 1960s disillusion. It takes the form of a discovery of new paradigms, in the theory of linguistics, in attitudes towards the study of culture, in telematics and computer science. A whole series of human and natural sciences have grasped, with enthusiasm rather than disdain, a new paradoxology and from it there is developing a rearrangement of the ways in which knowledge is compiled and accepted. In the era of postindustrialism knowledge is changing its skin and perhaps enjoying a new status. What I wish to address is how that change in the condition of knowledge is bearing down upon journalism, upon the special kinds of knowledge that pass as journalism and the ways in which journalism relates to all the other evolving forms of knowledge.

There are many ways to approach the new condition of knowledge. One may extract images of it from the works of contemporary poets and novelists: Borges tells of the emperor who requires a totally accurate map of his empire and leads his nation to ruin because the whole population is employed in drawing the map. One may seize upon a moment in the history of science: the Heisenberg principle of uncertainty is infinitely transferable from area to area, since it enables us in a flash of insight to see how no one may know a fact and the implication of a fact at the same time, since the knower is himself/herself situated within the field of scrutiny. One may take a social/

* This paper was delivered as a lecture at the Gannett Center for Media Studies, Columbia University, New York City, in June 1987.

historical perspective and describe the events of that pivotal year, noted by Virginia Woolf, of 1910 when a whole series of assumptions and beliefs seemed suddenly to collapse throughout the Euro-American world: cubism becomes the new exemplar for representation of the world.

What has occurred, by stages, during the century in all of the arts and sciences is a gradual acceptance of the implications of the collapse of the idea of the practicability of exact knowledge. Laplace offers us a model of the real which suggests that anyone who knows all of the variables affecting the workings of the universe at a given moment in time can predict its future. For a century or more most people probably believed that all the systems of which the universe is composed followed such a finite and essentially knowable course. Atomic physics and quantum mechanics helped us to realise that to *know* the condition of one of those systems completely would entail a consumption of energy as great as that within the system. We cannot map the world completely, we can only steer through the universe moving, perhaps, from one pool of fairly exact knowledge to another within a miasma of unknowingness. If you want to have complete control over some part of the universe – whether your own family, or a factory or a nation – in order to make it perform its function more perfectly you will destroy the organisation in the very course of getting its measure. These enticing paradoxes are the new commonplaces of official knowledge, of science and engineering. Newton and Laplace have been long dead. And yet we retain areas of social knowledge and specialisms within the observing professions which appear still to cling to the idea that the world can be reassembled and dissected and reduced to a stream of information known as news. The survival of the idea of objectivity or some approximation to it within the media, is a fact with far-reaching implications for the future of journalism.

The origins of new conceptions of knowledge lie also of course in industrialism which is itself a means of knowledge as well as a form of economic organisation. Each successive wave of the industrial revolution has in effect incorporated a new area of social activity. It was first formally noted as substitutive of traditional means of manufacture, especially of iron and cloth. It applied via engineering and chemistry new ideas of science and as it moved from stage to stage it provided a series of interim statements of the relationship between humankind and nature itself. The history of industrialism provides a register of altering conceptions while being an account of the implementation of those ideas. The industrial is also a form of human organisation and the 'inventions' which characterise it are human as well as physical. Thus, in the construction of the canals there was developed the forms of non-participative capital conglomeration which were adapted to the building of railways. There is a nexus which spreads throughout a society upon which industrialism feeds as much as upon physical materials and as much as upon scientific knowledge.

Industrialism spread from extractive to manufacturing spheres to transport and agriculture. However, in our own time there have occurred important eras in the evolution of industrial civilisation which we have somehow failed to identify as part of the same historic process. We have seen the arrival of industrialism in the years just before and just after World War II in the sphere of food manufacture; the packaging revolution was itself a stage in the development of the industrial order and the establishment of modern lines of food supply have been as important a change in history as the agricultural revolution which preceded early physical industries. However, in more recent years we have watched, under the rubric of computerisation, the industrial system spreading to the sphere of information and knowledge itself. When we look at the changing status of knowledge it helps to think of information having become, in the late 1960s and 1970s, a kind of crop produced within industrial society which is now farmed and packaged, collected and distributed by sale or lease, in the same manner as other commodities within the industrial economy.

The industries which provided the principal imagery of the last eras of human history, since the 18th century, no longer exist as central to economic life. The smokestacks have not yet disappeared. Many of them have merely moved from developed to developing societies. But where they formerly existed as dominant they tend now to be taking second place to the industries which are based upon the manipulation of information. Certainly these latter are occupying a very large segment of the workforce and the process of automation within the information sector of industry is producing the same kind of economies of efficiency that were achieved in the 1920s by the conveyor belt and in the 1950s by automation of equipment.

But what are the implications for knowledge of this alteration in its mode of collection and storage? Clearly those forms of knowledge that are easily adaptable to the new machines will tend to be more avidly and easily pursued. The new body of socially accessible knowledge will inevitably be that sector which is or will be computerised. In the last century large areas of knowledge became exoticised as different relationships evolved between different zones of the world. The area of easy transportation was the 'known world' and the more remote unlegitimised areas of human settlement took on the aura of the exotic, the scientifically invalid. Today, we can feel, within the decaying areas of cities, the presence of cultures whose knowledge has fallen out of the zone of legitimation, who are unrecorded as creditworthy, who lack computer skills and computer access and who become marginal and frightening, subjects of social concern and journalistic scrutiny, but on the outside of the dominant routines of media perusal and representation. Information stored by antique methods is becoming or is inevitably to become lost or marginal, together with the people whose knowledge it is, whose identity is contained in the memory by reason of those systems.

But the computerisation of information must cause a further and more important disjunction – that between knower and known. Knowledge has become and will become still further exteriorised, as it becomes commoditised. Our relation with a package of sugar or of rice which we recognise from the publicised brand label is different from the sacks of sugar and rice inside the store into which we once dipped with a scoop and which we handled before we purchased. So is our relationship with information which we obtain by renting it from a wholesale database provider, from the

99

information which we acquired as part of the *training* of our minds. In the development of knowledge as an exterior essentially purchasable service there lies an entire revolution in education. The training of minds by means of the inculcation of information is becoming obsolescent almost by the hour. Information is no longer the goal of education and knowledge no longer the goal of information: both are subject to valuation and purchase. That applies whether the information concerned is entertainment, educational, scientific or administrative. And yet this shift is not the result of computerisation in itself, so much as the result of a series of alterations in human organisation and human need which are today expressed in computerised functions. We are needing our minds less in the ways in which we formerly needed them; we need them of course as much but in order to perform different kinds of mental activity. Inevitably that must produce – must have produced and have been produced by – a new range of priorities within knowledge. That is not to say that we are turning into some new kind of automata; perhaps we are being enfranchised, released from unproductive mental drudgery. But there is no pure substitution. The exteriorisation of information entails a different relationship between the self and the environment.

To gain some purchase on the nature of these contemporary changes it is useful to look back at the worlds of knowledge before and after the impact of Gutenberg's invention of the printing press based upon 'movable' re-assemblable type. In pre-Gutenbergian mode knowledge was felt to be something which had to be *recovered*, which had been lost or existed in a constant process of being about to be lost. The transmission of information entailed enormous intellectual effort. For one thing, all the forces of nature conspired against its survival. Paper would crumble in time. Parchment and ink would fade and grow brittle. Stone inscription would in time be worn away by the elements and by conquest. Kronos was the enemy of knowledge. Of course, memory was of supreme importance in such civilisations. Whole techniques of memory were perfected which have now been very largely lost themselves. Being forgotten was the almost inevitable fate of everything which had been discovered, every human achievement. It was also a kind of cure, a process which cleaned the world of information and enabled learning to be renewed. None the less the whole of intellectual effort was concentrated upon acquiring the means of knowing and the material of knowledge. Those who possessed learning were essentially looking backwards, rather than concentrating upon the construction of new truths.

The chirographic era was one which concentrated upon formulae of language and in cultural forms within which information could be held. The great epics with their endless repetitions were the encyclopaedias of tribes and nations. The data did not exist outside the language which expressed it and protected it.

The new learning of the Renaissance was inextricable from the Gutenbergian technology. Printing was not the *cause* of a new attitude towards and new forms of learning. It was an indispensable facilitator, itself the *result* of changes within human needs in a certain group of societies. It, too, rendered certain forms of knowledge exterior to the mind, including language itself, of which the grammar and vocabulary could be recorded and fixed. In fact fixity was the great quality which printing conferred upon knowledge – calendars, sidereal charts, ecclesiastical practices, navigational material, all of these for example became fixed and therefore internationally exchangeable. Whole ranges of information became commoditised. Vernaculars could displace Latin after their grammars were explicitly established. *National* knowledge acquired a salience which it had previously lacked. Fixed information could be compared and analysed and sent on to different parts of the world. The spread of printing was as rapid in fact as the dissemination of computers in our own time, and the political, business and diplomatic implications were equally pronounced and equally drastic. The nature and location of capital altered with the coming of printing, as it has done with the creation of computerised markets. Knowledge became subject to a process of progressive augmentation. The image of knowledge was of something in the future, which would be acquired and could be acquired, by dint of mental effort. It was possible to record and reproduce the texts which had been inherited from previous generations with relative ease. The priorities of intellectual effort now lay elsewhere, in the production of new knowledge to fill the capacities of the press and the market for printed goods.

Knowledge became the question mark in the sky. Mental training was less directed at retaining large quantities of information and more at developing those mental habits which enabled knowledge to be calculated rather than simply transported. Opinion was the resultant of the strands of information which a single mind had absorbed. Through the contrasting of opinion, through argument conducted upon recognised principles, truth could be established. The era of Gutenberg was one in which the law could achieve new status in human society; politics became subject to opinion. Knowledge could belong to individuals rather than whole societies. Knowledge could be compartmentalised among groups of professionals – lawyers, merchants, tradesmen could share identical blocks of printed data. There were tools which could reduce knowledge to a condition of certainty. The search for objectivity through argument became a major mode of intellectual activity, where, in a chirographic society, the repetition of certainties expressed formulaically had been the comparable locus of forensic skills.

That expresses something of the altering status of knowledge before and after the development of moving type. What can be said about the current transformation in the processes of communicating information as a result of computerisation? I think one must begin by looking at the idea of modernity itself as it has emerged in this century. In literature and in painting, as in the sciences and in human studies, there was an attempt to draw out of the world the things which could not by their nature be seen and create some new form of explicitness. Picasso's cubism was just such an attempt – it said something about objects which underlay perception but which previously had been inexpressible. In Joyce one sees a similar literary quest. The modernists were trying to show that there are aspects of reality which are invisible until some new technique is used to demonstrate them. Modern movements in architecture could probably be cited, and, more than any other form of human endeavour, psychology itself. Freud taught us about the things which could never be said previously about the human psyche and the human condition which we could still find ways to say: analysis could make the invisible visible.

The Victorian conceptions of knowledge were rather different – they were explorers, attempting to accumulate knowledge rather than pierce it. One can perhaps see what is meant here by taking the project of Proust and comparing him with Joyce: Proust took the same language as Flaubert and Balzac, Victorian descriptive prose, but used it in an attempt to make the unknowable about the human spirit knowable. Joyce, like Picasso, like Freud, adds an extraordinary new means to the available techniques for making the un-presentable presentable. The avant-garde in art and cinema shared this same quest: they saw the task of the century as that of discovering, bringing out the hidden but to do so they realised that extreme emphasis must be placed upon finding an altogether new means for doing so. You cannot separate the things that Joyce is struggling to tell from the linguistic technology which he brings to the task. The content, if you like, is *in* the method. The vision is *in* the idea and method of psychoanalysis, *in* the dislocation of forms and cubism, in the way in which paint is applied and the shapes and surfaces of buildings assembled. The content lies in the very text of the writer itself.

In the context of modernism, the new knowledge is to be found in, if you like, the interpretation. The whole impetus of modernism comes in a way from the discovery that you cannot get beyond the interpretation if you are looking for the truth. The building exists in the style of itself. James Joyce's vision is to be located in his extraordinary language.

The current movement known as postmodernism is a kind of extension of this process of change into science and philosophy. It consists in a concentration upon style, upon the surface of things as ends in themselves, as objects of knowledge. In both art and commerce we are witnessing the working through into a phase of mannerism of the central tenets of modernism. The postmodern movement concerns itself with a reworking of the self through a reworking of taste by manipulating taste itself. The process of interpretation is becoming, as it were, a central intellectual endeavour.

If we go back for a moment to an earlier view of knowledge as necessary to be acquired as a training of the mind we can see the roots of the contemporary transformation. Intellectual techniques were created and developed in the process of acquiring knowledge. But where knowledge becomes separated from the intellect in the computerised society knowledge loses the function of being necessary as food for the mind, as the content of the mind. The intellect becomes a tool, a technique, rather than a storehouse. Vast quantities of information are available to the mind to work upon, to browse through, to adapt and cross-reference. The intellect becomes a mode of thought, the location for a succession of modes of thought. The acquisition of knowledge is not a necessary prerequisite for the training of the intellect. There is a parallel, at least a kind of metaphorical parallel, with the shift between Proust and Joyce. The latter locates the self in the text rather than as

102

an object of the attention of the text. The self of the information age emerges from the versions of the world which are available: it is hidden and revealed in the interpretations of the information made available.

There are many aspects of this self of the postmodern era which can be glimpsed as one looks at the newly emerging conception of knowledge. We have in the West begun to learn, for example, not to see our selves as a culmination of history, as the Victorians saw their selves. Rather, we are intent upon a recursive re-exploration of the past; we are relatively free of ideology moreover – detached because of our very success in releasing ourselves from being a culmination of history. Where the Gutenbergian era of information strove towards the creation of a language of politics and of justice which approximated to the language of science, the two have parted company in this century, often disastrously. The new language of justice is one of nervous approximations: we know that justice is buried in language, in the ways in which phenomena are labelled and subjected to moral amplifications. The media have been the tools of great re-engineerings of political and social consciousness: feminism, anti-racism, consciousness of the Third World, total reversals of popular thinking in the West about China and now the Soviet Union, all of these shifts in belief and attitude have been attempted, not by patient reworking of personal and collective conceptions, but by quite rapid media operations, biting deep into prevailing belief patterns. The self is prepared in the late 20th century to accept these reversals; it is happily subject to the layerings of interpretation which are the stuff of our new conceptions of knowledge.

This willingness to adapt to sudden changes in political belief is a counterpart to the kinds of alteration which production technologies have made possible. A century ago the telephone, the icebox, personal transport seemed eccentric acquisitions; mass production rapidly wore away the sense of differentness; innovations were disseminated slowly at first until we became conditioned to change itself, or certainly to the pace of self-alteration necessary to maintain the endless flow and exchange demanded by the economy in a high technology society. At first people could not imagine the kind of society in which they would require the telephone in every home, nor the washing machine, nor the refrigerator. But the rapid changes in consciousness occurred without the need to imagine; the idea of each social shift was spun from the manufactured objects themselves. In the computerised economy, as we know, the flow of changing taste and demand is constant, without great gaps of time between each succeeding layer of techniques and goods. We accept six different modes of mechanical sound reproduction in a single lifetime and dozens of changing patterns of music. Sherry Turkle speaks of the arrival of the computer as a means for refashioning the self to respond to a new kind of fantasy: gone is the rule-driven world of learning via print which creates a kind of mental safety and in its place comes a medium of writing which forces the self into forms of risk – each act of expression is an interpretation, a version where change, through correction, is never at an end. There is no reason to end the text. It is compounded of imprecisions, enriched rather than spoiled by alteration.

For several centuries science has been perfecting the rules by which a Cartesian universe has functioned. It has been likened successively to a clock, an engine, a living self-correcting organism, as the theories of science have succeeded one another. But as the forces of determination seemed to be almost completely delineated, that Newtonian, Laplacean world seemed to disappear in favour of one in which the nature of matter and the role of matter began to diverge confusingly. Of course, the laws of nature have not failed, but they have been found wanting. As René Thom puts it, pools of determinism survive without catastrophe, within a postdeterminist universe. In this perhaps crudely labelled 'postmodern' period science has preoccupied itself with the things which remain undecided; it has explored the conceptual frontiers of precise control and examined the dilemmas which are bounded by imprecise knowledge. In fact, in this age of disillusioned science knowledge has come to seem the very process of producing the unknown. Disillusion is its prime quest. It has become natural within our culture for circumstances to be in conflict with known variables. Within their own local circumstances the laws of inherited science remain; it is in attempting to construct the universe from them that we go wrong. Sherry Turkle talks about the contrasts[2] between the French and the American schoolroom's attitude to essay-writing and captured something of this new climate of knowledge: it has become impossible to train the mind by the use of processes which insist upon a perfect linking of premises to conclusions – interpretation is both technique and goal.

Let me take an anecdote adapted from René Thom's own account of this change to illustrate the way in which the deterministic view of nature remains true locally but not in aggregate. Imagine a dog which will bark or bite if it is teased in a certain way; imagine also that the same animal will take fright and run away if you approach it in another way. Now, if you adopt both modes of behaviour simultaneously and to the same extent, what will the animal do? The more intensively you apply the principles which have been learned the greater the uncertainty. The story offers a useful image of the state of knowledge in the computerised age. We live with a vast number of variables, not just two. And there is a vast number of 'dogs' on which they are applied. In any situation, in international affairs, or societal relations as well as in science, economics, medicine, there are innumerable variables at work upon innumerable situations.

It is still possible to look at the world as if the Marxist theory of class conflict were operating: there is plenty of evidence for it and often the determinism of Marxism provides an intellectually satisfying historical explanation for a given flow of events. At the same time you can adopt the Parsonian model of the social world with its endless self-correcting mechanisms, spreading out wider and wider into history. As you pursue the resultant of the various unpursuable variable forces you realise that it is impossible to examine them all simultaneously. You can use one explanation of history or another and each in turn will seem to work. But as you try to look at all the variables in operation in any society which is the subject of your enquiry you realise that you are looking at something which is essentially random. You cannot, in social as in scientific affairs, pursue successfully a chain of causation, even though, in microcosm, the lines of causation can be observed. Researchers into the relations between the media and violence in society are the perfect examples of scientists who have fallen into this maze.

Of course, behind this train of thought there lies an argument about journalism, about its techniques and its possible goals. Journalism is one of the observing professions, which has, over the years, acquired a range of skills or procedures which are both useful techniques and means of social self-protection. Their professional role is a 'strategic ritual', as it has been called by one researcher. That is, the journalist can hide behind the procedures of news-gathering and offer the world an essentially unselfenquiring but satisfying explanation of what he or she is doing. Within the world of the newsroom the test of accuracy and veracity appears complete. There is no collapse of objectivity as radical reformers and alternative journalism of the 1960s suggested. And yet journalism operates within the same world as the other observing professions and faces the same crisis. The journalist's world cannot be deconstructed and recomposed out of facts, any more than the world of the chemist or the anthropologist. The same uncertainty principle, the same unknowabilities are at work.

I am suggesting, therefore, that there exists an unconscious contemporary crisis in journalism, which has not yet worked its way through the new issues and problems of knowledge. There are ten ways to describe a fire, twenty reasons for an industrial conflict, thirty versions of the reasons why a set of disarmament talks breaks down, countless 'causes' of a kidnapping – all the explanations being equally compelling if one adopts a different time frame or asks a different question or looks towards a different range of consequences. That has always been the case, but in the past the available explanations have been narrower. Today we have access to many more of the possible simultaneous reasons for events. The computers are full of data, all equally available, all ascertainably 'true'. Journalism has not failed in the sense of being unable to grapple with these or being unaware of them, but in failing to talk to readers, listeners and viewers as if the world were compounded of uncertainties.

The reporter has been trained to speak as if he or she knows, as if the world were still knowable. Moreover the journalist speaks as if from a completed personality, as if the speaker of news could have no doubt: the journalist hops from topic to topic from day to day; the issues shift from pollution to equal opportunities to political corruption to poverty to conflicts within other countries and in every story there is a fixed point of certainty, as if the reporter were telling not enquiring. There is a certainty of circumstance and a certainty in the telling. When we, the non-professionals, see a traffic accident, or watch a street fight, we simply do not know the explanations or the way to lay the blame or discover the cause. We may try to act as truthful witnesses, but we actually do not and cannot know: our testimony can be torn to shreds and even then the lawyer on the other side will at best achieve a convincingness not a total certainty. And yet journalism feels it must deal in such certainty; it shrinks from an approach to the world which is the same as the lay man or lay woman's. The contemporary self is improvisatory, aware of itself as its own subject, a discourse about the idea of what it might be: we exist as a series of choices, a sequence of wonderings. That version of the self is scrupulously absent from journalism and yet I believe it is essential if journalism is to find a voice that chimes with the state of contemporary knowledge.

What has held journalism as an international practice together over the last twenty or thirty years have been the grand narratives of modern history: the Cold War, the gap between North and South, the division of Europe, the frozen debate between capitalism and communism or socialism. These great chapters of history have been the background in every other decision and political choice. We have not had to question the nature of defence or of weaponry, the need for social welfare programmes, the ideals of the welfare state or the great society, as forms of social self-defence within Western societies. But in the last years the great barriers between the old Soviet Union and the West have fallen away. In the space that is suddenly becoming available all sorts of new problems and opportunities arise. We have forgotten in Europe that our huge social welfare programmes were actually, historically, a result of the Cold War: they were there as a result of political choices and political battles but also as a way of rendering European societies acceptable habitats at a moment when Soviet society constituted an enticing proposition to populations which were inhabiting devastated cities and shattered rural communities.

The European Community rose from a desire to prevent further wars within Europe. Japanese prosperity itself is based upon a political project designed to make communism unattractive to the Japanese voter. These grand narratives are buried inside political practice, they live now as unargued beliefs within our contemporary historical explanations of the world. As they begin to erode their usefulness, completely new kinds of politics become possible and desirable. For example, the wave of 'privatisation' now under way throughout the OECD countries, from Japan and Australia to Finland and Britain is transforming the role of the state in our societies; it is breaking through whole ranges of long-accepted beliefs about social security and state-supported education and health provision. The results may be good or bad or just inevitable. What is suggested is that journalism of the last thirty years or more has been founded upon certain deeply rooted narratives of why and how the world is; today it is being offered a new range of stories within which some other background narrative is buried but it is not yet explicit.

As we read the stories of the great ideological upheavals in the old Soviet Union we may have sensed that they had a counterpart in an ideological upheaval taking place in the West. In both cases populations are instructed that prosperity must be paid for, that uneconomic enterprises must be closed, that only competition will give society the efficiency in production that it requires for its own good. And yet journalism fails to make those connections and to work through the implications: the stories are still locked into the older pattern of belief that is crumbling. The world after the grand narrative of the Cold War is a much harder one to report on and in. The heroes and villains have lost their heroism and villainy; they are all locked into the same constraints, from which journalism might in fact help to release them. It is not unlike in some ways the era after Waterloo when suddenly travel became possible again in France and Germany from Britain, and vice versa, but it was still uncertain which way intellectual and political belief would go.

A great geopolitical system had collapsed which had offered moral explanations so deep-rooted that they provided a side to be on for everyone on every question. A new set of narratives were gradually constructed and a new kind of journalism based upon national struggle and class struggle came into being. Nineteenth-century journalism revolved around newspapers which belonged to political parties which in turn supported different classes and factions within the nation state. The newspaper geology of Europe followed the political geology and the evolution of art and culture and philosophy was held in the same structure. All the movements from Marxism to mesmerism, from imperialism to Fabianism, belonged to journals and to newspapers and vice versa. That set of prevailing assumptions in time dissolved and, with new technologies, a new media system evolved. Today, we are in the course of dissolving a world of two autarchies and evolving a world – it would seem – without orthodoxy and without a search for new orthodoxy. That may be a transitional phenomenon, but towards what we cannot say.

In a world of changing knowledge which is moreover a world where the economy is formulated around knowledge itself as a commodity the roles of journalism are of course quite crucial. News-gathering skills are spreading way beyond the confines of public media; they are increasingly being harnessed by all sorts of micro-systems within the information economy and by a host of subsidiary enterprises. Political organisations, lobbying groups and companies, advertising and public relations, administration of all kinds, all of these and other sectors are in search of new tools which turn out to be essentially journalistic. All of them require analysis of events, information about personalities and groups, accounts of public perception. Journalism may or may not constitute a profession in the way that law, medicine, finance do, but it offers a special perspective on the world; it sits at the centre of a series of social inhibitions and political forces. It collects and surveys data from the standpoint of known institutional discipline. It is this perspective and the procedures which emanate from it that are the legitimising mainspring of journalism and the object which other observing practices within a modern society wish to use.

Journalism has also acquired a kind of generalised validating function, a way of selecting and labelling events and personalities and issues as salient. What journalism has always lacked is a sense of itself as a grand text, a living continuous flow of material reflecting and feeding the *mores* of a society. The individual stories are part of that grand text, as the parables and prophets are all part of the single grand text of Scripture. Every story is compounded of generalisations. Every item of news contains moral and mythical elements which crowd in upon it. So do the images of television and those conjured up in radio. A story about an injustice entails a narrative of justice. A story of a murder is based upon a narrative of the sanctity of life. Stories about corruption are implicitly about honesty, and about the prevalence of dishonesty – they are not just tellings of stories about single events. The crisis to which I refer is a crisis resulting from a contemporary failure of journalism to become self-aware, to sense the taboos and the truths concealed within itself.

Like the other observing professions journalism is encumbered by its own techniques, loyalties and abandoned aspirations – like them it is a series of improvisations none of which gets closer to the real than any other.

Notes

[1] See Michael Schudson, *Discovering the News – a Social History of American Newspapers* (New York: Basic Books, 1973).
[2] See Sherry Turkle, *The Second Self – Computers and the Human Spirit* (London: Granada, 1984).

2

What Are the Arts For?*

> *The secret of life is in art.*
> Oscar Wilde
>
> *'Tis to create, and in creating live*
> *A being more intense, that we endow*
> *With form our fancy, gaining as we give*
> *The life we image.*
> Lord Byron
>
> *All art is quite useless.*
> Oscar Wilde

So what *are* the arts for? Dozens of answers to this question have accumulated over the centuries and nearly all of them remain in some sense alive and active in us today. All of the answers have accompanying ideologies or derive from different sets of general ideas about the world. Any new answer we try out in our own time will therefore probably reveal a good deal about our beliefs and attitudes – perhaps also about certain hopes and fears – even some which remain unexpressed or unconsciously held. There are, however, some hyperactive notions at work in our society today. We should begin by identifying them.

Some people think that a knowledge of the arts 'humanises' (presumably other) people. But do not terrorists also listen to Bach, perhaps to take their minds off their work? Many people believe that the arts help to develop the inner life of an individual, adding to the furnishing of soul and self, building that bulwark necessary against the social world. But then it is hard to separate politics from art for very long; artists and politicians have never been able to keep away from each other. All nationalisms, for example, begin with the arts, with the emotions of loyalty to the collective roots and origins of peoples as these are expressed in narrative, in music, in craft, in costume and other artistic activities. And were we not brought up to believe that the Fuehrer also enjoyed his ideologically correct music? And have not all princes and governments in history taken up the arts as ways of making themselves and their power manifest in the world? Politicians certainly use art and artists

* This paper was written as a discussion document for the Arts Council of Great Britain in February 1992.

certainly use politics but surely here we have stumbled over another inevitable by-product rather than the real objective of art.

One can be tempted to revert to simpler answers and say that the arts in all their forms, from architecture to carpet-weaving, are really there to entertain us in our varying degrees of connoisseurship and sophistication. That one becomes hard to sustain when you consider how a great deal of art in its time failed to entertain or even detain its intended audience: if art does any real work at all it is often only after decades or even centuries of scholarly raking over. There is perhaps an interplay between society, artist, critic, curator and patron which justifies different kinds of work at different times and places, although that does not really help us to answer our question.

There are also some powerful ideas abroad which concern the value of the arts in dealing with present-day practical needs of society, in the struggle for feminist advance, for building the confidence of ethnic communities, of gay and disabled people, people in hospital, people who live in the regions, people who live in the streets, the promoting of tourism, the pulling off of coups of diplomacy, and so on. We have to be very careful not to offend any of those who are most passionate about these causes, while drawing attention to the fact that there is probably no real solution to be found *in the arts* to all or any of these real ills or requirements. The arts can indeed be used for many purposes, but is that really the same as describing the use of the arts?

I

There is no known human society without *art* but every society finds its own parts of social space in which to locate this diversity of activities, presenting them to itself as religion, business, craft, entertainment, therapy, politics. In our society they have come, most of them, to be lumped together as 'the arts'. The arts embrace things we make, things we admire, things which move us and amuse us and include a heritage of materials which we value for the evidences they present of what human beings can achieve, and can express. All of the living forms of art exist within great continuities and traditions of skill. They pervade every aspect of our lives, influencing the way we move, speak, think and feel. The arts exist as *influences* which are exerted in the minds of people who may not even be conscious of the sources of their resulting attitudes and tastes. In our society (but not in all societies) the arts are also associated with a sense of moral progress and also with the concept of excellence – that is, the doing or creating of something at the highest possible level of perfection.

As individuals we may choose whether to preoccupy ourselves with the arts, but they will enter our lives none the less. We can confront them passively simply as consumers or we may adopt a more dynamic pose and develop our knowledge about selected forms of art progressively throughout our lives, allowing them to shape our inner life. It is easy to mistake an interest in art for a hobby; but the arts are not hobbies, for they cannot simply be set aside as spare-time activities. They alter the whole nature of our existence, if we let them.

The homogenised label 'the arts' came to be applied in all of the industrialised societies, at that very moment in their history when this mixture of cultural crafts and professions was moving to peripheral status in the lives of most ordinary people. The arts were associated with what had come to be widely labelled the bohemian. It was only then, when they were seen at the margin of the life of the modern economy, that their shared characteristics became apparent: the arts came to appear to be modes of expression or communication which emanated from a particular kind of temperament. At the same time a barrier came down between the arts which were deemed 'fine' and those deemed 'popular' although this boundary has become blurred in our own 'consumer' form of society when almost every cultural activity is permitted to qualify as 'art'.

Today equally important though somewhat wavy lines tend to be drawn between those kinds of art which require money from the state to survive and those which do not, between those which are able to function within the mainstream economy and those which have to be subsidised by someone, if only the artist. These divisions have come to assume an enormous importance to us in the 1980s and 1990s.

Of course, a constant and complex interaction takes place between the commercial and non-commercial sectors of the arts and paradoxes abound. Opera is not commercial, but theatre often is commercial; subsidised orchestras make recordings for commercial record companies; public galleries purchase pictures from private ones, at market prices. The lines of dependence and support are paradoxical and often hard to distinguish. The arts are and have always been associated with great acts of public benevolence, benefactions arriving from private individuals for the benefit of the general public.

The arts have acquired as their collective role, that of being *avocations*, preoccupations pursued outside our economic lives. An involvement with the arts, therefore, in itself entails a special kind of decision and self-definition. The opera-goer, or the poetry-reader, or the connoisseur of painting and sculpture places himself or herself in a special relationship to the world, even to the extent of expressing a belief about a preferred condition of the world. The very terrain of the arts represents something foreign to what is felt to be the 'real' in the lives of the majority of people.

Until a century ago a great deal of discussion about art and its role concerned itself with the task of defining and describing the kinds of pleasure, the precise species of emotion, which painting or music or fine buildings evoke. There was great interest in the psychological operations of the tragic, the comic, the sublime. The mystery of art seemed to lie in the way it worked upon us and the way that great artists seemed to be able to see further into the human spirit – often prophetically – than ordinary people. All the philosophers in history have grappled with these questions; Aristotle thought that art functioned as a kind of gymnasium of the emotions – it made you work through the range of your emotions as an athlete systematically exercises limbs and muscles.

111

With the admission of more and often new art forms and cultural activities to the realm of the arts it has become difficult to say what really are the emotional and moral functions they perform. We seldom hear people say, for example, that they attend the opera or stand and listen to the local brass band simply in the hope of being spiritually transformed by the experience, although often they do feel this. One important notion, that of the sublime, in the sense in which painters over the course of centuries employed it, has fallen into disuse. We tend to talk about 'sheer pleasure' without trying to delineate very precisely the kind of spiritual benefit we mean. We use the term 'imagination' fairly loosely today, where formerly poets have tried to make distinctions between several different imaginative functions, giving them different labels.

Today the arts have become inextricably entwined with other more political and material motivations – their purposes have been extended to embrace questions of national status, the promotion of tourism, the expansion of the economy, the enhancement of the environment, and the curing of dozens of newly identified social ills. But thousands will still queue for the Promenade concerts every summer and crowd into Hyde Park to hear a free recital by an international opera star: curiosity and marketing have played their part, but still there clearly exists a latent desire for forms of gratification – however threadbare the inherited terminology for describing them – which only the arts can supply. The arts today although they live at the periphery of society have come to occupy a large terrain and to reside there in profusion. Even the most popular of newspapers will report daily the doings of great personalities from the world of the arts, and review exhibitions and performances. Moreover, the arts have been to a great extent released from the complex snobberies which beset them in past times.

Religion occupies another such terrain, having been similarly removed from a central, governing role in the life of society. The respective territories of art and religion have drawn apart from each other, even though the arts – paintings, statuary, stained glass, music, dance, poetry – have been the means by which religious beliefs have always been promoted and confirmed; religious art, however, has become captured by 'the arts' and is felt to be separable from the meanings and purposes which gave rise to it.

In trying to grapple with the issue of the 'arts' and their uses in the context of today one quickly realises that much of the necessary vocabulary has been disabled. It is no longer possible to refer to operations of the emotions which once as it were belonged to art and the experience of art, and which were the reasons for and the justifications of art; the very benefits provided by art, which were once capable of being carefully, indeed artistically, described are today incapable of being easily talked about. The arts are subject to a kind of dislocation within the modern self and this is reflected in the available language; there are lost instinctual connections between things which may one day be restored. Today these considerations are consigned to a mental category labelled mystical and tend to be shunned by the rationally minded. But the mystical is inseparable from art.

II

In the ancient world it was thought that art functioned through the imitation of nature and that the pleasure derived from art emerged from that fact. This notion of art as 'mimesis' lasted in different variations for thousands of years. But the ancient world did not really see art as proto-photography. When a Greek sculptor presented a human body in stone, thus 'imitating' what he saw in nature, he was indicating not a living individual so much as an arranged geometry of shapes and surfaces which the beholder would immediately recognise as the *perfected* essence of the human. The conception of mimesis was connected with the conception of the ideal. There was a unity between the mathematical and the aesthetic which was consonant with the profoundest of Greek beliefs. The pieces of art which survive can however still inspire in us sudden glimpses of what might have been going on in the mind of the Greek onlooker. It involves effort and learning on our part to recover for ourselves some part of this lost inspiration.

Although it has been the vivid and powerful ideas of the Greeks which have again and again re-inspired art and the ideas surrounding art in the Western world, Eastern religions have provided simultaneous and remarkably similar explanations. For example, Japanese thinkers twelve hundred years ago emphasised that while esoteric truth by its very profundity defied expression in writing, it could be effectively communicated in painting. Art was essential to the communication of truth. The splitting of Western culture from Eastern resulted in the latter being seen by the former as mystical and exotic, while Western civilisation has more and more tried to validate itself as a civilisation of rationalism and empiricism.

In medieval Christian thought art was normally felt to demonstrate the relationship between creator and created world. Thomas Aquinas said that the arts instructed tacitly through beauty, providing a sense of the order of the universe while Roger Bacon explained that painting possessed an ability to lead the faithful in an undemanding but effective way.

Most of the conceptions which are at work in the way people talk about the arts today are discernible in the great aesthetic debate of the 18th and 19th centuries. John Locke had argued in 1690 that all our knowledge stems from sense perception and experience, implying that we are by the nature of our minds' method of working 'lookers-on' of the world. Joseph Addison in his *Spectator* essays reveals how Locke's psychology influenced attitudes to art when he writes of the Polite Imagination that it enables a Man to be 'let into a great many Pleasures', giving him indeed a 'kind of Property in every thing he sees'. This way of seeing was connected to a theory about the improving mental operations of art (which survives in many forms of discourse about art today); the implied passiveness of the senses and imagination towards art and the world was the very thing which the Romantic movement at the end of the 18th century thoroughly rejected.

At the turn of the 18th and 19th centuries new ideas began to be explored concerning the nature and psychology of artists. For thinkers like Lessing in Germany and Coleridge in England art lay in special psychological powers which were creative, personal and expressive. Coleridge wrote about 'that pleasurable emotion, that peculiar state and degree of excitement that arises in the poet himself in the act of composition'. Old ideas about the mimetic role of art were relegated. Artists were thought to express their inner lives through their creative genius; to express artistic 'intentions'; to symbolise – and express – their epochs. Audiences just have to come and admire and make the effort to keep up with them if they are to benefit from what artists do and say.

Communication and art are made separate under the rule of Romanticism which emphasises the private inner-world operations of the latter. John Stuart Mill said that rhetoric was heard but poetry overheard. To Alfred de Musset poetry was a 'sob overheard'. Baudelaire said: 'For us the natural painter, like the natural poet, is almost a monster.' Art came to entail an extreme display of egoism, and came in time to be denounced for this by among others Leo Tolstoy, who believed that, on the contrary, art should help in the cause of the redemption of the masses. None the less the romantic notion of the artist still exercises a powerful influence over us, even those of us who affect to have discarded it.

Historians offer us plenty of explanations of how this convulsion in aesthetic ideas came about; there are economic and class theories available: the age of aristocratic patronage of artists had ended. The novel had become firmly established and hundreds of writers found ways to open up consciousness of the inner life through the development of their characters; the notion of the personal became primary. Art was being made to justify itself and explain away its own seeming irrelevance to the industrial transformation then under way. In the 1780s Samuel Johnson had proclaimed that artists were 'the legislators of mankind'. Shelley a few decades later found it necessary to explain that they were now 'the unacknowledged legislators of mankind'. (John Arden in our own day has gone one stage further and declared the arts to be the 'secret police'.)

What all the Romantic theories of art have in common is the idea that it is an 'original' author or artist who generates the work of art and who as a person is fused into the meaning of the work. From this it follows that the original intention of the artist is somehow recoverable through an understanding of the artistic practices and genres of the time of the work's creation. Indeed, to understand the work it is essential to discover this intention. But there are obvious limits to our ability to 'know' a work of art to this extent and in this way. If art is treated as a kind of cultural time capsule, then it appears to have no purpose, no *work* to do, other than to lie in wait for people who come to fathom its meaning and then, if they can, proceed to admire it.

III

Most of the 20th century's many strands of questioning of the role and purpose of art have emerged from attempts to deal with this problem. If it is impossible to say what Keats *meant* or Leonardo da Vinci or Beethoven, then how do we evaluate or define or analyse works of art of our own day? For these too will soon find themselves in that wilderness of infinite interpretation. Every artist who has ever lived has used the materials, the skills and the real or metaphorical languages which have been created by other artists or just by society in general. Artists no longer seem to be the long-term moral owners of their own products. Art seems more and more to be social in character – in a complete reversal of the romantic view.

Art has become detached from the artist and has come to be treated as a thing-in-itself, available for the extraction of an infinity of interpretations. The meaning of a work is therefore variable, depending on the circumstances in which it is received – rather than those in which it was made. The whole burden of art, especially literature, has been shifted to the receiver, and a new 'reception aesthetics' has evolved in the late 20th century. It is now the audience which brings the work of art into existence; the audience in the 20th century is thus no longer the breathless Victorian/Romantic admirer, an essentially passive receiver. The meaning of a work results from a dynamic interaction between artist and user.

For the prominent American critic Stanley Fish the meaning of a work belongs to one of a number of 'interpretive communities' who arrive by consent at acceptable interpretations. For the late French critic Michel Foucault works of art, 'texts', give rise to widely accepted 'readings' which solidify into traditionally accepted modes of understanding until, rather like scientific theories, they collapse after waves of steady subterranean scepticism and give way to new readings. In the last few decades we have come to feel that it is impossible any longer to define a work of art or force it to release to us any permanently accepted meaning. Every individual work seems to dissolve into the totality of human culture, without the security of being explicable in terms of the life or attitudes of an enduring artist.

The traditional 'canons' of seminal works have disappeared in many art forms. There seems to some critics no longer to be any point in endlessly arranging paintings or symphonies or novels in ranking order in an eternal competition for aesthetic prizes. Audiences are no longer expected to 'appreciate' the works laid before their eyes and ears by authoritative specialists. Instead, we study the structure of works of art, we 'de-construct' them, we the readers read our selves into the texts. Understanding art seems to have reached a kind of stalemate between psychology, anthropology and social history. There is an extreme relativism, even an anarchy, in theories of artistic interpretation akin to the dilemmas which now engulf (and enrich) scientific theory. In the theories of Mikhail Bakhtin, the Russian critic whose ideas have come to the forefront of attention in the 1980s, a text disappears into 'dialogism', every statement containing the spoor of other statements and bound seamlessly and inextricably into every work of art, into every attempt by an artist to articulate a thought.

A work of art is no longer believed to be explicable in terms of what its creator wanted it to be or mean; no longer explicable in terms of the biographical or psychoanalytic personality of its creator; no longer explicable through analysis of the structures embedded in the work; no longer thought to be the emanation of its own contextual political and historical circumstances, nor able to be interpreted through an understanding of the formation of the genre of which it is a representative.

Works of art are no longer even explicable as tools of radical action, as was thought by the influential Marxist critic Althusser in the late 1960s, their meaning consistent with their ability to carry out the role of subversion of contemporary values: the older notion of avant-garde has also subsided with the ending of the nineteenth-century antagonism between bohemian and bourgeois values: the artist is no longer seen as divine transgressor. That rather satisfying conflict between art and society has, it would appear, ended. With the death of Marxism in the 1980s the spark of outrage, as Denis Donoghue describes it, flickered out, for the time being at any rate. The roles both of artist and of audience have become normalised. Aesthetic theories are seldom offered as explanations of their work by contemporary artists.

So the attempt, it would appear, to explain in a straightforward way how the arts work ends up in a series of exploded theories, which mark the landscape dangerously like abandoned mine shafts. And if you cannot say how the arts function, how can you say what they are for? A work of art is not and cannot be – as anyone who looks today at the ceiling of the Sistine Chapel will be aware – synchronous with the wishes of the artist. It does not exist, primarily, to seek out ways of causing pleasure in an audience: Andy Warhol has brought home to us that whatever an artist *does* becomes art. Art does not, necessarily, have to bring us to any important truths: look at the rows of Madonnas and Annunciations hanging in our galleries, torn from their context and their original purpose. It has retained all of these functions for those who want them, but in late-twentieth-century society art, as they say, is somewhere else.

IV

The problem is that art transgresses all the modern boundaries between public institutions and private life. We sense the lack of an easily articulated *theory* linking the visible roles of art in public (cinema, industrial design, state visits, national galleries) with its personal nature (spiritual benefit, arousal of pleasure, training of the senses, mental excitement). The writer Jacques Barzun, in his book *The Use and Abuse of Art*, has said that today even though art is a public institution, 'it is an institution without a theory. No coherent thought exists as to its aim or *raison d'être*'. The problem is not so much the excess of available theories or 'coherent thoughts' as the fact that the question today has come to be shrouded in modern inhibitions, in particular the taboo against using in public the language of spiritual matters. Art suffuses every artefact in our environment – sometimes in negative rather than positive senses – but its real utility lies in the way it helps us in those aspects of our lives which people now find it hard to discuss. And as soon as we do try to speak of them we run into questions of justification within the context of the instrumental state ('taxpayers' money').

It is extremely hard to battle with the view that all matters which pertain to art are personal and therefore beyond the proper province of the state. It depends on your view of the state as much as upon your view of the value of art. One perhaps needs to start dealing with the question by pointing out that the extreme anti-subsidy view is unhistoric. Heads of state and heads of government have always felt the support of the fine arts to be a duty, not merely to art as such but also to themselves, and to the state. The extreme view, now current in certain quarters, that art should be supported only by individual and commercial patronage is based upon a misunderstanding both of the traditions of art and of the traditional role of the state.

A change has taken place in the Western economies over the last twenty years. A steady process of 'commodification' has spread rapidly. Today matters of health and welfare are being pushed further into the private sector of the economy and it is natural that the support of the arts should be under similar pressure. If art is treated as a series of objects and services, which perform their function only when possessed by individuals or organisations then such a view follows automatically. It is only if you hold the view that all art is ultimately social in its purposes (i.e. if you believe that its existence improves the world) that the use of public, central, governmental funds seems inevitable and therefore appropriate. If every piece and process of art is eternal – in its consequences if not in its 'artefact' state – then its possessors at a given moment are its stewards. Whether they are individuals or organisations matters little, if it is the work and its intended effects on the world which are the objectives.

In the traditional world, a painting or a piece of music would be thought to have as its purpose that of communicating the sacred vision – or the tragic or comic vision – of a whole society. It served its function as a work of art in a public space, within the mind and spirit of a group living in the society concerned. So general was the vision served that the artists of those societies would not necessarily be known to history by their names; they saw themselves and were seen as part of gigantic and eternal processes. The stone-carvers in a cathedral were not seen as individual artists as are those of a later day. The emphasis on creativity in times nearer our own has resulted in the loss of this cultural common ground. Instead, the unknown artist has been relegated to the status of 'folk artist', while the commissioned individual artist has become primarily the named maker of legally specific objects, not the channel of an experience. The art is what he or she does rather than being something which passes from the community through the artist into the artefact.

William Morris and John Ruskin both, in different ways, tried to reckon with this problem, that of the arts in the manufacturing economy. They proclaimed the unity of craft, art and work and tried to restore the position of the artisan in society as in art; they raised the consciousness of art within industry, constantly expressing indignation at the inhumanities of a machine-based civilisation. 'No machines will increase the possibilities of life,' exclaimed Ruskin. 'They only increase the possibilities of idleness.' Many new lines of influence emanated from their ideas and their activities. One of these has led to the opening up of what one might call the art of participation. Here both craft and art become the means by which people may express themselves, not necessarily for the benefit of industry or society so much as to fulfil a kind of personal civil right.

Another concern which originated in mid-nineteenth-century humanism is the issue of 'folk art'; today this has receded into a confusion of anthropology, primitivism and charity. Folk art arrives in industrial societies as commodity; it generally has no artist's name attached, although it may entail objects of great monetary value. Oriental carpets are found on the walls of art galleries as well as on the floors of finely furnished rooms. Decorated pots from Third World countries may be exhibited or used in kitchens. Our respect for artisans and their products forces us to cross the line between art and manufacture, between the causes of beauty and utility, and experience again the paradoxes which Morris and Ruskin so indignantly tried to clear up.

The relation of artist to audience is that of an individual through whose solitude a higher purpose of society is attempted. A Beethoven or a Mozart, a Matisse or a Gauguin produce materials which are meant to communicate between the deepest feelings discerned by the artist in himself and those discerned in the ambient society. The artist works by trying to transcend the common experience in a way which enables others to join in his vision. That vision thus becomes a common property, although it is expressed in terms of artefacts which are, in our society, treated as personal properties. In the history of art there are periods and places where the individual's role and rights in art have been emphasised to the point of contradicting the social dimension; but there have also been situations in which the social utility of the artist's vision has been excessively developed, to the point of undermining art. In the course of the 20th century some truly terrible aberrant notions of the role of art in society have been inflicted on the world.

Only now for example is the truth about the role of art under communism beginning to become clear. The Soviet Union has passed through a series of stages in the decades since the October Revolution, in regulating the relation of artists to the new state. At first the Revolution took the avant-garde as its especially protected species of art, encouraging a conscious spirit of novelty and a futuristic view of society and art. Then after a brief time it came to espouse forms of art which more directly supported the new regime and worked for the establishment of the new political doctrines in the hearts and minds of the population. The doctrine of Socialist Realism was offered to the arts by the Bolsheviks as their particular gospel in the 1930s and then began the harnessing of artists to the task of propaganda; sometimes the results were absurd, but gradually they turned to horror.

After a further period of years, however, a new generation of artists (the previous one having been largely liquidated) was obliged, paradoxically, to abandon all enthusiasm for communist ideology and even for the doctrine of Socialist Realism itself for that was too often found to lead to the production of politically inconvenient work. Artists were now made simply to express what groups of bureaucrats from time to time demanded. Art was deprived even of the use of the imagination; the aesthetic which prevailed was the aesthetic of banal obedience. Art became subject to the form of government we call bureaucracy, one which had abandoned the belief even in its own official ideals, even though they were inscribed on walls everywhere.

Under the Nazi regimes a different and perhaps even more terrible role was staked out for art. All of its skills were developed, lavishly financed and given full official status but made to glorify the regime and its leader. The profoundest of the artist's skills – that of communicating direct to the heart – was perverted to the task of the exploitation of the public emotions of loyalty to a regime which slaughtered on a scale previously unknown.

In the 1960s, throughout Western Europe and North America, there took place a revival of socialist thought and with it also of a socially purposive view of art; the context was new and the social ideals were also rather novel, being led by aesthetic as much as economic slogans. The vanguard were mainly students and intellectuals rather than workers. The result was a rekindled interest, shared by people of the right as well as of the left, in cultural and social freedoms, including sexual liberation. A new generation which gradually abandoned the political content of the movement was left with a rekindled interest in matters of style in music, dress and in life generally.

V

It was in the 1980s and 1990s that a new materialism (characterised by some as a new philistinism) arrived, and introduced a somewhat bitter note of disagreement with the cultural doctrines which had been at work in Britain for a century. The cultural settlement of the 1960s was now challenged from the right. The new values stressed the importance of individuals and families; there was injected into the political atmosphere a revived spirit of self-help, or at least a powerful argument for people to take control of their own circumstances and destinies rather than look to the state. The arts were not in fact sent into further retreat in this era, so much as expected to revamp themselves, and accept the new insistence that subsidy should be minimised and commercial activity maximised. The new class of entrepreneurs, especially those associated with the 'Big Bang' when the City deregulated commercial activity, unlike previous generations of newly wealthy, showed an interest in art itself, but also as a focus of enterprise, as part of available experience, and in particular as a source of influence over style and taste. It is difficult to disentangle all the threads of argument, but in the 1990s we end up with a mixture of ideas and aspirations all centring on the arts and the institutions which house and support them.

The public doctrine which had come to prevail after the war – and which led to the foundation of the Arts Council itself – was one which favoured the mass provision of art as a kind of public health service for the spirit. The Arts Council descended from the wartime Council for the Encouragement of Music and the Arts (CEMA) and was founded for the purpose of developing greater knowledge, understanding and practice of the fine arts and to increase their accessibility to the public. That series of rubrics continued really until the 'new politics' of the 1970s shook the whole world of broadcasting and the arts by making a new series of demands upon it.

The Arts Council mission was a simple one and related to inherited views of what the arts were and why they were wanted, which are traceable, like the BBC itself, the British Film Institute, and other cultural institutions which were founded in and around the 1930s, to the ideas of Matthew Arnold, who more than anyone else had in the late 19th century laid the basis for the ideals of public access. Arnold has noted, as he trod the classrooms of hundreds of Victorian schools as the country's first HM Inspector, that two armies seemed to be lying in wait at the Victorian street corner for the children who were now (after the 1870 Education Act) being provided with literacy, that starting-point of access: one of the armies was of revolutionaries and the other of pornographers. To protect the newly literate it was necessary to create for them a constant and plentiful supply of Culture, which Arnold often described as 'sweetness and light'; the alternative course would be to permit them to be attacked by the evil of Anarchy, the opposite of all that Victorian society hoped for from its first literate working-class. All of the instruments of twentieth-century popular education and culture have evolved from that simple realisation, and the founding of the Arts Council was itself an example of the same endeavour.

The spreading to the masses of the personal experience of the arts was one of the great causes of postwar social democracy, espoused by all the major parties in Britain. The ACGB became locked into the fabric of the society, though not as effectively as the BBC. As its resources grew, so did the dependence upon it of an ever larger tranche of the artistic activities of the country. It created colonies, though not contented ones. Each increase in its governmental support entailed arguing all over again the general case for state support. Much of the wartime thinking about the new organisation was provided by J. M. Keynes, the economist, who had seen its role in slightly patrician Bloomsburyesque terms, as a set of opportunities rather than a system of nationwide provision. In this respect British policy differed greatly, as it always has done, from that of the European societies, East and West.

It was in the 1970s that a new and different set of demands and a further revision in the prevailing view of the role and purpose of art sprang up; these ideas were the political outcrop of the street politics of the 1960s. This movement was spearheaded by the Livingstone-led Greater London Council but sprang at root from the inability of the earlier Labour Government to find a way to implement the 'new politics' of mass participation. As the long-standing programmes of nationalisation and welfare provision got bogged down or slithered into unpopularity the retreating adherents regrouped around the cause of culture; in this they were greatly influenced by the rediscovery of the writings of the 'young Marx' who had – in the view of his 1960s re-interpreters – emphasised the importance of ideological practice or the creation of radical consciousness through cultural instead of (perhaps in addition to) purely economic and political activity.

That 1970s injection of energy into the political debate about culture is still being slowly absorbed into the dominant political culture of Britain; it has spread to all of the parties in fact, raising as it did the whole range of issues of social equality and economic opportunity. The arts were seen as ways of compensating the deprived – women, black, gay and disabled people – for the deficiencies of society, but also as a new location for expressing themselves and forcing society to give them a fuller sense of their own identity. The arts were being treated instrumentally, not in the same terms as Matthew Arnold nor in those of Socialist Realism, but rather in the name of a revised political humanism. It is still unclear whether the arts are really able to yield all that is expected of them in this respect. Certainly one can say that the Arts Council was not founded with so vast an agenda in mind and has never been invited by government to undertake so onerous a set of tasks. None the less, that agenda remains in the mind of some – and this 'some' represents a very large proportion of the arts constituency itself – and the Arts Council remains the only available institutional tool.

VI

The new view of the arts broke through the divisions between high and low in art and also led to an enhanced demand for access of all kinds to the media and to art. It led to an exponential growth in expectations, but paralleled by only an arithmetic growth in resources, and this created a gap which is still expanding nearly two decades later. There was also a 'new politics' of the right, which demanded responsible public financial accounting before all else but which came to accept the underlying case for the broadening of general access to the arts. The debate spread from area to area of public policy, local and national, but notably in the field of education. Here a new project for a National Curriculum shows evidence of the impact of the debate but the opportunity was offered and rejected for education to take on a major responsibility in preparing a society for the experience of the arts.

Matthew Arnold ended up by losing the argument: practical economic skills now occupy the foreground of educational policy rather than 'sweetness and light' – it is to prosperity not to the development of the spirit that public policy now looks in the fight against the diabolus of anarchy.

More and more, however, expenditure has become the crucial issue, and the debate has used but partly concealed the various survivals of older aesthetic doctrines. British society was being trained in a new and urgent discipline of public accountability. The politics of the arts became a politics of justification. In the context of a society intent upon resurrecting – or, rather, instituting – the power of markets, a general process of commodification took place in national life, embracing the arts, as it made its way into a wide range of institutions and attitudes.

Markets were thought to be not merely convenient instruments for setting prices, but have been elevated into being the actual means for creating a new democracy of taste and choice. Through markets will come solutions to the 'new' range of social problems, or thus many believe. It has been accepted that the arts should work in aid of the same social causes, and on the basis of public money, but will also have to be harnessed to the economy through commercial sponsorship, benefaction, better management and charging.

The public funders of the arts have – wisely or not – accepted each fresh burden of self-justification. Feminists have demanded that the arts express the values of the new womanhood and reject the locutions of male chauvinism. Advocates of cultural diversity insist that the arts institutions broaden their view of what is fundable to include work indigenous to a wide variety of ethnic minority communities. Gay people have made their demands upon the resources and the language of the funded arts. So have disabled people with a powerful lobby demanding participation as artists and as audiences on a basis of equal and effective provision. These may well prove to be significant contributions to art, and the arts need not be limited in range or variety. But what of the arts funding system? If the Arts Council and the rest try to respond to all pressures – promote the arts as economic regenerators, as a magnet for tourists, as 'business', as a panacea for social and cultural inequalities – they may end up not adding anything to art. The policies of the more enlightened local authorities may provide a partial answer, but the arts and media funding system will need in the future to face up to some hard choices which it has shirked in the past.

There are many other politicised expectations which have grown in intensity in the 1980s and which the existing arts institutions are being called upon to fulfil. Britain has, for example, been tortured by its excessive metropolitanism for many decades, generations even. The boom of the 1980s entailed intensifying the economic bias in favour of the more prosperous Southeast of England and the discontent of those living in other regions with their general level of provision has been made increasingly manifest. The reallocation of public arts funding has, therefore, been expected to redress these inequalities. The success of this policy may well have been as limited as critics allege; but within the existing level of resources, such redistribution can only be at the expense of existing provision in the capital.

Nor has that been all. Many of the pressures of justification have not been to encourage the arts to present themselves as resources of spiritual progress, so much as sources of exports and national economic revival. The arts are invited to argue their case in terms of tourism as a justification for their public funding. They are pressed to prove their case as commodities rather than experiences. All artistic works communicate with publics, if they do, through exploiting areas of common allusion, through the deployment of languages and styles which bind them to the people whose vision they express. It is difficult today for example for English theatre to work with 'tourist' audiences, large sections of which do not speak English as their first language. The whole culture of theatre in London is altering under the pressure of being made to serve as a tourist industry.

The arts institutions have been forced at government- and lobby-point to try to address this great range of non-arts-related social and economic issues. This has redefined and greatly enlarged the number of 'arts' while raising the question of what they can reasonably expect to achieve in a society such as ours. It is now the arts with their inadequate resources which are being made to carry the weight of the new radical egalitarianism, rather than other larger agencies within the working and the welfare economy. The new responsibilities are all well argued and in society's terms fully justified. But the resource implications have never really been addressed. A quart of 1990s social aesthetics is being squeezed into the pint pot of a 1940s institutional conception.

The inspiration of the Keynsian Arts Council was to provide for those people, largely working-class, who loved opera and ballet and classical music but had little access to them. It knew, as the BBC and the framers of the 1944 Education Act knew, that there was a much larger task to be done, that of bringing everyone into the compass of the (fine) arts, but the Arts Council was not equipped for this much greater role. Half a century later, however, the same basic institutional framework is trying to cope with a greatly broadened view of the role of the arts as well as the range of the arts. Politicians, professional and lay, are really today dreaming of a generalised social service of the arts, without considering the institutional means for delivering it. We still have as our central institutional tool the patronage model of the Arts Council. And of course it can only offer up one cry – 'more!'

It is as if the Victorians had asked the dame schools to prepare a generation of teenagers for university entrance. It is like inviting the managers of the stagecoach service to provide for the age of mass tourism. It is like asking barbers to provide a national health service. It is more than a problem of strategy. It is one of conception. A vast task of preparation, of training, of mass education and sheer thinking out has to take place before society and arts both are ready to fulfil this new range of mutual expectations. This is a task wholly beyond the capacity of the arts funding system as currently conceived. It is not clear that a new, grand synthesis is possible. It is all too clear that it is not possible without a major injection of new money, and that it is a task that the Arts Council and its sister organisations are not equipped to attempt. We have been led by the aesthetics of the present century into the belief that the arts, all of them, are for everyone. The politics of the century has converged. But not the economics. Nor the administrative system. Perhaps not the arts themselves.

VII

Thomas Carlyle over a century ago, in *Past and Present*, mocked those who tried to create political gadgets which could be used to cure all of society's ills at once: he called them Morrison's Pill. In Britain of the 1990s Morrison's pill is its arts, pounded in the pestle and mortar by the apothecary of public policy now for nearly twenty years. At the dawn of the 1990s the arts of Britain are a much trampled battlefield, many of the institutions drained of energy, resources depleted, and many groups reorganised into a condition of bewilderment.

What then *are* the arts for? Clearly they *can* be asked to deal with all of the tasks that society chooses to set them. And it is difficult for them to reject roles which give them purpose and poise within a society. They are today irrevocably fixed within a subsidy economy, though with a considerable admixture of private to top up public funds. But the central and regional funding framework derives from a 1940s conception of the limits of possibility which is trying to fulfil the much grander Arnoldian ideal. There is a conflict between a never fully spelled out vision (putting culture in place of anarchy) and the resources. That is not to say merely that government (or, really, society as a whole) provides inadequate funds, but something more serious: that we are asking for one thing and paying for another, that we have accepted the rhetoric of one position on the arts but are paying for another.

It may well be that local government, particularly in our major cities, will be able to respond effectively to the call for provision. But that leaves a vital, if limited, area which has received too little attention in recent years: a real commitment to the operations of art itself. And so a new strategy has to begin with that commitment, a formula of rededication to the spirit of art, to the spirit in art, from which contemporary aesthetics and contemporary politics have so long withdrawn.

There is so much of course that the arts institutions can do whatever their resources. In looking for a new strategy this might be the moment to concentrate on neglected essentials and long unstated priorities. The arts can restore something of what we have lost in the transition from citizens to consumers, from souls to purses. They can protect us against the bewilderment which accompanies a preoccupation with the littleness of life. They can transform our sense of what is real. They can help us, all of us, in the words of Byron, to 'live a being more intense'. Is that not enough?

3

Books to Bytes

*The Computer and the Library**

Technologies establish themselves in civilisations by offering opportunities that later turn into inevitabilities. New institutions then arise and others survive according to the stage at which they adopt the technologies concerned. The institution of the library is now passing this transforming era of new information technology. It has arrived in the world of librarians somewhat slowly compared to the speed with which it has become integral to such institutions and industries as travel, the newspaper and financial services; these are all, in the late 1980s, well inside the phase of transformation.

In the first part of this chapter I shall say something about the longer term, the truly historical forces and trends that are implied in the arrival of these new technologies of knowledge, calculation and text. In the second half I shall look in greater detail at the experience of the library as recipient, user or victim of changing technological circumstances.

The impact of electronics upon our ways of creating, storing and disseminating text goes through our whole culture, since the composition and use of text permeates everything we are as a civilisation. The electronic transformation of the text does not, however, displace our values; nor does it identify, so much as superimpose itself on, what has gone before. It is useful to remind ourselves what the traditional method of printing itself offered our culture when it arrived some centuries ago.

Printing and Processing

The advent of printing meant that unified, identical blocks of text could be shared across different times and different places. In fact it provoked a heightened awareness of differentness in Western culture and fed this sensitivity into our intellectual practice. Of course, Gutenberg's invention also rapidly made possible the standardisation of important statements and documents, and with this came such familiar phenomena as calendars, dictionaries, charts and maps, diagrams and price lists. It became possible to institute shared systems for recording and measuring time and distance, size and quality. With printing there rapidly arrived a kind of fixity in language itself; the mainstream vernacular could be settled and its offshoots and

---

* Delivered in summer 1985 as a lecture for the Gannett Center for Media Studies, Columbia University, New York City.

dialects registered as derogations from a norm. Alphabetic order suited the printers, as did Arabic rather than Roman numerals and formal, predetermined systems of punctuating written text.

With such fixed norms there arrived newly appropriate mental skills and qualities. The formulaic and ritualistic patterns of pre-Gutenbergian culture gave way to a new, codified system of thinking in which knowledge moved beyond mere retrospective recovery of the past and became instead the product of an endless process of progressive augmentation. Through the comparison of text with text, one arrived at new knowledge, what Francis Bacon called the 'Novum Organum', a new world of thought based upon the accumulation of factual understanding. Indeed, the chief characteristic of typographic culture as a whole is perhaps the prevalence of the very idea of objective knowledge: the knower became separate from the author, and that which was knowable became a detached, social property, validated by reference back to the author as ultimate authority.

As I argued earlier the essence of the electronic system, the computerisation of text, lies in the reduction of all symbols to the dots and dashes of the binary digital code. The bit and the byte replace the letter and the word as the basic units of the system. Out of the stream of digitised pulses that are sent through the telecommunications system one can extract any symbol; the bit stream carries music and voice, text and image.

Moreover the stream never concludes. There is no last edition, but an endless series of opportunities for changing meaning and text, for alteration and revision. The stream can be stored in many places, and its very ownership is increasingly open to question. The distinction between manuscript and revision, between manuscript and publisher's copy is hard to determine. In the blurred choices that offer themselves to a text once it has entered a word processor – between becoming a personal letter, a personalised circular, an institutional document or a freely available file in a database – much of the Gutenbergian fixity of mode, meaning and possession is dissolved. Gradually the word processor, like the typewriter, is becoming transparent within our culture; that is, it is rapidly becoming indispensable, playing a role so automatically in our lives that we are not sensitive to the fact of its differentness from the technologies that preceded it.

At first, for instance, there seemed to be a kind of social deception entailed in sending fifty people letters which, apart from tiny 'personalised' alterations, were identical to the point that no one could be sure whether he or she was the only recipient. We no longer think that the loss of that traditional Gutenbergian distinction is a deception, or even that it is particularly bad manners. It is simply an opportunity offered by the word processor which is ours by right if we own the technology.

Mind and Text

It is still hard to tease out and identify precisely the mental qualities that the new systems encourage at the expense of the old ones. We are to a great extent our text systems; our values are heavily influenced by them, so much so that it is hard for us to conduct the self-scrutiny necessary to examine them. The search for knowledge in typographic culture was physical: to find out something you had to lift and shift heavy objects, fill out cards and carry them about, wait on line for access to stacks and shelves, ride from one building or institution to another. Of course to research via the computer also has its physicality, but the nuggets of knowledge are already in some sense stuck together. Knowledge in this new system shares much of the mathematical relativity from which it was born. Its certainties are interim versions of an unending text, to the totality of which the computer can give us access.

In passing from analogue signal to digital we seem to be passing also from the objective view of knowledge – which has been in decline throughout this century for other reasons – to the relativistic, endlessly interpretative view of knowledge. It is a final working through into our culture of the relativity doctrine with which the century began.

Gradually the new technology, together with its attendant baggage of assumptions and shifted intellectual attitudes and practices, is moving through all the organisations and strands of our culture. Its impact has of course regional and national differences; it adapts and superimposes itself – it does not displace and uproot. Physical toil, together with the mystique of toil, are passing from many parts of our society and attendant culture while various forms of mental toil – probably containing a higher element of frustration – are taking its place. In the place of the low-paid drudge who did the heavy humping about of metal and wooden objects, there sits the consultant, highly paid and dependent upon one or more pieces of costly but ephemeral technology. It is a different age, a computerised or at least computerising age.

The computer plays a strategic role in the reorganisation of all the institutions in which it arrives. It is not a silent visitor, but an active agent of change, bringing with it the inexorable sense of its own modernity – inexorable, but with incalculable consequences. Like an epidemic, you cannot be sure where it will strike or what it will spare, only to return later. The reader will readily see why I have chosen the library as my case study, for while the computer has arrived in the library, it has not transformed the institution or its practices – not quite yet.

The Library as an Institution of Universal Knowledge

A hundred years ago the public library would have been listed without question as one of the institutions that lay at the foundation of a modern society. A universal public education system, a structure of local government, a freely elected legislature and universal access to knowledge would all have been considered necessary elements of social progress and of freedom. The school, the town hall, the parliament and the public library were the buildings which between them constituted the visible infrastructure of citizenship. A fifth institution, with its counterpart visible edifice, would in many countries have been the newspaper.

In recent decades we have seen all of these institutions undergo a steady process of change under the influence of modern electronics and the media.

None of them has altered fundamentally, however, much less dropped off the list of social foundations – except perhaps the public library, which in many places today is more important as part of the machinery of welfare than of citizenship. The public library is no longer a political institution, no longer a crucible of social equality and a resource for political change. It is, however, as I shall try to explain, the potential location of a dramatic cultural change of a different kind. But in the present and the recent past the public library has failed to modernise to the extent that other organisations have in meeting the challenge and the reality of the computer revolution. (The library has also simultaneously become one of the early victims of straitened finance in local government. It is low in the local political pecking order, and often, in universities, near the bottom of the list of financial priorities.)

The library once suggested to its surrounding community the constant possibility of access to the totality of human knowledge. The campus library, at least in the major places of learning, aspired to provide a modern counterpart to Alexandria by attempting to offer its readers practical access to the reality of universal knowledge, as, for example, by the institution of interlibrary loans. But very few universities have managed actually to collect more than a fraction of the thirty million or so titles which have passed through the printing presses of the world since Gutenberg first set up his press in Mainz. Oxford and Cambridge muster about five million volumes each; several US campuses better that by nearly double, and the University of California claims holdings of fifteen million titles. The dream of universality long ago became an illusion and if pursued would quickly become a nightmare.

For much of the 20th century there has been neither a political nor an economic incentive to maintain the status of the library as a social enterprise, in part because self-education has diminished in glamour and frequency with the rise of mass availability of university education. Dependent upon public-sector cash in recent decades, the librarian has diminished in professional status, although the image has probably changed more drastically than the reality. While the librarians have had to make do with the micro and the PC, the library associations and think tanks have been dreaming of a mainframe future. Concurrently, a politically invisible pressure for rapid self-enhancement has been building up within parts of the library profession.

The Problems of the Traditional Library in the Computer Age
It is not the failure of the dream of total access to information nor even the inability to keep every town supplied with up-to-date access to all the prevailing strands of thought and learning that has caused the institution of the library to falter. The problems of the library in our day are problems of servicing and preservation. Printed information is stored on rapidly deteriorating materials riddled with acid and, a great section of them, in the course of self-consumption. The microfiche and the microfilm have not succeeded in becoming acceptable substitutes for conventional books to the majority of readers. The cataloguing systems in many major libraries still today are based on the Dewey system, devised in the 1870s when most areas of current

knowledge did not even exist as subject headings. All of the modern sciences are hopelessly split across dozens of Dewey subject headings. The cataloguing systems in use have not developed equal and compatible methods for the filing of films or moving-image materials, partly because book libraries and librarians still base all cataloguing upon authors' surnames, which do not in fact even exist in all literate human cultures. Moreover while the encyclopaedia has undergone all manner of modernisation in recent times, the library has neither followed nor adopted any of its example, nor has it pursued the alphabetic subject approach to the listing of books.

Faced with their shortcomings, the librarians have not looked to other institutions with comparable problems from which to derive revolutionary solutions, but have fled to the stacks and taken refuge in their professional mysteries. Rather than concern themselves with the needs of their customers, libraries have gone in the opposite direction and announced that their readers must be trained before being permitted to enter. The collections have been expanded, but at the price of declining accessibility to the user. And yet we know that forty per cent of all the books in the major collections have never been asked for. The library has faced the age of the computer but has attempted to make its technology exclusive rather than participate in the dynamic discoveries that have eased, for example, the lot of merchandisers, spare-part manufacturers and others who have to manage a myriad of different items.

In the United States, librarians' training has been based on the dictionary-style listing of authors and titles, a method thought to be a simple and user-friendly approach to the organisation of collections and to the retrieval of knowledge. In Europe, librarians have based their operations more on the classificatory structuring of knowledge, on the analysis of subject matter; it was once thought that this helped them deal with enquiries more easily, without it mattering which subject a librarian was actually trained in.

Today, however, a user unfriendliness is apparent in all the cataloguing systems, and both traditions of librarianship need and are searching for a line of common development in computerisation. How do you guide the readers to what they want? The computer specialists have not yet produced a proper subject retrieval system, and if librarians have been blind in the past to the difficulties of the various cataloguing systems, the computer specialists are still somewhat blind to the issues raised by library searching. Somewhere in the logical systems of the computer is the key to a new, knowledge-searching librarianship which would combine the best of the American and European traditions. Despite my perhaps rather unfair strictures on the achievements of the library profession in this generation, there is a great deal of innovative work under way that could one day restore the library as a front-line institution of society.

The Learned Journal
To trace the evolution of present-day changes in librarianship one has to look back at the history of the scientific journal, a form of publication which goes

back to seventeenth-century France and which had not changed very greatly in function or in form until the advent of computerisation.

In the 18th century there were already as many as 800 scientific journals, all of them selecting manuscripts from the learned societies and circulating new knowledge and controversy. Half of these were published in Germany. By the turn of the 20th century there were around 10,000 journals, and by the middle of the century that number had grown to 50,000. By the start of the present decade the number had doubled again to 100,000 and was growing by several percentage points a year. In volume rather than number of titles it was probably growing even faster.

As a result, the abstracting of learned journals itself became a booming industry. Even two centuries ago there existed para-journals that specialised in summarising the contents of other journals, thus enabling interested scientists and learned societies to keep up with their respective fields. In fact it was the societies rather than individual publishers or libraries that undertook to maintain the flow of abstraction publications. (To be fair, librarians in the learned societies were the pioneers of this movement.)

It was this secondary information system which first identified the computer as a necessary tool. A number of the abstracting and indexing services established in the 1950s started searching a decade later for ways to publish and circulate their materials from library to library via computer typesetting. By 1964 Medlars had come into being, a system by which the *Index Medicus* could be searched by computer and the full text of abstracts subsequently mailed to enquirers. By 1971 Medline had arrived, which supplied the same data off-line to subscribers.

At the same time certain libraries, under the leadership of the Library of Congress, were searching for a computerised cataloguing system, and the resulting standard, entitled MARC (Machine-Readable Catalogue), has dominated library cataloguing for the last two-and-a-half decades. At first it was a method for cataloguing newly arriving material, and it spawned many derivative systems: United Kingdom Marc and Library of Congress Marc among them. REMARC (Retrospective Machine-Readable Catalogue) made it possible for a great retrospective project to commence on an international basis, and some 3,000 libraries started to capture data concerning their listed holdings. Quite quickly, tens of millions of records have accumulated, forming something like an electronic bridge between the lost reader and the vast totality of printed information.

Gradually a whole series of newer technologies arrived to act as the girders and rivets of this great bridge. Videotext, videodisc, facsimile, electronic publishing – all these and others make it possible for information about information to be gathered more rapidly, interrogated more thoroughly and interestingly, and recycled back to enquiring readers instantaneously. Hundreds of private databases feed back into these methods, offering collections of up-to-date information which have perhaps never passed through the form of the book or journal.

The Changing Library

One can say that by the start of the 1980s the linkage between the world of today and the vast book collections had been made, but the book collections remained just that, museums, as it were, of printed artefacts. Although the new technologies assisted and supplemented the traditional library, they had not changed its essentials; while they helped readers get to the books, they did not and have yet to find ways to get readers to the information itself. Consequently the librarian remains a custodian of objects, although there exists – in the air as it were – the vision of a new kind of librarian, a technician of information search and brokerage. The professional journals of library science have for years now been heralding such a change, but the reality is not yet with us. It is beginning to be clear, however, that at some future stage the library could develop a new and wholly updated cultural role in the growth of the technologies of information. It is interesting to look at the steps which would make this possible.

Computer specialists who have concentrated their attention upon future developments in library systems have tended to emphasise the knowledge role of the library rather than its creative and imaginative functions. They have tended to envisage for the immediate future an era in which the evolution of expert systems will interact with the work of libraries, a period during which the library's materials will provide nuggets of expertise and information ever more efficiently and in ways that will help the processes of research. In this approach the computer absorbs the knowledge in a whole field of expertise and helps to use it intelligently. This vision is an early stage of artificial intelligence, one envisaged even in Alan Turing's theorems of the 1930s, which showed how machines might be made to handle symbols much as humans do in the process of thinking.

Advanced thinking about libraries today, however, tends to look one stage further, toward a time when computerised knowledge systems will begin to interact directly with human beings by sharing, in one form or another, the use of natural language. This form of artificial intelligence depends upon building into the computer the power not merely to reason in an abstract way, but to analogise, absorb and use metaphorical links and to suggest connections between patterns and ideas in the way that scientists do in their most creative moments. In a sense this is what people do in libraries. The ability to browse internally, as it were, after browsing externally, is the skill or function that some envisage for the next generation of computers.

There is an important group of American computer scientists working at a national level on imagining the library or knowledge systems of the future. One of them, Professor Marvin Minsky, one of the fathers of the field, refers to the future process as one in which the books in a library will 'speak to one another'. Professor E. A. Feigenbaum of Stanford University, at a lecture in England a couple of years ago, scorned the libraries of today as mere warehouses, even the so-called 'electronic' ones. The real computerised library would function as a consultant. It would not need even the intervention of a human reader, but could help another library deal with a problem, raising the questions entailed in a given issue of research rather than just answering a direct inquiry. The computerised library of tomorrow would give advice rather than just check quotations from published work. In this sense it would develop the present-day advisory functions more than the curatorial ones of the librarian.

One can see the value of such a resource in, say, medical research, which needs to call upon the whole corpus of past and present scientific research in the course of pioneering new developments. But it seems to me that this form of futurism, though highly practical and not too speculative by any means, suggests a further usurpation of the traditional roles of the library and librarian, rather than a rededication.

When computer scientists are invited to consider the future of libraries, they assume them to be sources of data rather than collections of texts that have a right to exist as texts and, at the same time, benefit from technological evolution. They think of the ways in which the library can be displaced or replaced, rather than brought into the present day, when the task of bibliographic organisation is becoming ever more intractable.

No one thinks that twenty years or more from now libraries as collections of familiar printed books will have disappeared, or even greatly diminished in number or scope. The problem is whether they will be ever more maddening to use.

The Next Stages in Computer Impact Upon Libraries

Certainly there now exist large quantities of machine-readable text, with larger amounts still to come that can be held in any convenient electronic form, from databases to optical discs. There is no need for many of them to appear in printed, much less in book-bound form. For shorter documents that do not need to be accessed very often, the database is certainly the solution. But for longer works and works that are likely to be required by groups of readers in many places over many years, there is unlikely to be any substitute for the printed book. I notice that one Canadian library is experimenting today with a system of printing sections of books and documents when readers ask for them, but it is not doing so very enthusiastically or in the belief that the practice will spread. Librarians there have calculated that a single loan by this method costs nearly 30 Canadian dollars, as compared with 75 cents for an average library or interlibrary loan. There are as well various other experiments under way today in the on-line use of texts, including one at Columbia.

Perhaps the greatest challenge to the librarian of the future is the fear that computerisation will permit infinite revisions of works that contain perishable or time-dependent information. Instead of bringing out an annual update of such works, the author or publisher would be – or rather is already – in a position to offer continual updates. The problem of a book that consists of lists of data is relatively easy to solve, but in the future the phenomenon of the unfixed edition will spread to a wide range of published works. One answer is to treat such a work as a database and offer the reader, at appropriate cost, the chance to log on to it.

But what happens when a publisher decides that the task is no longer financially viable? Who then holds the database for purposes of public record? And at whose cost? Who holds the copyright? Who protects whom against acts of plagiarism from such a work? The librarian will begin to confront the full effects of the post-Gutenbergian age, when the fixities of text and authorship and their fusion into copyright law will begin to dissolve. The cumulative notion of knowledge will gradually give way to a more interpretative, haphazard conception of knowledge and its boundaries, leaving the librarian to pick up the pieces while still maintaining control of a vast, pure Gutenbergian backlog.

Of course, the current efforts to which I have referred – creating on-line catalogues, full-text abstracts of journals also held on-line, and other initiatives – will very soon now reach a kind of fulfilment. That in itself will resolve some of the difficulties. Virtually all major library catalogues, back to the beginning of the age of printing and even beyond, are already available on-line or will be available very soon. With the cheapening of computer storage and the lowering of telecommunications costs relative to volume of traffic, it will become easier to gain access to these bibliographic records throughout nations and across the world. With the arrival of CD-ROM – the hard disc containing very large quantities of data in an internationally usable format – it will be possible, and much cheaper, for libraries to send out their whole collections of bibliographic data to other subscribing organisations. The compact disc will thus become the basis of a new form of periodical publishing in which time-sensitive material can be constantly updated and accessed by computer with great sophistication.

Moreover, as libraries around the world improve their listings of subject headings, following the present lead of the Library of Congress, browsing through catalogues of one's own or some other library's will become possible again, electronically. New ways to find one's way through the complex forest of subject definitions within the catalogue will greatly ease the task of the researcher, or at the very least of the researcher who has access to the full panoply of technologies. The new developments will also help to bring American and European libraries in closer touch, since the European approaches to subject classification have been, as discussed earlier, different from the American.

Until now database searches have been based upon the existence of keywords, terms selected by author or cataloguer, by which a researcher can stumble across a relevant work. That method has now itself become a bugbear of research, since library databases are now so large that it is no longer helpful to know the number of references that exist to a given word, combination of words, or phrase. New forms of searching through strings of cognate terminology are evolving, and these should help protect readers from the sense of being constantly swamped and ever more hopelessly out of touch with the information they desire. More and more it will become the responsibility of the publisher rather than the librarian to decide the terms, i.e. the subject heading, under which readers should be able to locate a work. This development will require a considerable international standardisation of approach, but it will free authors and publishers from dependence upon remote librarians' conceptions of the subject areas under which readers of the future will be obliged to search for their information.

Unravelling the Gutenbergian System

So far I have referred only to developments that extend the natural or normal functions of the librarian as collector of works. We have considered only functions such as cataloguing and cross-referencing. But under the impact of new printing and publishing methods that entail the computerising of text, many familiar forms of publication – including possibly the learned journal itself – may well become on-line services and forego the printed form altogether. There exist several systems for circulating the text of entire articles, and these may well come to take precedence over the conventional journal format. The library subscription to a given journal would then cease to be the purchase price of a physical object, but become a subscription to a database to which the ordinary reader would then have to negotiate access. The library might well never hold a hard copy of any of the material. The problems of how to lend such material, how to charge for it and how to share costs and revenues between library and publisher have scarcely begun to be tackled on the scale at which they will present themselves within a decade or so.

The library will also find itself, paradoxically, turning into a kind of print-house, since readers will want to create more and more of their hard-copy material within the library and then remove it. In most countries, librarians already have sorted out the legalities of photocopying for library access, but they may well not be prepared for the vast increase in the volume of intra-library printing and copying that is likely to occur. The library has been preparing itself for the tasks of highly sophisticated on-line bibliographic search, but it has not prepared for the possible aftermath, the demand for printed, physically readable materials.

In such circumstances it might begin to matter less and less where a particular text is actually kept, although the computerisation of full-text material is likely to be restricted to journals for a very long time to come. In due course, however, one might foresee the computerisation of special collections of older material. Libraries around the world will decide between them which ranges of work they will be responsible for. Indeed, the cumbersome problems of conserving, sometimes restoring, paper-based texts, problems which are now beginning to confront all well-established libraries, might be resolved by systematic computerisation of full texts, accomplished through international cooperation and made universally available on-line.

In Britain the whole of the pre-nineteenth-century collections of printed materials is held on-line. Schemes exist for putting on-line as well the vast collections of early manuscript materials that could never be published in conventional format. The *Thesaurus Linguae Graecae* exists to protect the whole corpus of Greek classic texts. There are comparable systems for French and other classical literatures. All of them are available to campus libraries, of course, and offer again a new vision of absolute access to the totality of text materials.

Another important development within library management – in the acquisition process – will also redefine the relationship between publisher and library. Today librarians consume a great deal of their time selecting, ordering and paying publishers for their books. In the near future the librarian should be able to order direct from the International Standard Book Number (ISBN) and pay the publisher by subscription, with the cataloguing information being read straight into the library system. This would entail further cooperation between publisher and library management, whereby the publisher would take on many of the tasks previously performed by library specialists.

One can begin to discern other areas besides publishing where the traditional disciplines of the librarian are likely to be redistributed as well. On the one hand, a large amount of library work will depend upon the use of databases, and it will become evident to the managements of libraries – whether they are local authorities, national parliaments, ministries or universities – that computer expertise should be centralised or shared at some point outside the library itself. While librarians will become ever more adept at the task of searching for information, it will not necessarily be appropriate for them also to manage the physical resources of the computer. There could be switches of staff and expertise within universities and within public administrations that contain libraries.

Libraries of the Further Future

Even as the role of librarians changes, libraries will retain their museological role as collections of physical works. The tasks of conservation will become more and more scientifically intensive, more dependent on specialist knowledge of chemistry and paper-preservation technique. One can envisage a situation in which the publishing industry, in order to ensure its survival and development, will take on much of the work of cataloguing and assign the physical control of library computers to consultants or to other industries, leaving the library as a centre for conservation (in major collections), search and research, and printing. The more sophisticated forms of library search are likely to become so experience-oriented that many librarians will become freelance consultants to researchers rather than employees of specific libraries, as they are now. The most important qualification for such a role will not necessarily be librarianship as such, but specialist knowledge about the organisation of contemporary knowledge. One hopes that those with such expertise will invest much of it in the on-line catalogues themselves, in making them more accessible and acceptable to non-specialists. At any rate, librarians of the future have a spectrum of new roles developing around a changing physical base.

It seems to me, however, that a further distinction will emerge between the popular library of the town and city and that of the university and research institute. The management expertise required by these two types of institutions is likely to bifurcate. If the library is to survive as a local institution rather than be absorbed into the functions of the bookstore, it will need to undergo the same kind of transformation that other consumer industries have in recent years. The popular library will need to go out and sell itself to its potential users and to find ways in which the transforming technology of our time – the computer – can help in that task. Perhaps when the librarians have completed the first stages of the more sophisticated tasks we have been discussing here, they will turn their attention again to their traditional role as facilitators of popular education and popularisers of self-education.

Now there is an obvious gap between such visions of the future library and its social role and the vision I referred to earlier in association with Marvin Minsky's work. There is a line of development produced by extending current events and another by thinking based on conceptions of artificial intelligence as yet unrealised in practice. Twentieth-century history contains many examples of technologies that arrived much faster than even their inventors predicted, as well as many others that simply never came to fruition. Certainly there is a competition between the library as repository in the Gutenbergian mode and the more revolutionary conceptions of the knowledge needs of the future. But the library has on the whole been slow to adapt and has thought less about society's needs than it has about making improvements in its own housekeeping methods; rather it has treated its professional convenience as if that were identical with the needs of society. Many of us commit that error as we try to envisage the institutional changes made inevitable by the advent of the new information technology.

4

A Century of Reith*

The BBC was founded in a different world from ours. In 1930 it was possible for Reith to think that the BBC model of 'rationalised nationalisation' could and should be applied to the railways, coal-mining, the steel industry and other services, without his being a socialist. When he thought about the relations between governments and broadcasting the neighbouring case histories would be those provided by Hitler and Mussolini. When he was accused of being unfair to the left his mind would perhaps turn to the comparable arrangements in Moscow or Madrid; when he pondered the problem of how to share radio time between the parties his context would be a three-party system, soon collapsing into a kind of coalition, the National Government, with active communist and fascist parties waiting hopefully in the near distance.

The BBC was none the less placed inside the same society which we inhabit today, and the infant institution was obliged to see its way around obstacles which we would find familiar. The leading politicians all recognised that the BBC needed to be independent but not *that* independent. There was a parvenu bourgeoisie which appeared to be in power, but the country's cultural models seemed to be based upon the *mores* and inherited customs of a faded aristocracy. There was an opposition Labour Party in constant turmoil, uncertain how to position itself towards Britain as a country. There was an official suspicion of all things artistic. There was a powerful group in politics who believed that things should pay their way. It was a naturally compassionate society in which there was a strong current of belief that the unfortunate could only be so somehow through their own fault. There was no accepted place or function for intellectuals outside the universities.

The new medium of radio had somehow to pick a path through a thicket of British distrust. Everywhere there lay intractable questions of doctrine, impossible conundrums of taste. In religion, in language, in the dress code of the staff, in positioning oneself towards the various manifestations of authority, in the treatment of monarchy and Parliament, unemployment and aristocracy the stance of the BBC had to be one thing to its audience, another to the political elite to which Reith necessarily played. The work of creating the BBC was, in Reith's hands, essentially a constitutional project, an experiment in the manipulation of the materials of the British political system. Those

---

* Written for *The Listener* on the 100th anniversary of the birth of John Reith, founding Manager of the BBC, July 1989.

who let him in the 1920s build radio inside an indigenous national monopoly – one which gradually became far more powerful than anyone had envisaged – did so because they thought he would exercise a convenient new form of mass social control. All of Europe was deeply preoccupied with such needs and schemes and Reith's was a milder, more democratic-seeming means to the desirable end of holding together in a thrall of simultaneous listening a mass society which lay still at the heart of a great Empire. Reith was trying to build a command structure for culture, a prefecturate in information and entertainment. His models were the marching army, the crusading Church, the management of great companies. He was concerned with political instruments, with how one might arrange to get one's own way in the context of the United Kingdom. The BBC was skilfully insinuated into the panoply of great institutions and its most valuable contribution to this society has been made because it has continued the exercise of that skill.

Read his summary of his own achievement composed in 1950 in an effort to dissuade the Beveridge Committee from proposing the breaking up of the monopoly: 'The exploitation and development of Broadcasting were (haply) under control from the outset: and in the public interest; without prejudice to entertainment functions, under a feeling of moral responsibility; moral in the broadest sense – intellectual and ethical; with determination that the greatest benefit possible would accrue from its output.' Later in the same document occurs again his much quoted phrase 'only the brute force of monopoly' which he had often used in the course of explaining his policies in office twenty years before. It is a curious invocation when one looks at it in the cold light of the 1980s. Not 'monopoly', not 'the force of monopoly' but 'the brute force', and 'only', as if the cultural benefits which he was enabled to bestow had demanded an organisational instrument comparable to those then being used in certain neighbouring countries of Europe. We know from Reith's diaries that he sometimes daydreamed about becoming a European-style dictator. The images and metaphors he used of the BBC were endlessly altered and improvised, taking coloration from outside events, but all directed towards imagining an organisation which could undertake the cultural control of a society. One cannot help a frisson of embarrassment in reading today the speeches which justified the early BBC at the time.

One has, I believe, to separate the cleverness of Reith's institutional achievement – the simple barefaced brilliance with which he established the BBC in the heart of the Constitution – from its insufferable cultural overtones. The senior management of the BBC invented an audience which did not exist and could never have existed, an audience which enjoyed being led through the profusion of tastes and interests which Reith's radio channels provided, an audience which would patiently listen while the BBC spread out its cultural wares in music, entertainment and talk. Of course, there could be audiences for all the separate elements but no universal Reithian public of nine million listeners ever actually existed. It was a political conception. The force which divides the audience of today into its countless simultaneous specialisms was not suddenly for the first time exerted in the 1960s, when the BBC moved to 'generic' radio. The audience of conscripts was a Reithian contraption.

The early BBC developed an institutionally driven and politically necessary image of an assiduous audience, one that was patient and persevered with material with which it was unfamiliar. Later, under Sir William Haley, the whole scheme became corrupted into a hierarchy of taste, in which the audience was supposedly led ever upwards from Light to Home to Third Programmes. The only context in which such a project, in Reith's or later versions, would work was indeed a monopoly and the domineering stance towards the audience of Britain developed by the organisation was one which a later generation would quickly reject or ridicule. The minute it got the chance, in fact. In the event it was the war which first broke the mould in which Reith had set the BBC though by then he was no longer there.

What seems to have taken the generation of the 1930s by surprise was the sheer influence of the BBC upon surrounding events, cultural, social and political. Until the arrival of the BBC music, entertainment and talk were all live phenomena. There were newspapers of course which supplied general information; there was the gramophone industry which had professionalised certain elements of music and in effect *mediated* the musical culture. There was the silent cinema, already dominated by America, which brought before the public a certain range of acting styles. All these were indeed media, in our sense of the word, ways by which cultural activity was turned into a physical product and marketed. But it was the institution of radio, via the BBC, which turned popular entertainment out of the home altogether, transformed it from the practised mode to the passively absorbed.

It was the BBC which put together what were in effect a series of quite different phenomena, different musics, into a single entity – music – catered for ultimately by a single broadcasting official. Moreover it was the institutional exigencies of the BBC which provided the final demarcations between music which was 'amateur' and music which was 'professional'. The concert hall and vaudeville and the gramophone industry had all exercised an impact but the sheer quantity of material used by the BBC, and the need to negotiate performers' terms across a wide variety of musical practices all forced or encouraged the organisation into a kind of monarchical role.

What was the case in music applied *mutatis mutandis* in many other fields. All the strands of a culture were made to pass through the machinery of an organisation of which the founder had determined that it would be universalistic in every possible way. 'Whatever was put into it,' wrote Malcolm Muggeridge of the BBC in his book *The Thirties*, 'must either take on its texture or be expelled, a waste product; though different meats were inserted, the resultant sausages were indistinguishable.' The material of prewar BBC programmes does not survive in great quantity but all contemporary reference suggests a listening atmosphere profoundly and consciously pressurised through the organisation; the audience must have been extremely aware of the BBC itself and of the fact that it expected their respect and gratitude for what it was doing to them.

Certainly, a wide pluralism was the goal but it was a rehearsed, agreed and scripted pluralism, all points of view offered for the listener's impartial consideration and the listener was expected to be in an impartial state of mind, *susceptible* to the BBC's objectives. As Muggeridge put it, 'the same gentle persuasion washed against the nine million, patiently wearing away angular opinions; like waves on a beach, ebbing and flowing, transforming rocks and stones into smooth round pebbles, all alike into a stretch of yellow sand.' Reith aimed at creating in the programmes a kind of simulacrum of his audience-society, an idealised, earnestly contrived aggregation of all their legitimate interests – and all of it in pure and sanitised form.

In its great discovery of the power of seriality the BBC found a way to wrap itself around the population; its programmes filled the hours and recurred at the same moments in the week, creating a new and memorable public imagery. Dance band leaders and comics, children's story-tellers and readers of the news, clerics and announcers, hundreds of fresh names and fresh images entered into the national psyche but all of them aura-ed by 'standards', exuding the sense of the prescribed. That was the force of the monopoly.

That, too, was what put Reith's BBC into a position which has never been effectively assailed. Not even by the present government whose plans, after years of determined iconoclasm, result in very little change indeed to the BBC. Competition among radio and television channels of the kind that engulfed American radio and horrified Reith and the British establishment of the 1920s and 1930s has never really arrived in Britain until today. So strongly entrenched is the spirit of monopolism in broadcasting in this country that over the decades we have merely granted a series of new specialist monopolies as the two media have developed: ITV has enjoyed a monopoly of television advertising, one which was extended to cover Channel Four when it was finally established at the start of the 1980s; the BBC has retained its monopoly of the licence fee; Channel Four's form of funding, an annual subvention from the ITV companies, is also a special revenue available to only one institution; in radio also most of the country enjoys no more than one BBC local station competing against a single IBA station. It has been a case of an evolution of monopolies towards the condition of pluralism. We have continued to fear the spread of channels for their probable cultural (and therefore social) consequences far more than any comparable country. That inhibition has done us incalculable good for upon it we have built a stable and profuse broadcasting culture.

Today a welter of new channels is promised forth, though it is now finally agreed that they will be encased by vigorously policed standards. A public authority will decide the geographical spread of signals. Channel Four will compete in the sale of advertising but not in order to make profits, for it will not function as a commercial company. Most of the foundation of British monopolism will remain, its durability sustained by the evident and long-standing popularity of the programmes that emerge from our system. One cannot help feeling that if Reith had lived through the long postwar debates over broadcasting he would feel at home in them, angry certainly that he was no longer in dictatorial charge but without doctrinal demur. The country has retained in fact everything which *could* have been retained of the Reithian model. True, we are moving towards the privatisation of certain peripheral elements (including the transmission system), but the whole system will remain subject to intervention in matters of content by public authorities. The economy of broadcasting is being remixed. Reith would find plenty of examples drawn from his own regime to justify an inextricably mixed economy of broadcasting. He would not of course have liked the products, but he would have realised that the consumer stance of the 1980s was another necessary 'cover' for the real project – protecting the institutional essentials and navigating them through the maddening shoals of political circumstance.

The only proof of the triumph of Reith is in fact the survival of the BBC at the centre of the broadcasting system and therefore at the centre of the whole national cultural system. One can see how the various stages were contrived, as Commissions of Enquiry and successive Ministers wrestled with the problem of what to do *next*. But for the Corporation to have survived and grown at every stage of the last seven decades as it has suggests that it enjoys a special strength. It has never lacked eloquent enemies and in many ways these have done it more good than its friends for the former have laid out the arguments and problems for the BBC to answer either by self-reform or refutation. The friends have often merely tended to smother the organisation in obfuscating flattery. Its American friends, in particular, have done it little good for they have misconstrued the BBC notion of 'quality' (which has been a political technique) as cultural snobbism, which is what BBC programmes stand for in the context of the American broadcasting culture.

So long as the structure exists and remains adequately (though perhaps unsatisfactorily) funded through the licence fee the BBC's channels can continue to dominate the broadcasting scene and the attention of the audience. By controlling a spread of radio and television outlets simultaneously it can operate far more flexibly than any competitor; by continuing – as its history demands – to raise a very wide range of expectations it also commands an equally wide range of supporters who know that no substitute source of patronage will ever exist. Even, therefore, in a climate of vigorous competition – actually because of it – the BBC retains widespread political support. Any project to demolish the BBC presents the demolisher with an increasingly difficult task of replacement. The scheme proposed by the Peacock Report of 1986, which suggested that an electronic marketplace for individual programmes was now at hand, has been permitted to die quietly. The present Government seems to have accepted the indefinite survival of the BBC even though this will render permanently impossible the vision of a private self-regulated market-based system which first inspired the current round of reform. It has faced, slowly, the real choices and waited while even the more fervent adherents of the vision have grasped the essence of the country's system: we enjoy a bargain, cultural and social, as a result of accepting a radio and television company to function virtually as part of the Constitution. So long as the BBC remains there cannot be a real market-based system, only a minor facsimile of one, constructed to satisfy the ideological needs of the moment.

An organisation however long it lasts needs no more than one founder, one Weberian charismatic. Reith was that individual, a demonic, and in human terms sometimes rather pathetic case. He could not live up to the ideals which founding the BBC in the way he chose had forced upon him. Once he was out of the BBC the magic departed from him; he could be seen through. The more we learn about him from memoirs and from his own diaries the less personally likeable he becomes. One wonders whether he ever derived pleasure from the programmes he provided for the pleasure of others. For Reith perhaps providing pleasure was mainly one means of enforcing an enduring authority into his institution. In show business he scarcely belonged. Of course, the BBC has bred its later Reiths but it has never been able to handle them. They have all been cast out, their reputations reconstructed internally to present them as eccentrics or extremists.

The paradoxes accumulated through long years of survival have been impossible to contain within the single personality of a Director-General or a leading group. The great teams break up. Always the exigences of the institution have overridden other considerations, not surprisingly as the interests of the institution have grown more numerous and concomitantly more perilous. The true end product of the BBC has always been – though it might seem cynical to say it – its own continued existence.

It has taken on many competing and complicating lives; it is both nationalised industry and bureaucracy; to the Annan Committee it projected itself as a foundation, to the Pilkington Committee as an academy of national standards; today it is adopting the language of a consumer business, and it seems only yesterday that it called in a consulting firm and began to adopt the language of a 1970s managerial elite. Tom Burns' classic sociological study of the BBC, not greatly admired internally, was subtitled 'Public Institution and Private World'. Each successive executive world of the BBC remains somewhat secret because it is a rehearsal rather than a total conversion, an improvisation on a theme of public service, no rigid system of self-belief ever grafted on because of the need for the institution to adapt and adapt again, one specialist language following the other.

Reith's institutional role-models have accumulated in a farrago of self-contradictions. The greater the tension between the roles, however, the more important the institutional rhetoric which must be deployed to make them seem to cohere. Hence an endless public dialogue between openness and closedness, the systole and diastole of the BBC's corporate life. The more 'closed' the institution the easier it is to manage its political life, but the more difficult to cope with internal debates; the more 'open' the style, as at present, the harder it is to explain purposes and policies to a staff which is inevitably more conservative than its management. That also is part of the heritage of Reith. In the last few years the BBC has come closer to political disaster than ever before but it appears now, again, to have won its Thatcher battle, as it 'won' Pilkington and Annan. The political staff work always wins out over the programmes. Programmes are the raw materials, sometimes even the waste materials of the institution, of which the real end-product is – itself.

5

Public Service Broadcasting Meets the Social Market*

When we talk about and often even when we practise the crafts of broadcasting we use the words 'public' and 'private', 'commercial' and 'independent' as sectors of the two media. In fact these terms are but the shards of old political debates, and the chewed bones of old doctrines which have become embedded in the language which encases these cultural institutions. As the years pass they have come to have overlapping meanings and as new policy debates arise they become often the convenient means of obfuscation. Listen to any internal industry discussion and you can hear how these words hang around like redundant metaphors waiting for something to signify, unemployable words insisting on secure work in out-of-date institutional machinery.

These and many other terms, however, are used to organise our thinking about the two media of radio and television. The issue, which has always been crucial, as to whether these media are public or private, independent or commercial, was thrown up by a dilemma, which goes back to the very technical and political origins of broadcasting; the issue was whether to treat radio and television as industries which provide the materials of a modern culture or instead as a set of cultural activities which pass through society via the apparatus of two industries. Which comes first? and why?

In the 1920s it was the wireless set manufacturing industry which asked government to set up a special company to send out material to the new audience and so encourage people to buy receiving equipment. The industry of manufacture left it to the new public body – which was poised often uncomfortably and sometimes even perilously in that vacant space between the governmental and the private/industrial – to deal with the difficult problems associated with the music and newspapers industries, theatre and, later, cinema – with all the software in fact. Both dimensions of broadcasting have of course remained on the agendas of government, and the official administrative framework which has evolved from decade to decade is still concerned with both supervising the content and finding the right organisational framework. Governments have from the start of course been notoriously highly sensitive to the content of broadcasting. Whatever solutions

* This paper was originally delivered as a lecture for the annual Manchester Symposium on Broadcasting, 1990.

were offered from time to time the basic decision of who was to use the spectrum and whether for personal or other benefit remained with government. No government has ever shed the responsibility however hard they have tried to relabel the problem. Even where a society has tried to reduce governmental involvement to the merest and most technical fragment, it has eventually found itself building a complex and often rather invasive apparatus of supervision.

These concerns of government have never been allayed, however the two media have matured. Unlike any other industry or art form radio and television have nationally accepted organisational form. Every change in technology was used as the argument or excuse for a fresh look at the institutions and professional practices and the sources of revenue. Britain, with what are surely two of the world's most stable broadcasting institutions has had no fewer than seven major public commissions of enquiry since the 1920s. France has passed through four dramatically different stages. The United States has almost never been without its courts and several governmental agencies being in the midst of quite serious rule-making and rule remaking.

In the last decade and still today attention is again being paid, right across the OECD countries and now in the re-emerging societies of central Europe, to the questions of how to reorganise radio and television with the intention, in many cases, of enabling commercial enterprises to enter into fields previously occupied by public interest bodies. The content of radio and television as well as the ownership of radio and television distribution systems (which have themselves become diverse) have today both become the material of extremely large and strategically important international businesses. They are likely to become even bigger between now and the end of the century. New means of distributing moving images through cable and satellite are being brought into commercial use and have to be provided with institutional housing. In Britain we have now settled some of these issues for a time at least, but, for reasons which I shall try to set out, we are on the brink of a further major discussion – around the future of the BBC – which could have the effect of altering the entire mechanism all over again in the latter part of the present decade.

I think the BBC should go on, as it is, with the licence fee as its main support; I think it ought to exist not as a marginalised and carped-at survival of an earlier era of broadcasting but as the central instrument of the broadcast culture, radio and television, as the largest continuing source of programmes, programmes which could find their way into all parts of the system which has now, for better or worse, been established. I think the BBC should proclaim its purpose and not apologise for it. I think those concerned about the state not only of the television medium, but of the state of mind of the country, should start the process of explaining to government how necessary this institution is. My argument is about the BBC but it will take a somewhat circuitous route.

In the 1980s this country became embroiled in the issues of deregulation, a term which had become used in the United States, more frequently by liberals than by conservatives, to describe the policy of making companies compete more vigorously in the interests of the consumer. To deregulate meant to remove the props of government and to sweep away irksome official interference. The end result was to make industries stronger through competition and to force companies to pass the benefit to the consumer through improved service and lower prices. The United States has had long experience in handling industries which are virtual monopolies and are therefore subjected to a high degree of supervision by government agencies. Such companies become greedy – so it is believed – and less technologically dynamic; the removal or alteration of government controls and the elimination by slices of areas of monopoly help pricing to become sharper and increases the willingness to innovate. Deregulation, however, does not lead to the companies becoming free of all rules. Far from it. New systems of regulation have to take the place of the old ones to ensure that the new competitive position continues and the new systems – though undoubtedly 'deregulated' – entail an extremely high degree of official intervention, through government agencies, the courts, the Supreme Court, even Congress. To prevent two complex multinational conglomerates which manufacture tens of thousands of items from forming an unobtrusive but illicit cartel entails an enormous machinery of constant investigation and invigilation.

The term was imported to Britain in the mid-1970s but more by the new right than the left. Deregulation in Britain was rather different from that of the United States, although the same term was used. The UK's deregulators wanted and have very largely achieved a reform in the country's management-workforce relationships; they wanted more industry to be available for private investment; they wanted companies to serve the consumer with greater keenness, with better and more competitive products and services and at lower prices. They wanted millions of people to start accumulating shares and other property. They were trying in fact to revive the whole industrial economy by ensuring better services and supports of all kinds, especially in the newly burgeoning field of telecommunications. The term deregulation acquired wider and wider usage in their hands. It had much more to do with changing attitudes, with creating a new class of entrepreneurs, with manipulating change in society at large than had deregulation in the United States.

The new Thatcher administration of the 1980s found itself dealing with an economy which was far more socialised than that of the United States and which had long lost the habits of zeal in business as this is noticeable in Japan and Germany and America. They were wanting to change in effect the prevailing belief system of British society, to make people admire entrepreneurial work and enjoy again the taking of risks through investment. Above all they wanted to rid British society of its torpor and of the influence of certain institutions, from the Coal Board and British Rail to the Post Office and the whole range of advisory quangos. For the British right in the 1980s the underlying quest was the conquest of institutions; deregulation had a very different aura from the process which had been taking place in Washington, D.C.

British deregulation and the parallel policy of privatising previously publicly owned or managed enterprises were accompanied by the discovery of enterprise culture, already deeply set in the United States. In Britain it was felt that there was taking place an enthronement of self-interest with its penumbral ethics and emotions. Deregulation was an assault upon institutions, indeed, a project primarily of passionate de-institutionalisation.

It seemed to the reformers that the target was the country's deep-seated practice of locking up large sectors of responsibility inside monopoly organisations which then proceeded to make up all the rules and ignore the customers. Perhaps the industry which has undergone a transformation most characteristic of the Thatcherite process is British Airways: it was sold off, slimmed down, forced to compete and go on competing, deprived of its special status, made to give up privileged access to routes and expected to smile at all its passengers; all of this it proceeded to do and few could doubt that the changes have been great and mostly beneficial.

It was the confrontation between Thatcherism and broadcasting which brought out certain contradictions lurking in the process. The Prime Minister, umbraged by what she took to be the BBC's habitual unfairness towards her government and shocked by what she took to be in ITV restrictive practices emanating from an entrenched monopoly, decided to put in hand a project of deregulatory reform. She took a step which she very rarely took during her years in office – she set up a public committee of enquiry, the seventh such enquiry in the history of British broadcasting. Unlike all its predecessors, however, the Peacock Committee was instructed to look at, not the future circumstances and opportunities of radio and television but simply the finances of the BBC. In other words she asked one question and one only – is there an alternative to the licence fee? The Peacock Committee's answer was no, or rather 'not yet by a long way', and in the course of giving its reasons it proceeded to examine the whole situation of broadcasting in Britain, ITV, Channel Four, cable and satellite.

The Committee was established in March 1985 and the reforms which the government finally brought about – which in the end scarcely affected the BBC – were instituted in January 1991 and only passed through Parliament just in time to meet that deadline. It was a long-fought struggle in which the supporters of high public service requirements in commercial television gradually won back the ground inch by inch and thus left the new Independent Television Commission with a much higher level of regulatory authority than the doctrinaire de-deregulators had desired or envisaged.

What has emerged is not the freewheeling public body which was originally going to impose a number of requirements upon each supplying company through contract and then ensure that it got its way, if necessary, through the courts. What has emerged is a new public institution, the ITC, watched over by the Broadcasting Standards Council with the help of the Complaints Commission; the ITC still looks to many people the mirror image of its progenitor, the IBA. There is to be an auction for the new franchises, of a kind, but only those contenders who have the right qualifications – and these are judged discretionally by the ITC – may enter the race; the highest bidder will win of course but the ITC may vary this requirement at its own discretion if one contender promises a clearly superior schedule of programmes.

What happened over the months was that a body which was to look like the American FCC, a purely regulatory, rule-applying body, turned into a broadcasting institution with powers of substantial editorial discretion. The new auctions began, as the extra-Parliamentary discussions went on, to look awfully like the old ITV franchise round. There are many wholly new players, but then there always were at franchise time. It is not at all clear that the new Channel Three will be very different from the old ITV.

Of course a number of important changes have taken place, not least the establishment of a separate Radio Authority, but the Annan Committee in the 1970s had recommended that. There are some new statutory bodies set up at public expense to examine standards and complaints of unfairness but these too are in practice somewhat similar to the institutions of public accountability recommended by the Annan Committee. What we saw during the post-Peacock legislative round was the slow collapse of Thatcherism as a reforming force. It was eroded not because it had run out of steam but because it simply does not fit the requirements of broadcasting – and by requirements I mean the things which *society* requires of broadcasting. The fact is that we all *want* radio and television to be regulated. All of us, including at the end of the day the deregulators themselves, want to have some kind of stake or say in this great machinery of influence over our time and our lives.

What became clear as the debate proceeded was that the more perfectly deregulation is imposed upon broadcasting, the more we lose of what viewers and legislators actually value – and that is the production of programmes which encompass a wide range of society's needs and interests. A succession of Ministers came to see that care had to be taken to keep the national programme production activity in existence, even though that meant sacrificing the nostrums of Thatcherism. Cinema in the 30s and 40s had undergone an experience which had seared itself into the national psyche; American films had rapidly swept away what had been a rather healthy and diverse film-production industry in Britain. Controls and fiscal devices had been introduced to steady the situation but they all slightly misfired unable to be of more than temporary service once the distribution industry passed into foreign control. The logic of total deregulation in British television would have been the same. And so, in the argument which went on between 1985 and 1990 more and more controls were subtly reinserted, partly in the proposed auctioning process, partly in the creation of supervisory institutions, partly in the rules governing adjacent mergers, hostile takeovers, forms of compulsory programming.

What in the end has been assured – we believe – is that the main businesses which distribute programmes through television channels will remain under local British indigenous control or regulation.

If you attempt to impose on broadcasting that same discipline which is very good for consumers in other industries – that is, the pressure on all prices to sink as closely as possible to costs – you get a competitive system in which the programmes are either forced to be cheap or bought in or honed down to the homogenised needs of subsidiary markets.

What Parliament and government came to understand was that it is difficult to create a transactional system in a medium which by its nature is non-transactional. It is easy to invent for viewers and listeners the label consumers, but they are not consumers of broadcasting in the normal sense of the word. Between the audience of broadcasting and the broadcasters there is no direct act of purchase and radio and television are social in character. They cannot ultimately be forced into being commodities.

To introduce market pressures therefore necessitated inducing the companies which supply programmes into a structure of commercial exchanges. Individual viewer choices could be made to influence them by making competition for advertising (not present previously in the UK system) take the place of normal competition between commodities. Instead of turning the programmes into the commodities which are bought and sold in a market, the would-be deregulators had to place the audience on the slab and make the suppliers bid for it, slice by slice. Of course, additional ways of supplying programmes are now possible, through cable, satellite and subscription, but these by the nature of their wares and of their technology can only be supplementary. You have to get at the bulk of the audience if you are trying to establish an open market in the medium of broadcasting, which as the word itself suggests, is distributed by randomly scattering its wares to society as a whole.

However, competition between advertisers on simultaneous terrestrial channels (the new Third Channel and Channel Four) would be an essential but is not a sufficient measure of competition. That might merely have enabled the new Third Channel companies to grow rich through holding privileged franchises particularly since Channel Four is limited to collecting (in competition with them) only enough advertising to survive – since it is not to have the full apparatus of shareholders and stock exchange quotation. So it was quite necessary to make the Channel Three companies and all the satellite and cable companies *unstable*, first by making them guess their profits in advance through the auction, and secondly by keeping them vulnerable to takeover if they allow themselves to become cash rich. The traditional assumption in Britain that channels competing for the same audience should be prevented from competing for the same source of income cannot be maintained in a system which is seriously attempting to make commercial operations compete to live.

There was a further snag in implementing the deregulatory vision, which is that the BBC, so long as it survives, is capable of denying, as the Americans say, anything up to half the total audience of the United Kingdom to its commercial competitors. There were well-grounded fears expressed at one point in the national post-Peacock debate that the BBC, with its ability to attract audiences with a large proportion of home-made programmes would end up with a preponderance of viewers, while the competing commercial companies ground one another into extinction, unable to set aside sufficient revenue for programme-making. The deregulatory vision is extremely hard to make real in a society which does not give its audiences wholeheartedly to the competitive machine. So, step by step, the vision faded and the system which has emerged can be represented as a continuation of what we have much more than it is a Thatcherite transformation.

Broadcasting's peculiar characteristics defeated the ideology. Broadcasting is social rather than transactional in character. It can be made to serve at the altar of Mr Hayek's doctrines only if it is reversed upon itself and the audiences become the goods for sale rather than the programmes. There remains of course the possibility of subscription becoming a good source of production finance for certain channels but by its nature subscription entails cutting out all those members of society who are unwilling or unable to subscribe. The object of universality then has to be sacrificed and the benefits – unknown since such a system has never been tried – difficult to discern. To take the broad out of broadcasting would be like taking the yeast out of bread. With a system based on private subscriptions for selected channels the best aspect of terrestrial television is lost; the bringing of knowledge and pleasure to everyone in any walk or station of life is sacrificed to a stifling elitism. Subscription can perhaps become a valuable specialist addition; but if it represents the heart of it, the system simply ceases to be national in scope.

One significant problem predicted by the Peacock Committee in a broadcasting system reformed along privatised and competitive lines was the need to 'find means of separate and secure funding of those programmes of merit which would not survive in a market where audience rating was the sole criterion'. The Committee recommended a Public Service Broadcasting Council, a governmental body to distribute money to radio and television companies in exchange for making programmes which would otherwise not be available; this was not to be an 'arts and current affairs ghetto' according to the Peacock Report, which was satisfied that quite a broad range of programmes would need help of this kind. It is significant that the Committee thought that Radios Three and Four would also require direct funding from the PSBC. If the most eloquent and thoughtful advocates of a pure market for broadcast products believe that Radio Four could not survive on commercial terms then how wide, I wonder, would be the range of the programmes which would be on offer in a system working entirely on subscription and competitive advertising?

In case you think that I am retreading very old territory and that the Public Service Broadcasting Council – direct government funding of individual programmes through a kind of television Arts Council – is no longer on the cards, let me refer you to a new pamphlet just published by Mr Damian Green, for the Centre for Policy Studies. While it offers firm support for a continuation of the public service principle it resurrects and enlarges Peacock's PSBC; it proposes that the PSBC be responsible for grant-aiding the production of high-quality programmes all over the broadcasting system; and it wants the PSBC to be given the whole of the licence-fee revenue to carry out this task. The BBC would get much of it at first but gradually have to sit up and beg with the rest.

So if one listens very carefully one can hear today the opening chords of a new policy tune, still very much in early rehearsal. It is a new sound in deregulation policy, and it is designed to gouge out that crucial remaining element of the public broadcasting system – the financial independence conferred by the licence fee. The PSBC would be a direct quango rather than an independent broadcasting authority and according to Mr Green, for example, it would require a staff of two hundred – just to carry out this task of overseeing and commissioning work from broadcasters who want to make serious and demanding programmes. Two hundred was exactly the number hired to run the whole of Channel Four during its early years.

So the notion by which public service broadcasting is made to survive outside the framework of an independent institution still lives on but in an even more high-handed form. A source of revenue – the licence fee – which possesses among its other virtues the benefit of being non-governmental would be transmuted into government rather than viewers' money before it passed into broadcasting. Another worrying aspect of this idea is that it hands over to a non-broadcasting body decisions about what is entertainment and what is information, what can and cannot be appropriately funded by commercial means. Unfortunately it would not be unworkable. It would be rather like the Public Broadcasting System in America; I recommend anyone just to look at the kinds and quantities of paper produced to make an application for funds to one of the US endowments which support the making of documentaries and other worthy films. The process is hideously politicised and the would-be programme-maker is turned essentially into a political lobbyist for the intended product. An army of professional factors and pushers for money has inevitably been encouraged into existence – a further layer of people eating off the product. A horror. Any problem you might have experienced with Channel Four is a picnic in comparison.

At the end of the Thatcherite era a doctrinal vacuum has developed in broadcasting, perhaps in the political agenda as a whole. It would be a tragedy if the 1990s simply continued along the same track which the previous decade had found meaningful even inspiring at times but in the end limited in its helpfulness.

During this decade of the 90s Parliament will be deciding the future – one might more accurately say the fate – of the BBC, and with it the broader issues of whether and in what form public broadcasting will survive. It is not the future of an industry which is at stake but the whole future of the medium. For the alterations which have been brought about during the Thatcher years in the running of commercial television are only able to exert half of their potential impact so long as the BBC, with two national channels at its disposal and a large guaranteed income, continues to attract up to half or even more of the audience.

So long as the BBC and the licence fee exist there remains a plural system in which the different elements can pursue different cultural goals, but all of them addressed to the whole audience of the United Kingdom. That I believe is a goal in itself, obvious though it may seem to many, and is worth fighting for. What is now at stake is the possibility of the continuation at the heart of British broadcasting of a large and effective programme producing capacity. There is a temptation built into the ITC system for franchise holders to spend less and less on programmes in order to survive in the commercial fray and in arguing for the BBC to be left fundamentally intact I am arguing for the continuation of an organisation which can produce a large·quantity and variety of programmes and which enjoys the tradition of political independence, strained though that has been at times over the years.

It is an odd experience to take out your battered copy of the Annan Report – that neglected blueprint for broadcasting which was prepared shortly before Mrs Thatcher came into office. Much more of it has been implemented than we sometimes realise. We face the 1990s with three television institutions. Radio has its own Authority as Annan recommended. There remains a system of dual funding whereby the licence fee remains a BBC privilege and only a limited competition in advertising between Channels Three and Four has been permitted. The latter in its new form, as a separate institution earning its own revenue but not distributing profits to anyone is in many ways closer to the Annan plan for Channel Four than the one Lord Whitelaw actually brought into being. Channel Five is not yet with us but will surely acquire a unique and specialist role, based on local and regional programmes. The final outcome of the 1980s arguments, before the battle for the BBC begins, looks much like the pluralistic system of the Annan Report. Even the Broadcasting Standards Council is developing along lines very reminiscent of plans put forward in the late 1970s. I am not suggesting that all we now need do is reach for those dusty, but probably well-thumbed, copies of Annan. But I am suggesting that we should look again at the benefits of the plural system for at this moment we still have it and we need it more strongly than before.

One problem of the 1990s is that of getting people to believe again in the value of public institutions. These are bodies whose policies evolve with the qualities and attitudes of the nation and can be mulled over and fought over as of public right. The BBC has long been belaboured for its haughtiness and the seemingly inexorable quality with which it carries out its self-defence. It has done much to repair this in recent years, though one cannot help feeling that if it had moved more rapidly and enthusiastically into the era of commissioning and independent programming it would probably be in a stronger position now and have more allies within the growing industry of television.

The argument of the 1990s is necessarily an argument with the BBC as much as an argument about it. The BBC in the 1920s and 1930s was the exemplar of the public organisation, the model for every quango and nationalised industry that followed. It needs today to provide the same kind of leadership in the context of our recently remixed economy. It has to find its own way to being prized to the point at which its political stability is reinforced. It has to offer society those qualities of responsiveness and accessibility which have become so important today, not merely in broadcasting. The BBC has, if it can find how to manage itself into the space, a very large new territory available, since the multi-channel system will no longer consist of two exclusivist camps. BBC programmes could be offered to other channels and networks. The BBC does not have to control every channel through which its programmes pass. It should see itself as the lynch-pin of a machinery of patronage. Its programmes will pass into millions of homes around the world and so back again through satellite into Britain, often in competition with

BBC channels. It has the opportunity of being above channel competition; and this would also be politically helpful since the retention of the licence fee will require a demonstration that the audience spread of the BBC and of its programmes is as great in the future as in the past. The more widely the BBC is depended on the easier it will be over the decades for the licence fee to be protected and to remain a BBC-dedicated form of revenue.

In the years of the 1980s we developed in this country a very narrow view of the role of democracy within the sphere of culture. We discovered the consumer. We discovered, again, the patronage of the ultra-rich. But we came to undervalue the work of all public bodies and they turned in our minds into the status of victims of a new public poverty. Whenever the Opera House, the National Theatre, the RSC, the BBC, the Arts Council made it to the front pages it was always about the shortage of cash. These institutions, instead of being seen, by governments, sponsors and attenders, as the long-term creators of society, came to be seen merely as carping beggars, endlessly demanding for themselves a right which society no longer wanted to accord them.

I believe that it is an understanding of the role and importance of institutions themselves which may hold the key to a new stage in the broadcasting culture of this society and perhaps, of other aspects of its culture. Institutions have their own traditions and histories and imperatives; they have policies and plans which evolve over decades. They influence those who come in contact with them. Cultural institutions are the receptacles of freedom. They perform functions of influence; they can foster new tastes which then come to improve what markets have to offer.

When the shrill ideology of deregulation dies down, we are left with a television and a radio in Britain with certain specifiable needs. They need, somewhere in the landscape of the medium, some secure organisations with secure funding, not liable to be swallowed at any moment by a predatory tycoon. They need to be secured within their own professional tradition, that is, to have access to the materials of the last sixty years of broadcasting, for these are the property of the medium of broadcasting in its broadest sense. They need a large and various training ground, for experiment free of commercial pressure – not only the experiment of the young and unversed but also the experiment which only those with years of experience dare to undertake.

They need also, however, a new justification, not merely an argument of preservation. That new justification is not hard to find, if the BBC can begin to see itself not as an exclusive holder of channels but rather as the vast foundation of which it spoke in the 1970s. In the 1990s it should be at the centre of the system, not surviving at the periphery as the deregulators have quietly hoped. What I fear is that the government of the 1990s will try to find a place for the BBC, but a narrow and confined one. I fear that every programme-maker with a vision will be made to beg like a trained animal for every scrap of funding, obliged to justify his or her thoughts to people with priorities other than programmes in their minds. I fear that the BBC will be made to survive but under occupation by accountants and if not accountants then civil servants. Those are the fears.

There are also hopes. First that a new kind of debate over broadcasting will characterise the 1990s in which we concentrate on looking for organisational techniques which will enable programme-making to proceed in conditions which support intellectual independence. I hope also that the BBC will now lead the debate and not duck it as it has done throughout the 1980s. It has much to offer, not only behind locked doors, and that is principally its own history and heritage. I hope also that the programme-makers will not all be transformed into a class of small businesses but will see their task as that of developing their skills to provide knowledge and delight, some of it for profit and some of it with no motive other than the pleasure of communication.

6

Licences and Liberty*

Anyone who has engaged professionally in broadcasting will recognise how it obliges one constantly to take positions, explicitly or implicitly, on a great range of sciences and specialisations. That is in the nature of the whole heterogeneous business. Once when Reith was interviewing a trembling graduate applying for a job he enquired whether the candidate was proficient in music. 'No,' was the reply. Then whether he was proficient in electricity. 'No,' was the reply again. 'Then you are applying for the wrong job,' said Reith, 'for those are the two things with which the BBC is principally concerned. Music and Electricity.' In broadcasting those who at one level are simply making themselves responsible for a communication medium automatically find themselves taking pre-emptive and far-reaching judgments not only about music and electricity, but also about politics, economics, psychology, defence, industry, whatever the subject of their programme. They exert a patronage over vast territories in which they cannot, in the nature of things, claim any proficiency. The judgments of producers, directors, researchers, represent a source of unelective social power and the whole endless debate about broadcasting since the 1920s has, at root, been about the process of legitimising, democratising, harnessing, mitigating, denying or undermining that power. Only relatively recently has the focus of the debate been economics. Most of the endless series of official enquiries have concerned themselves with structures and public accountability, with essentially political issues.

It is temporarily fashionable in Britain to analyse everything in terms of money, as if income and expenditure represented the reality of things rather than a measure of them. So let me start within the vogue and begin by saying something about the financial framework of broadcasting in Britain, for it does not fit easily into normal methods of economic analysis.

The Financial Framework

In radio and television no transaction takes place between supplier and market. It is a system for the gratuitous distribution of a highly differentiated series of goods and the decisions which shape the system and those goods

---

* This paper was originally delivered as the third annual lecture of the John Logie Baird Centre, set up jointly by the Universities of Glasgow and Strathclyde under the directorship of Professor Colin MacCabe. It was given on 7 July 1985 at the City Chambers, Glasgow.

have always been and always will be far more political than economic in nature. The right to disseminate information and entertainment through the ether is a privilege granted by authority to a company or institution. There may or may not exist competition among a group of suppliers; there may or may not be the sale of advertising time as a method of revenue. The primary market of viewers and listeners will, none the less, receive the product without a direct transaction. Broadcasting is similar to the supplying of water, similar to the state education system, to defence, in that it exists first by political decision, and a system of revenue is built around it. The licence to operate is granted ultimately by the powers that be within a society; they decide how the service concerned is to be paid for, and on what conditions its managers will have to work.

At the end of many decades of slow building of broadcasting institutions, the British system has evolved a nexus of three interlocking monopolies, supervised by two quasi-governmental boards. The three monopolies are first the licence fee, paid by viewers wholly to the BBC, with its spectrum of radio stations and two television channels; secondly, the monopoly of television advertising time on two channels granted by the Independent Broadcasting Authority (IBA) to over a dozen commercial franchises; thirdly, the monopoly of the special levy paid by those companies to the Channel Four Company. Nowhere in our system does a group of entrepreneurs compete against another group of entrepreneurs for a single source of revenue. That is not an accident. It is the deliberate result of all the thinking and planning of the last sixty years.

Within the BBC, radio and television compete for a share of the licence fee, news competes against drama for resources, current affairs against light entertainment, production against administration. ITV companies compete against the BBC for audiences; they compete in international marketplaces for programmes, and also to sell programmes. None the less, ITV's unbreached monopoly of advertising time is basically unaffected by anything other than its concomitant obligations to the public authority, the IBA, which dishes out and withdraws its licences to operate. The precise share-out of the available audience between BBC and ITV also does not affect the revenue of either party. Advertisers do not mind whether ITV also does not affect the revenue of either party. Advertisers do not mind whether ITV has 45 or 50 per cent of the audience, although they might if there were a competing outlet for their advertising. Channel Four's audience similarly has no influence upon its revenue, which is decided year by year by the IBA. Only in the very longest of runs could alterations in audience size affect the revenue of any channel, and the alterations would have to be dramatic, so dramatic that they would have been remedied by administrative changes before any financial cataclysm could intervene. Of course, there are many factors which can influence the income of ITV, such as the general state of the economy, the levels of consumer spending, but the day-to-day audience of programmes is not among them.

In Britain the instinct for monopoly runs very deep, certainly within the whole culture of broadcasting. Even in industries where the process of privatisation or deregulation has been recently imposed, it is interesting to see how patterns of rationalisation and corporate takeover help to eliminate the steady day-by-day slogging out between company and company. Perhaps this will change, but in broadcasting we still have our familiar atavistic system of carefully demarcated monopolies.

From the moment when Reith, founder of the BBC, in a characteristically Hobbesian phrase, declared that 'the brute force of monopoly' had created the great diversity of the BBC's programmes, the attention of broadcasting administrators has been unswervingly concentrated upon the belief that competition for resources would narrow and corrode the programmes both of radio and television. Any proposal for introducing a measure of financial competition has always been turned down. We do not even have in Britain competitive programme journals. Competition for audiences has, however, been extremely, indeed somewhat bafflingly, fierce, especially since the introduction of ITV in the 1950s, but possibly earlier since there was a certain amount of concealed competition between the BBC of the 1930s and the overseas commercial radio stations of Normandie and Luxembourg.

Much of the *talk* about broadcasting, in Parliament, the press, before special committees of investigation, has centred on the issue of pluralism, the breaking of monopoly. The whole drive for commercial television in the 1950s was camouflaged as a campaign to break the monopoly of the BBC. What was done, however, in the funding of ITV, of BBC2 and now of Channel Four, was to bring about an extension and duplication of monopoly, disguised as economic pluralism.

The explanation of our disingenuous approach to broadcasting structure lies surely in a deep-bred fear of the cultural and social results of out-and-out competition between channels. If each broadcasting outlet fought for its life when it fought for its audience, then, it has always been believed, the diversity would go out of the system as broadcasting managers chose material which was known to be able to command large audiences. Competition would bring about a breakdown in the service of minorities. It would homogenise the rival channels. This belief has been maintained for half a century and the Annan Committee, a decade ago, upheld the dictum that a competing channel should never draw its income from the same source as its direct rival. The Annan Committee was right. There is no broadcasting system in the world today which does anything but underline the validity of this view.

There are those today who believe that a little experiment in *financial* pluralism would now be timely. They are, in my view, wrong in their failure to understand the nature of the licence fee, and its implications for the institution which is built upon it, and therefore of the other institutions also which have been built as a response to it.

The Case for the Licence Fee
The licence fee is a very simple device for funding a non-transactional medium. Television is not the same as cable, nor as pay television, nor as video or

satellite, which are all by their nature transactional media and the kinds of material they can offer – the culture of those media, if you like – bear witness to their different economic nature. The audiences can purchase their wares one at a time. The licence fee is a price, adjudged from time to time by government as ultimate enabler of the whole system, for a total service within which a large element of financial redistribution is entailed. Large sums are spent on certain kinds of programmes, small sums on others, without reference to respective audience sizes. Popularity of programmes is not linked, in either direction, with the cost of individual transmissions. Furthermore, the costs of the transmission system itself, that is, the engineering of the television channel, are equalised, via the licence fee system, between urban areas, where transmission costs are a few pence per head, and rural and mountainous areas where the cost can be many pounds or even tens of pounds per head.

The licence fee also conveniently submerges capital and revenue into a single annual payment. It is a poll-tax of a kind and regressive in a way, since rich and poor pay the same sum, but it is also very highly redistributive by its nature. If you examine a truly commercial system like that of the United States, you will be struck, as everyone is, by the large number of channels in the inexpensive urban areas, by the predictability and sameness of the programmes of rivals. But if you penetrate to the hinterland, you will be struck also by the very small numbers of channels which reach a very large proportion of the population – it took decades for television even to reach certain parts of the country. That is because it is not deemed economic to provide local transmitters and local stations in places without large or prosperous populations.

If this poll-tax of a licence fee is mixed with advertising, as it is in several European countries, then the faults rather than the benefits of both methods of revenue-raising are emphasised automatically. Advertising will tend to diminish the redistributive elements, or act as a disincentive, while the licence fee will appear increasingly to be unfairly subsidising a commercial operation. Why should the licence fee remain the property of one organisation, in other words, if advertising fails to remain the exclusive property of another?

There exist other important and unnoticed differences between the two funding methods. The ultimate decisions about the size of the licence fee are taken, of course, by government, by politicians, after consultations with a variety of relevant persons. With advertising, the real decisions on the placement of cash are taken by people who measure audiences or who believe the results of audience measurement. These measurements have the same kind of precision as pre-election polling. Better methods are constantly being devised and tried out and complex though interesting technical arguments take place concerning the comparative reliability of methods. Happily, we have never chosen to use these systems to replace elections in the political sphere. It is one thing to sample an electorate and enquire about preferences in politics in a given week. It is quite another to sample television receivers, which may be switched on without anyone being in the room, or with people in the room who are not actually watching, who may be asleep or playing cards or listening to music on headphones. It is fortunate that in Britain the measuring of audiences has been carried out not to decide the levels of revenue for any system, but merely to satisfy curiosity and to feed institutional rivalries. In a truly competitive commercial system the measurement of audiences through crude methods of sampling is paramount; programmes, channels, whole companies even, can be swept away through the presence of unknown statistical bugs. In America vast quantities of investment in pilot programmes are regularly junked on the basis of ratings divergences well within the margins of statistical error. It is the extension of roulette into culture. The undoubted benefits of advertising are swept away when advertisers are hunted by competing channels.

There does exist a third possible way of paying for broadcasting and that is funding direct by government. Not a voguish system of finance in 1980s Britain. The danger in such a system is not so much the interference of politicians, but the operations of civil servants. The levels of accountability and the techniques for distributing, withholding and calculating direct government grants should be in themselves sufficient to deter a nation from embarking upon the direct grant. Ask Canadian broadcasters or Australian what it's like to try to run an organisation of public entertainment tied to the government's purse-strings. Treasury officials and movie producers belong in different worlds, and neither can explain its actions in terms of the values of the other.

However, the real argument in favour of a unitary licence fee lies elsewhere. It lies in the potential of the nature of the unitary institution funded by it. The extraordinary flexibility of the BBC has been at times obscured by its own insistence upon secretiveness towards the public and its traditional refusal to treat itself as a truly public resource. The arrival of competition in the 1950s gave it a kind of short-sighted justification for behaving simply as one of two rival concerns. Its staff, as they became used to moving from side to side of the industry, came often, though not always, to ignore the differentness of the BBC. Trades unions, governments, management consultants, newspaper critics, advisory boards, all came to accept the idea that the BBC, the television services in particular, was destined to struggle for audiences for ever against ITV, slowly sacrificing the special ideals inherited from the founding era, as the exigences of modern times forced compromises upon the organisation. That may be to paint too extreme a picture, but it has been a constant tendency, under constant pressures. The licence fee, however, is both symbol and infrastructure of a potentially very different relationship with audience and society from that between ITV and its audience. For the BBC must be a public resource of a special kind. It should not have to justify itself in the same terms as its rivals. It should not want to do so. It has been a simple choice on the part of its management that has resulted in its behaving since the late 1960s as but one half of a duopoly.

True, it is difficult to fit the BBC into an industrial or a bureaucratic typology. It is different in kind from its rivals, and it has different, utterly different duties. It has never been able to find the appropriate analogy for itself among other institutions, because there isn't one. It has chosen various role models over the years.

The Changing Roles of the BBC

In the 1930s Reith came to think and feel about the BBC as if it were a kind of national church, its producers a priesthood and himself a kind of cardinal or pope, at times even perhaps a messiah. Certainly as charismatic institutional founder he left behind a system of governance in broadcasting which remained basically intact, as Asa Briggs shows, for several decades. Like many charismatic founders of organisations he left behind essentially a bureaucratic structure ministering to a set of purposes which had been repeatedly spelled out over a course of years. The BBC was run partly according to the principles of modern 1920s management which Reith had discovered during his years in America, and which a number of successful British firms in the private sector had also espoused – also, some, such as the Post Office, in the public sector.

The BBC, in its era of pure monopoly, was a profession, an industry *and* a kind of ecclesia. There simply were no other broadcasters or managers of broadcasting in the country. There was no other organisation competing for its special source of funds. The institution exercised the right to make its entire range of cultural and artistic choices. Unfortunately, most students of broadcasting history have concentrated on special issues such as the General Strike, the treatment of Churchill, the handling of industrial and international affairs in the 1930s. The BBC's principal role in this society was as a mass entertainer. It lived in people's hearts and minds because of the music it offered and the drama and comedy. Of course, the BBC's values were clear and it was, no doubt, as establishment-minded in its entertainment policy as in its news policy. But the true points of comparison are not services such as today's Independent Television or Radio News or Channel Four, since no such rival bodies existed. Its points of comparison were Hitler's radio services and Mussolini's and the rapidly growing American networks, and it worked out its relationships with government and other heads of state, with other institutions of the society, in silent comparison with those other nations' broadcasting systems. Perhaps the BBC didn't do much, or not enough, to enhance democratic liberties in these islands, but it didn't really have any other system to emulate. It concentrated its energies on entertainment; and the products of that chief era of monopoly – the 1930s and 1940s – in British mass media content, and here I am thinking of cinema and the popular press as well as radio, stand up very well to contemporary international comparisons. What it learned institutionally at that time was how to survive within a parliamentary democracy, how to marshal silent social forces to support it, how to build a constituency as we might put it today.

In the years since World War II, the BBC has passed through a series of phases and has offered the world a number of quite different accounts of itself. The paternalistic values and hierarchical system of Reith gave off by the late 1940s a distinct aroma of elitism and it is from a succession of different versions of elitism that the BBC has been trying to escape ever since. With the arrival of commercial television in the late 1950s, an era of contrived populism was born, the era of Mr Macmillan, of economic populism. One response to ITV, within the BBC, was the fostering of the belief in professionalism. By being a professional, the broadcaster shared something with the people who worked over in ITV. The BBC became more of an employer of professionals than a church with a priesthood. In the 1960s the controllers of the BBC had also entered a phase of professionalism and the BBC, in the television service in particular, came to think of itself as a management. Lord Hill, Chairman of the BBC in the Wilson years, brought in a firm of management consultants and suddenly the familiar section heads were transmuted into a new managerial structure, with new titles and different budgets and terms of reference. The great age of managerialism has emerged: in the Thatcher years, staff and management have come to see themselves as an industry. It is very fashionable today to be seen to be running an industry.

During the 1970s another half-blurred metaphor was invoked to describe and justify the ways of the Corporation, that of the foundation. For several years the sage figure of Noël Annan loomed across the whole landscape of broadcasting. The Annan Committee's deliberations became the supreme focus of all intellectual strivings. In its evidence to Annan the BBC officials argued eloquently that the Corporation was a great 'foundation'; the phrase helped to smudge the debate over Channel four which has indeed emerged as a kind of foundation, providing its airtime and its cash to external companies new and old who present their cases to its commissioning editors for selection.

The BBC has, of course, been and still is all of those phenomena; a kind of church, a management, a profession, an industry, a foundation, and it has been, exclusively, none of them. In an industry which offers material to a public without payment, the relationships created are different, utterly different from those which operate within a normal system of exchange. Institutions of broadcasting are simply not like companies or firms, however much one is drawn to analogise. All one can say to define the indefinable nature of the BBC is that it is a national institution.

To be a great institution it must lead. It must intervene in area after area of national life and, therefore, must build the public trust and support necessary to fulfil such a role in a democratic society. The licence fee link is not a commercial privilege of a management called the BBC, but an opportunity granted to an organisation to enhance the life of a free society through the use of a communications technology. That does not mean that the BBC is confined to one grandiose Reithian method. There has been a series of evolving organisational systems for producing programmes and the licence fee does not necessarily force the BBC into the hidebound retention of any one of them. Indeed, I believe that a new model is evolving, pioneered by Channel Four, which would help the BBC live within its ideals – perhaps live up to them more closely – and live within the licence fee.

Until recent times the argument in favour of the BBC and the licence fee has been an argument for a kind of total system. The BBC and its supporters have believed that it must, as a single organisation, operate in every field of broadcasting endeavour. When there was talk of local radio, then the BBC decided it must go into the local radio business. When there was talk of commercial breakfast television, then the BBC had to go into that business also. Satellite offers us the most egregious current example. Naturally, the licence fee has been stretched further and further in terms of its political acceptability. Now we have in Britain today a government more willing to make drastic changes than its recent predecessors, less willing to accept traditional arguments. The continuation of the BBC within the licence fee is threatened as a result directly of the BBC's need to sustain the great variety of existing services it has chosen to develop, at the quality which the audience has come to expect, at a time when commercial rivals are in a position to pay higher wages than their staff. A large family of chickens have come home to roost. They need never have been hatched.

Systems of Broadcasting

We are evolving at this end of the century a broadcasting abundant in channels, and possibly abundant in material also. I say broadcasting, but I include the various forms of so-called narrow-casting which appear before the viewer on the same screen, though they emerge from a variety of companies and technologies. There exists a case for a national programme-making centre using television channels so long as these remain dominant modes of communication, and that must mean for many decades yet. Once programmes are made and used, however, they have today a variety of possible after-uses through the new technologies. Now, one further great virtue of the licence fee is that it is available directly to make programmes; the great vice of what I call the transactional systems of electronic communication is that the payment made by the viewer is used first to cover the cost of exhibition and distribution. In the case of cinema, the first person to be paid is the cinema proprietor, the second is the distributor, while the producer stands at the back of the queue and hopes to make a profit, if at all, only from a large range of products, taken together. The producer stands at the same place in the queue in satellite, cable and video, where distribution takes up a very large proportion of the customer's payment.

The licence fee has been a wonderful programme-making revenue because the other elements of the system do not take priority. But the licence fee would be undermined in this respect if it were to be frittered away on the hardware and the technology of expensive distribution systems. The concentration of the licence fee within the BBC conceived primarily as a national programme-making centre, with other companies and other channels competing around it, is among the greatest of arguments for our existing system. The real issues of today are the nature of the future BBC, within the proliferating world of new technologies, the priorities which its management enunciates, the purposes which it announces to the world. A vast reinterpretation of the BBC is necessary – a rededication is how I would put it – not a dismantling.

What *should* be a matter of public discussion is the stewardship of the BBC, the choices which it has made over the last decades, and its planning for the future. We should not be engaged, as we are, in the shadow of the Peacock Committee, in an argument over whether to add advertising revenue to a rather high licence fee. Broadcasting has evolved a variety of modes of operation, the BBC's vast mega-production house being but one of them – and in the next stage of my argument I should like to look back at the evolution of some of these.

If you look through the history of radio and television in this country, you can detect two great watersheds, separating three great eras. I like to call them the three cultural systems of broadcasting, though these do not correspond precisely to the 'three ages of broadcasting' of which Brian Wenham writes. The first era was one of the total institution, during which Reith sought to construct a BBC which itself recruited, trained and employed all those who provided the material of the broadcasts. The BBC constructed eleven house orchestras. It had its own repertory company of actors. It employed many of the major writers of the time on its staff. When confronted with problems of religious doctrine, it published its own hymn book. When looking at the problem of dialect, it established its own idiom of pure English. In the field of engineering it tried for a long time to create or modify all its own technology. It even attempted to develop video-recording, on its own, in its workshops. There are vestiges of this now curious approach at work even in the present day.

This approach, however, collapsed under the impact of the new cultural pluralism of the 1960s. It was simply impossible for the BBC to sustain a totalistic attitude towards every strand of the culture in this no longer homogeneous society. It had to admit pop-music and rock to its schedules; where Reith might have tried to hire staff rock groups, the BBC of the Hugh Greene era established the compromise of Radio One. Where Reith tried to fit the range of national tastes into an evaluative pyramid of services – Home, Light and Third – the Greene era developed a policy of cultural outreach; it invaded the cultural ghettos in the search for talent. It harnessed a wider range of energies, but enveloped them in the BBC. The irreverence of the mid-60s was incorporated into the then daring late-night programme, *That Was the Week That Was*. The toddlers' truce, that period in the early evening when television disappeared from the screen, to help parents put their children to bed, was filled with magazine programmes which attempted to colonise the multitudinous strands of audience taste through a pot-pourri of snippets.

But above all, the Greene era, the second cultural system, as I call it, recognised that the harnessing of an intelligentsia could not be undertaken in the Reith mode, though its harnessing was still essential for the political protection of the BBC and the development of the medium itself. The BBC, and the ITV companies also, perhaps indeed led by them, deliberately sought out the new talent. The ITV companies fostered a different style among their producers. Rather than searching for writers who would work within the system of prescribed values, the new BBC of the 1960s, competing with the first commercial channel, reversed the doctrine and sought out the writers, in the knowledge that they would shape a new set of cultural values for the institution. Johnny Speight could not be truly co-opted. Nor could Dennis Potter. Nor could David Mercer. The BBC started to work within the community of writers as a great impresario, and with remarkable results. The Wednesday play was the Globe Theatre of the period. The BBC assimilated the implications of the new cultural system, and after publication of the document *Broadcasting in the Seventies*, started to dismantle some of the more unworkable parts of its heritage.

The third of my systems of patronage is the one inaugurated by the Annan Committee and Channel Four, a system based upon the recognition that society is a kind of cauldron of activities, controversies, aspirations, talents and that it is the task of broadcasting to turn the vexations into opportunities, to go out and seek, not talent so much as meaning and message, not to recruit already existing ability to make programmes, so much as register situations which should be transmuted into programme material, in fact evolve talent in a different way. The rubric Innovation, which is crucial to the personality of Channel Four, is a term capable of expressing both much and little; Channel Four has used it to develop new strands of expression, has sought out the unexpressed, has stimulated not just half-suppressed communities, but has given them the confidence to use the medium of television as if it were theirs. It is a task which Channel Four has initiated, but which is capable of still wider exploration. Indeed, I think that the commissioning of independents represents a third cultural system, because I think the process can and will transform the entire face of broadcasting, not as an additional option, but as a new dynamic force.

It seems to me that the public service broadcasting of the future will build upon the relatively small and new independent movement of today. It is sometimes treated, correctly, as one part of a television industry. It is already more than that. It is on the way to being a new institution of the society. A relationship between licence fee and independent community is the necessary next step in the transformation of television itself. It will take many years only because the BBC will take many years to convert and will have to transform its whole system and arrangement of staff and resources to adapt. The proposal is not one of convenience, is not meant to be. What is at root being proposed is a different kind of television, the introduction of a range of new professionalisms, if you like – a different management imbued with different motivations. The BBC of the future would not, however, be an unhistoric transformation of the present body, but a continuation.

The Future of the BBC

When you take, for example, the Corporation's galvanising role in spreading the use of the computer through this country, you see how a national institution, using television, can play a strategic role in a society. There are many such examples – perhaps the current Doomsday Project is among them – where the BBC, by reason of its whole history and position, is able to undertake major interventions in the life of a society, way beyond the mere provision of a series of programmes.

I am not just saying that the BBC should or could solve all its problems by commissioning works from small groups and independent companies. I am suggesting a considerable reorientation of the BBC, a shifting in its whole stance towards audience and society, a switch from an organisation whose chief end-product sometimes seems to be its own continuation to one which sees its role as that of making a series of interventions, using radio and television, in the life of a society.

Perhaps there is no area in which the institutional self-orientedness of the BBC is more aptly illustrated than in the matter of television archiving. It is an area in which I must, as the person responsible for the national collection of moving images, in my day-to-day capacity, declare an interest and you may wish either to discount or perhaps give greater credence to what I have to say, on that account. The BBC, as the major national television institution, has accumulated over fifty years the largest historical repository of moving image documents in this or any other society. On several occasions official committees and influential individuals have pleaded with the Corporation to acknowledge that its collection is more than the private production library of a television company. After a period of time historical records of any kind become progressively social, national or even international property. In the moment of its origination the Magna Carta was a local legal document – it has now become a major relic of international historical significance. Such is the way of all signifying artefacts which encompass representations of life and manners. These collections of artefacts continue to surrender their encoded store of meaning over the centuries. We use them and we honour them in the process of registering ourselves as members of a continuing civilisation.

The Corporation has argued that its sole responsibility towards its collection was that of an organisation which might need to use the material in future programmes. Access has been denied. Attempts by other friendly parties to create an access service on behalf of the BBC have been solemnly rejected. The BBC's argument in its own defence is extremely important to my general argument in this lecture, for it says that the licence is provided for the purpose of making programmes and cannot be used for the purpose of creating what would become an accessible national resource, available presumably far beyond the BBC itself. Recently Stephen Hearst, an adviser to the Director-General on policy matters, argued in *The Listener* that there should be a national collection of television materials accessible to television professionals so that each generation of producers should be aware of their own professional heritage. Of course he is right. It would be an important advance. But why is this massive heritage the moral property of one profession of a few hundred people? Why should it not be acknowledged as a major source of national and international history? Of course, the rules of copyright would not permit access to be developed as easily as to the national collections of books or music. But the performing unions have long now recognised archival and cultural rights to the after use of their members' work. There exists within the National Film (and Television) Archive a growing though terribly inadequate collection of television programmes and the uses to which this is being put, even within the proper but painful constraints of copyright, are both inspiring and instructive. Progress will continue to occur. The ITV companies and Channel Four have been slowly building up with the National Film (and Television) Archive a wonderful collection of their work.

On 1 January 1985 the NFA established a new basis for the collection and one can now say in respect of those two channels that for the last six months little, if anything, which should have been kept has been lost. All of it is being preserved at broadcast standard, as well as on inexpensive and easily available cassettes. Does the BBC really have to refuse to participate? And because of the licence fee? The licence fee is not a payment to a production company, but surely the foundation stone of a national resource; the licence fee rather than a justification for not archiving offers, it seems to me, a reverse argument – it provides by its nature an obligation on the receiving organisation to operate precisely as a national resource. The BBC's treatment of archiving as an excrescence or luxurious irrelevance illustrates the way in which it is habitually unable to recognise its own historical achievement. In insisting that it is really just one part of an industry and that it must always appear to be prudently cheese-paring it is selling itself short.

The licence fee places the BBC irrevocably inside the public sector, but insulated from government. What we pay for through our licence is the BBC's liberty, because that underpins our own liberty. The greatest thing the BBC offers us is *its* independence. We need it to be strong in the sense of being invulnerable to political and commercial interference; we do not want it to behave as a private bastion. Its haughtiness, which has increased exasperatingly with the years, is a denial of the true purposes of its independence. The BBC, as the principal instrument of public service broadcasting, requires its strength to withstand attack, not to protect an interest. Politicians should feel free to attack it but know that it will reach its own judgments on policy. Its largeness and wealth are necessary so that it will never cynically incline to the wishes of the powerful. It has seldom done so. But its financial weakness in the present decade, allied to its incessant desire to enter and dominate every field, makes it more and more likely that one day it will fall victim to the depredations of an unscrupulous politician. The more often the BBC is obliged to press the Prime Minister of the day for rises in the licence fee, the more politically vulnerable it renders itself.

There are various ways in which one can order the elements of the argument about the BBC's independence. Licence fee, political pressure, inflation, growth of services, size of staff, public service – those are the elements. Does the BBC need to undertake every branch of broadcasting and narrowcasting in order to maintain the size of its audience overall, in order to have the licence fee raised, in order to pursue independent courses of action? I believe the argument works the other way round. The BBC offers us its independence of operations as the chief return on our annual investment in the licence fee; the larger the increase it demands, the more politically vulnerable it renders itself. It follows, therefore, that it should operate always within a licence fee that is not excessively politically contentious. The BBC's scope should be defined by the available fee, not the other way round. It should not expand its staff beyond the number necessary to operate as the supreme national institution of broadcasting. As the new media arrive, it should, more and more, stick to its last of programme-making and not seek to operate one transmission technology after another. Its programmes could well, in any case, take up a major part of the channels of cable and satellite, and not only in Britain.

The BBC's chief resource is its staff and the way in which its extraordinary range of responsibilities increase their skills. But it must recognise also the way in which the skills and professions which make the moving image are now spreading across the country and are no longer held within one or two institutions. The power of the licence fee is just as great if exercised via outside commissions as via in-house production. The freedoms which are conferred by the licence fee are capable of being spread and multiplied. The authority of the BBC is not attenuated through the provision of work to independent companies. On the contrary, the BBC, if it operated indeed as a great national foundation, would be helping to sustain the levels of excellence, the spread of voices, the cultural nourishment of the nation. Wherever television programmes are being made, there should the BBC be, offering resources, protection, experience, influence. Wherever national policy is being discussed, in the ethnic communities, in the new cinema industry, in the cable industry, in the satellite industry, there the BBC should be, looking for opportunities to help, to make strategic interventions, to experiment, to collaborate, never simply to incorporate or to dominate. I am trying to suggest an alternative line of corporate development, not put a plan to cut back, to economise, to make do. I am suggesting a reinterpretation of the BBC's political, moral and cultural purposes to suit a period of time – our time – in which the use of moving images is no longer the mysterious exclusive property of one agency or two, but a general means of communication. I am suggesting a vast range of new roles and new skills, new places in which the BBC should appear as stimulator, animator. I am suggesting that it abandon the policies of the fortress, and I am suggesting that the licence fee, in its purest form, unadulterated with advertising, is the most important democratic instrument we possess.

In fact, the BBC and television generally have probably been the greatest of the instruments of social democracy of the century, more important than the health service, than national insurance, than the state education system combined. We spend more time with television than we do, as children, with our teachers. We spend more years watching television than we do drawing our pensions. The medium dominates the sources of the message and its penumbral power is vast and barely understood. Somewhere in the space between the audience and the screen, representations turn into realities. To describe and analyse these processes will be the work of many researchers, most of them not yet born.

Amid the swirling changes in technology and in prevailing doctrines, we have to hold fast to the rock of public service broadcasting. We need the established institutions because they either are or can be rendered accountable. Through them we, the inhabitants of the society, will have some access to the new and still little understood processes by which societies are today controlled. That is why we need the BBC more than ever before to carry out its fundamental mission still. But to do so it will have to undertake massive and continuous self-reform. The other institutions of broadcasting and the new devices will indeed only find their true role in the new conditions when the BBC has found its.

Index